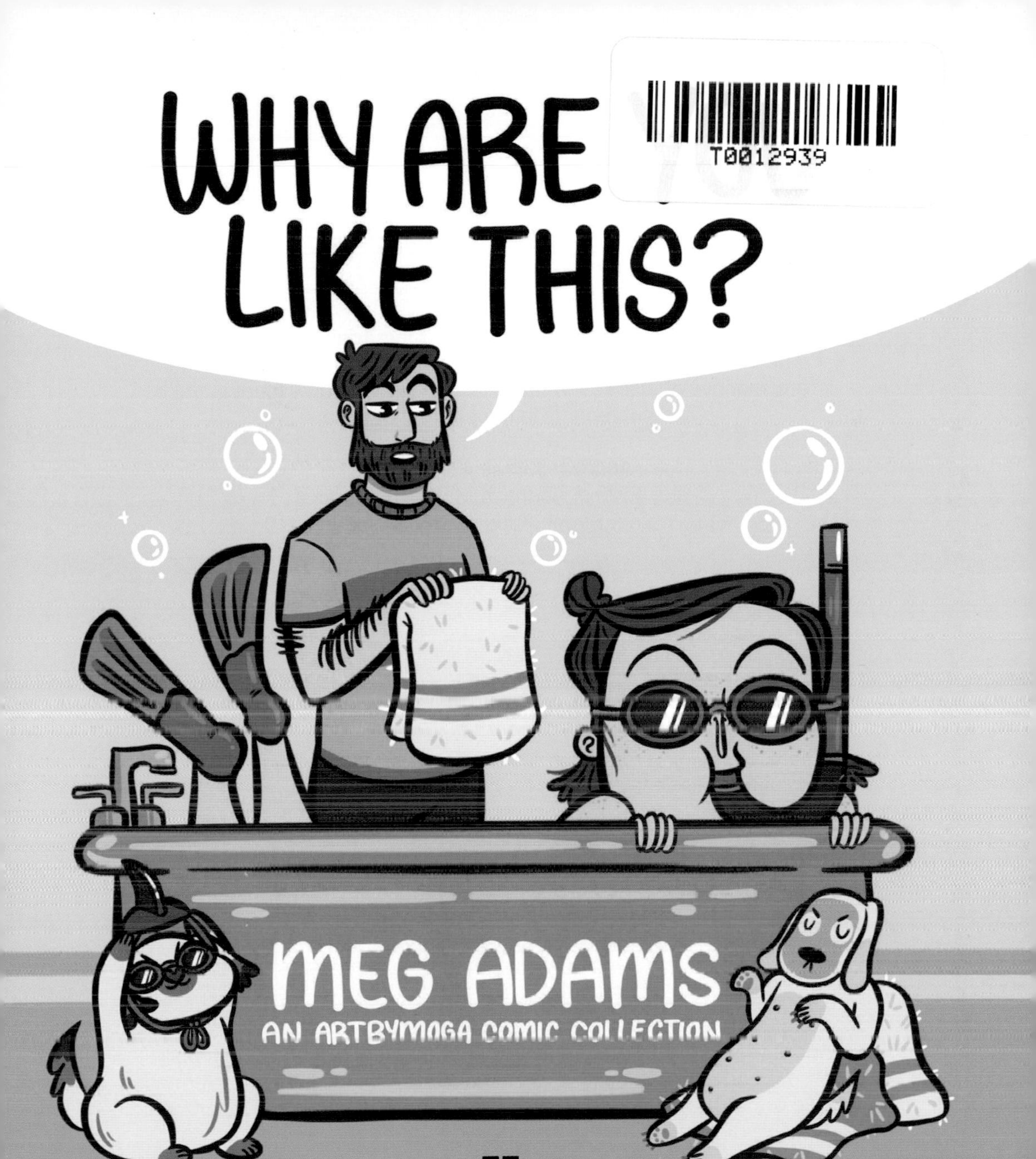
WHY ARE
LIKE THIS?
MEG ADAMS
AN ARTBYMAGA COMIC COLLECTION

Andrews McMeel
PUBLISHING®

Andrews McMeel Publishing
a division of Andrews McMeel Universal
1130 Walnut Street, Kansas City, Missouri 64106

www.andrewsmcmeel.com

23 24 25 26 27 TEN 10 9 8 7 6 5 4 3 2 1

ISBN: 978-1-5248-7426-1

Library of Congress Control Number: 2022941313

Editor: Patty Rice
Art Director: Julie Barnes
Designer: Tiffany Meairs
Production Editor: Jennifer Straub
Production Manager: Chadd Keim

FOR CARSON

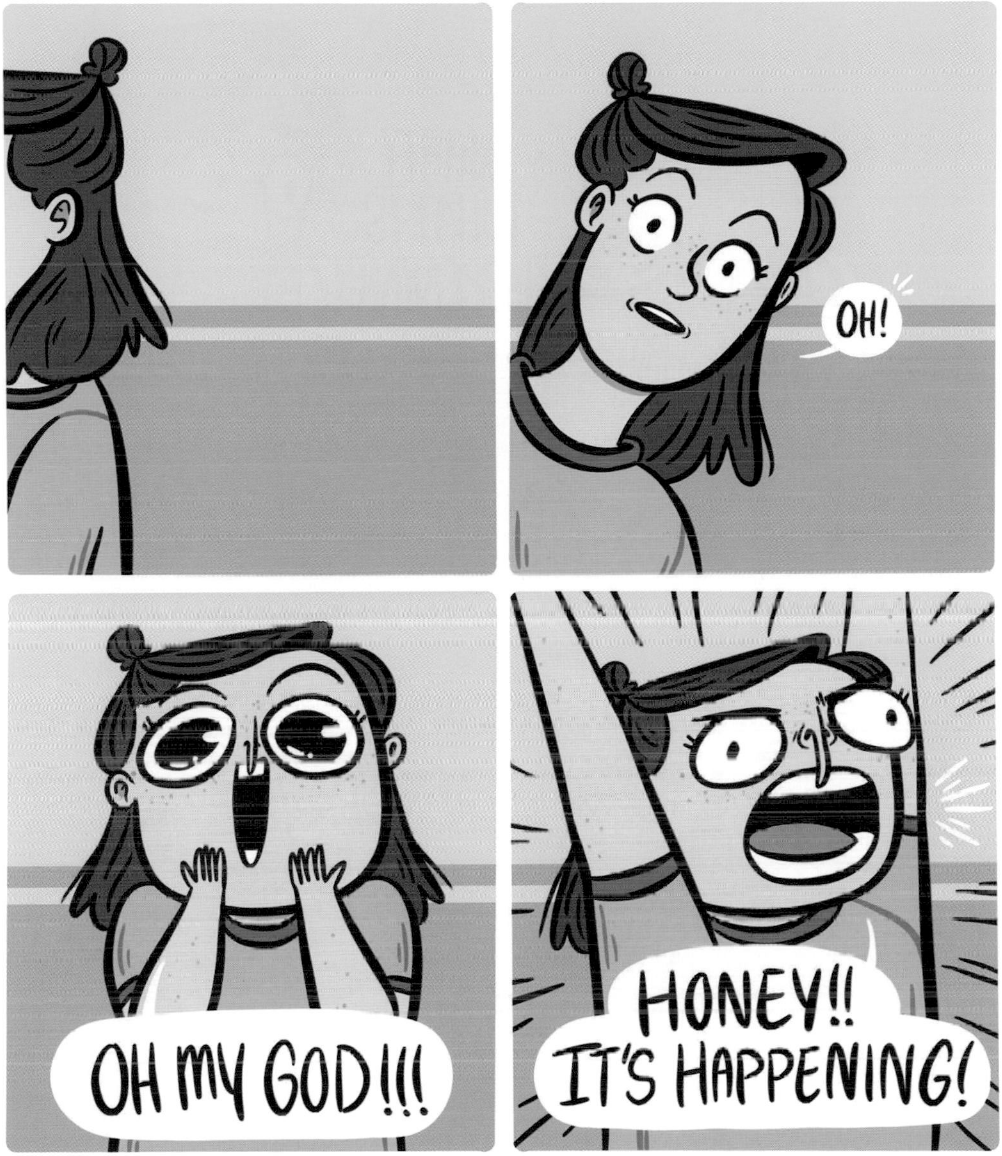
OH!
OH MY GOD!!!
HONEY!!
IT'S HAPPENING!

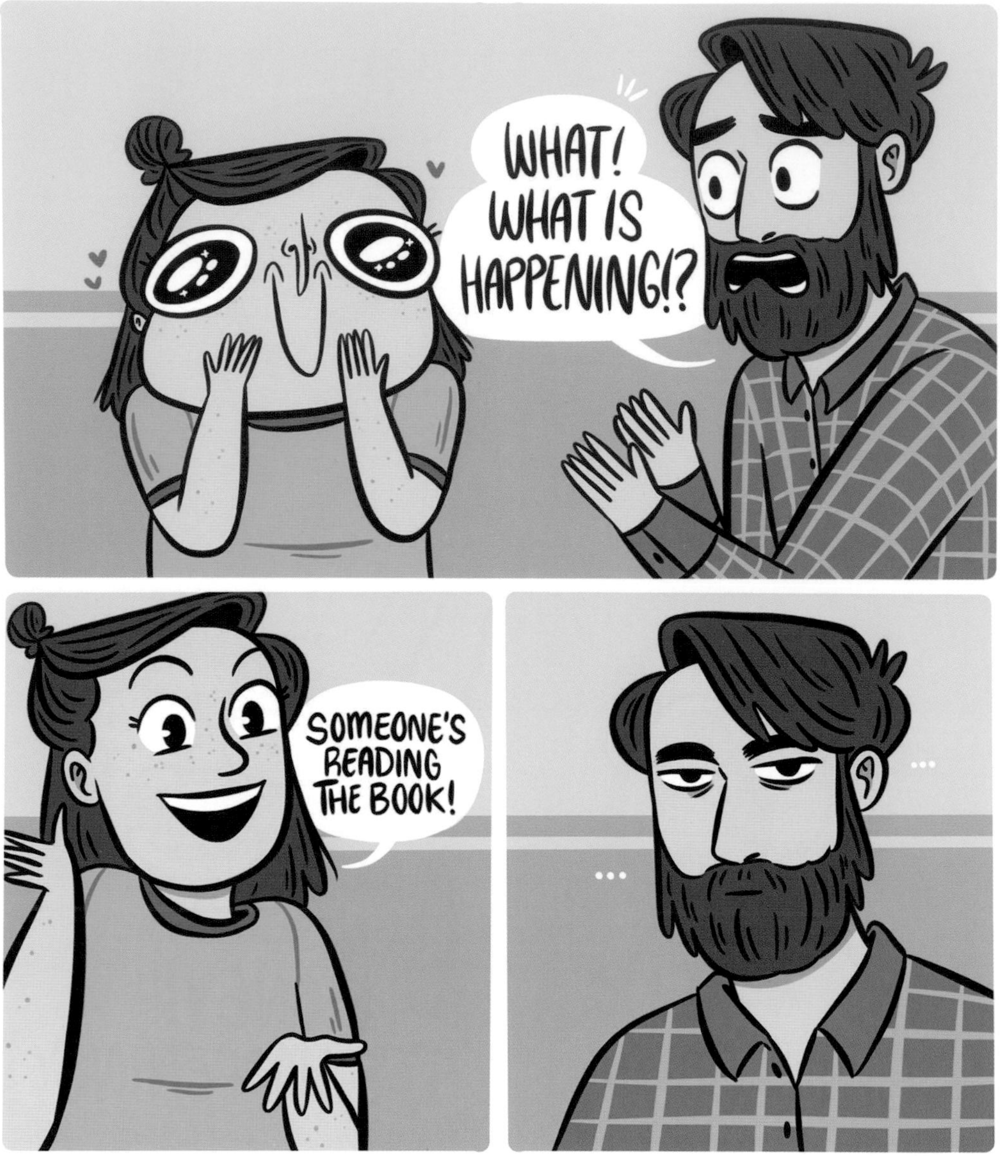
WHAT! WHAT IS HAPPENING!?
SOMEONE'S READING THE BOOK!
...
...

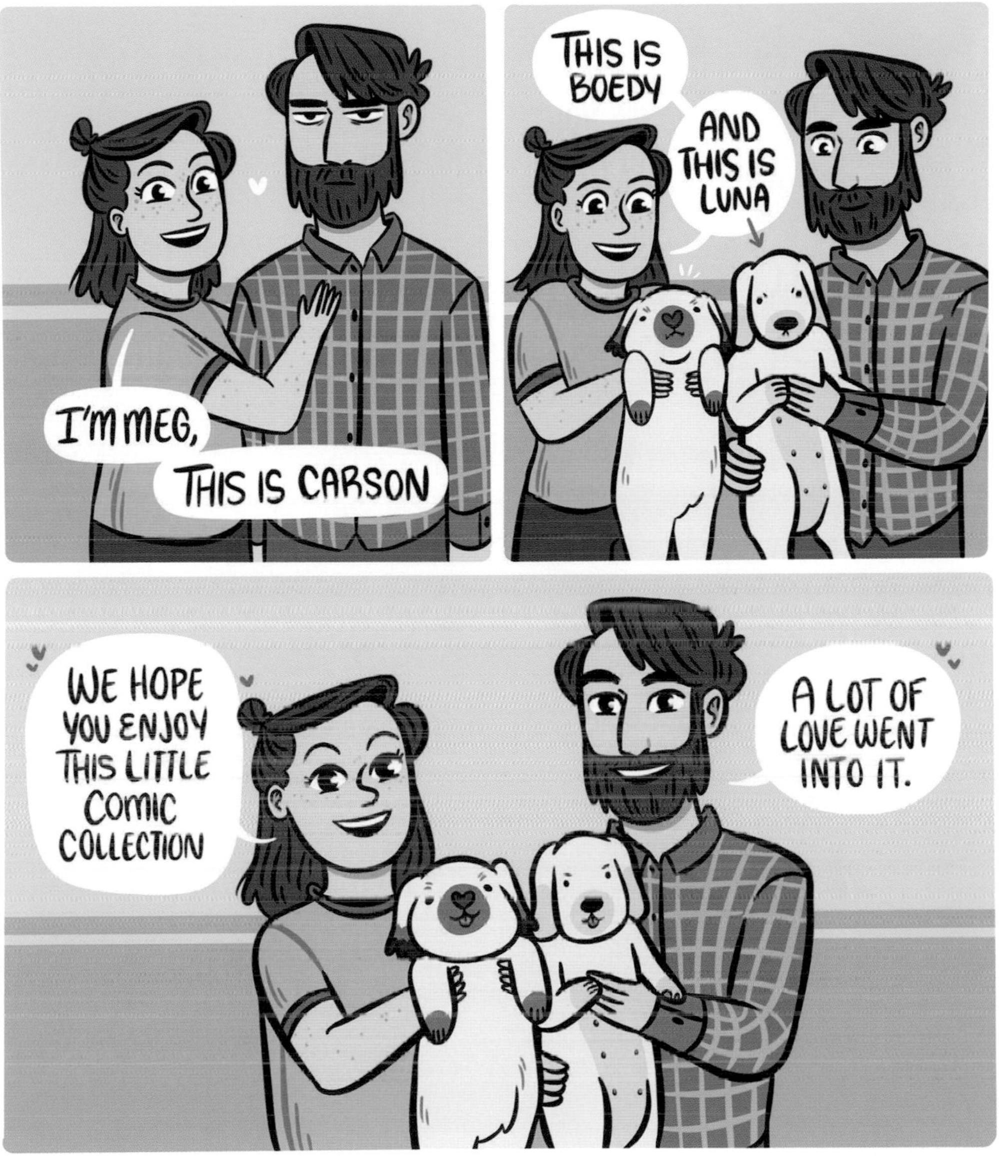
I'M MEG,
THIS IS CARSON
THIS IS BOEDY
AND THIS IS LUNA
WE HOPE YOU ENJOY THIS LITTLE COMIC COLLECTION
A LOT OF LOVE WENT INTO IT.

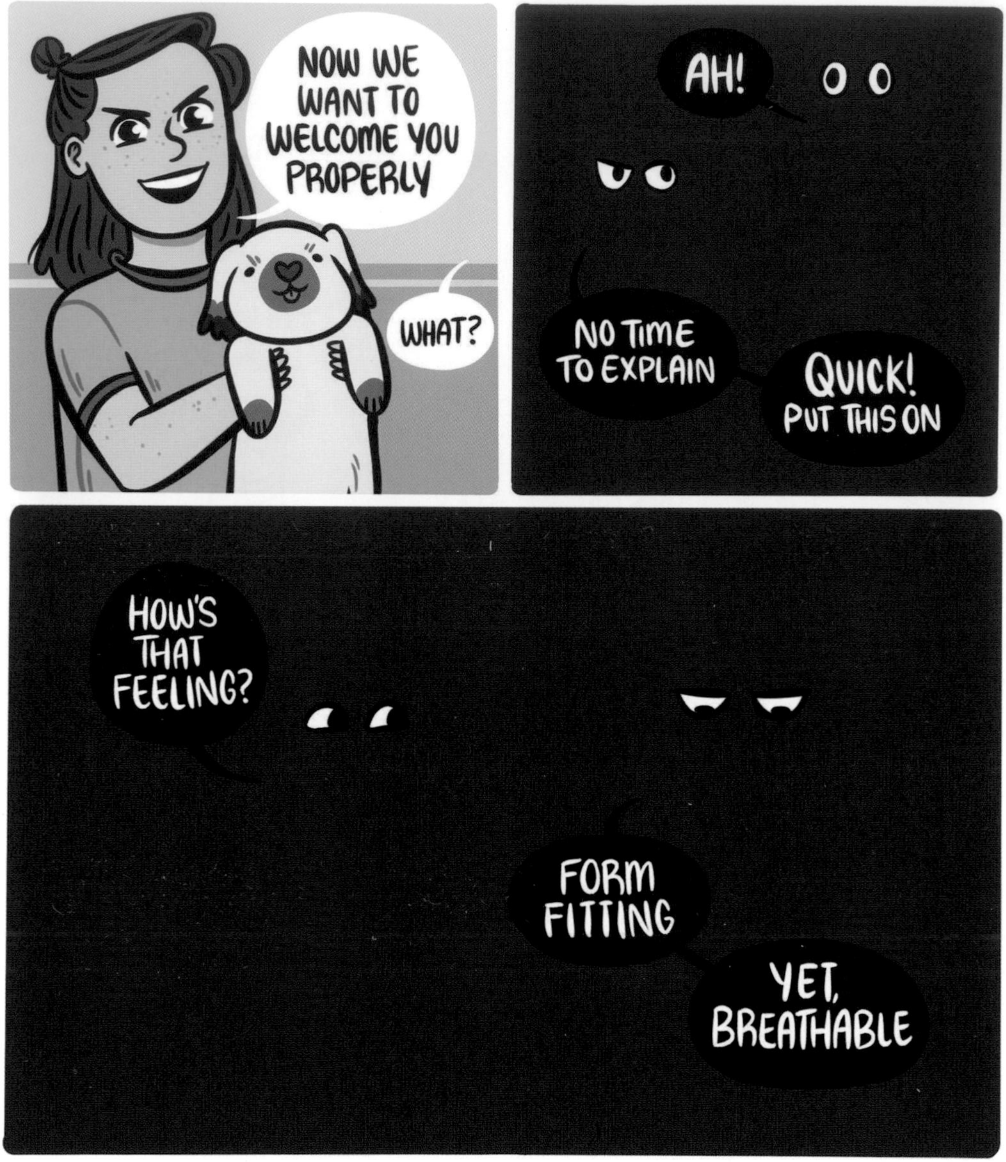
NOW WE WANT TO WELCOME YOU PROPERLY
WHAT?
AH!
NO TIME TO EXPLAIN
QUICK! PUT THIS ON
HOW'S THAT FEELING?
FORM FITTING
YET, BREATHABLE

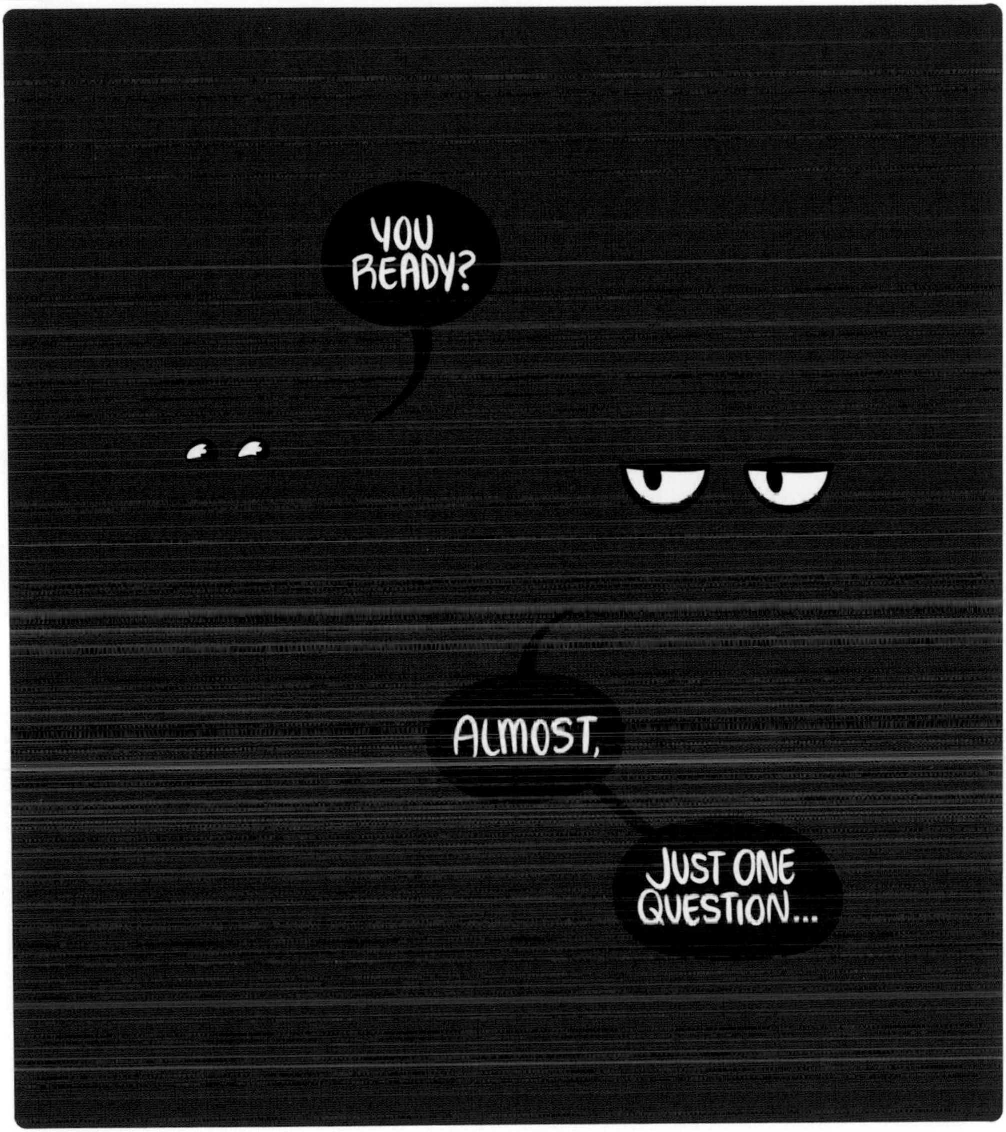
YOU READY?
ALMOST,
JUST ONE QUESTION...

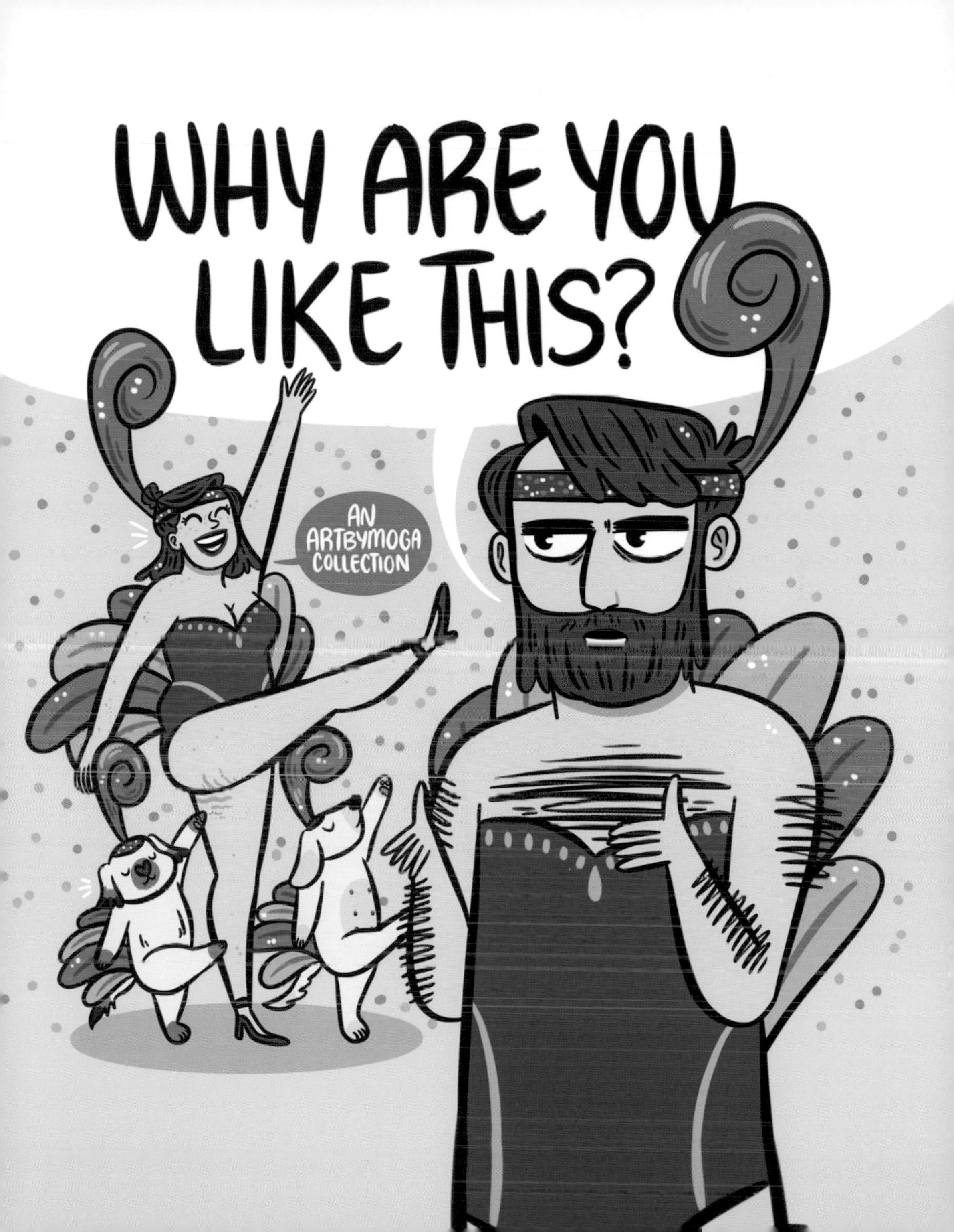
WHY ARE YOU LIKE THIS?
AN ARTBYMOGA COLLECTION

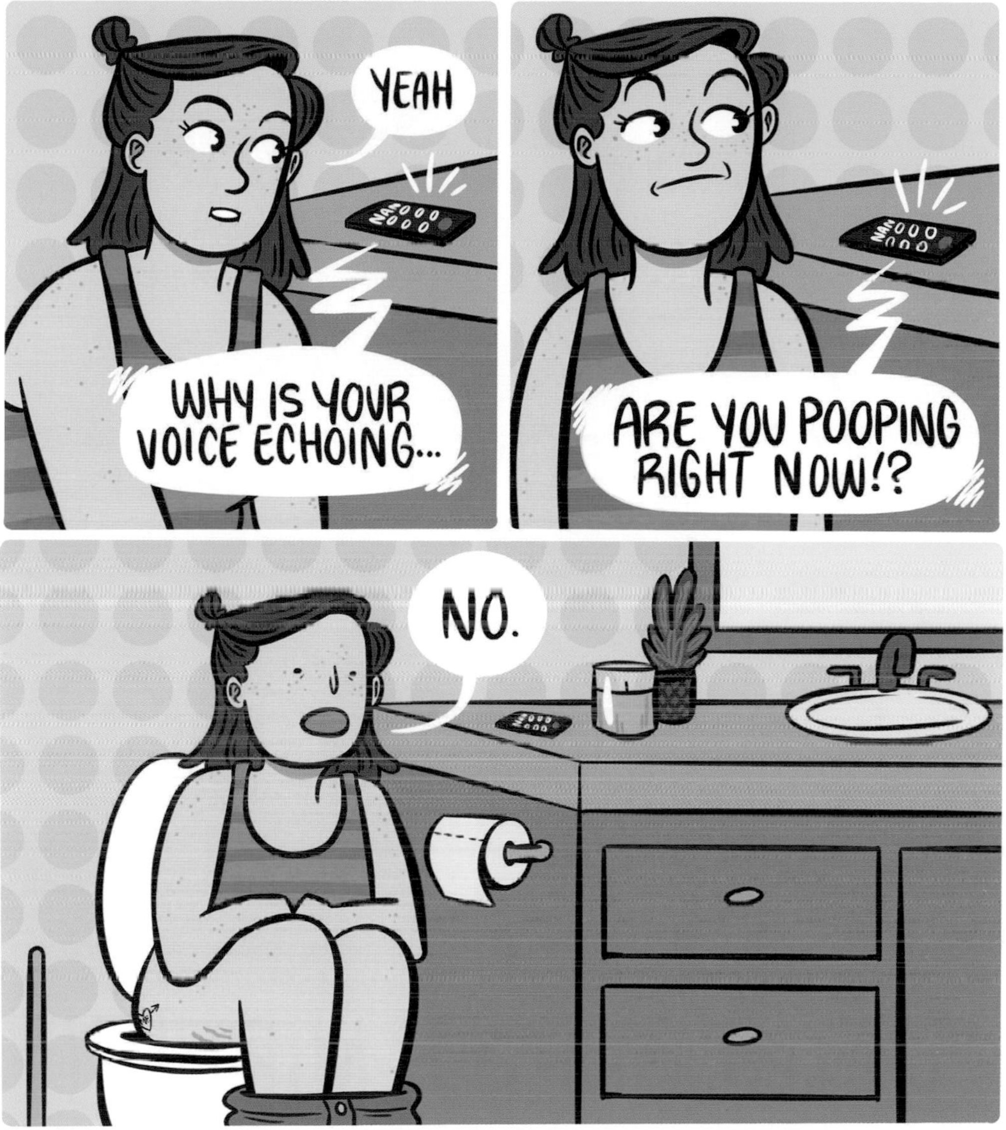
YEAH
WHY IS YOUR VOICE ECHOING...
ARE YOU POOPING RIGHT NOW!?
NO.

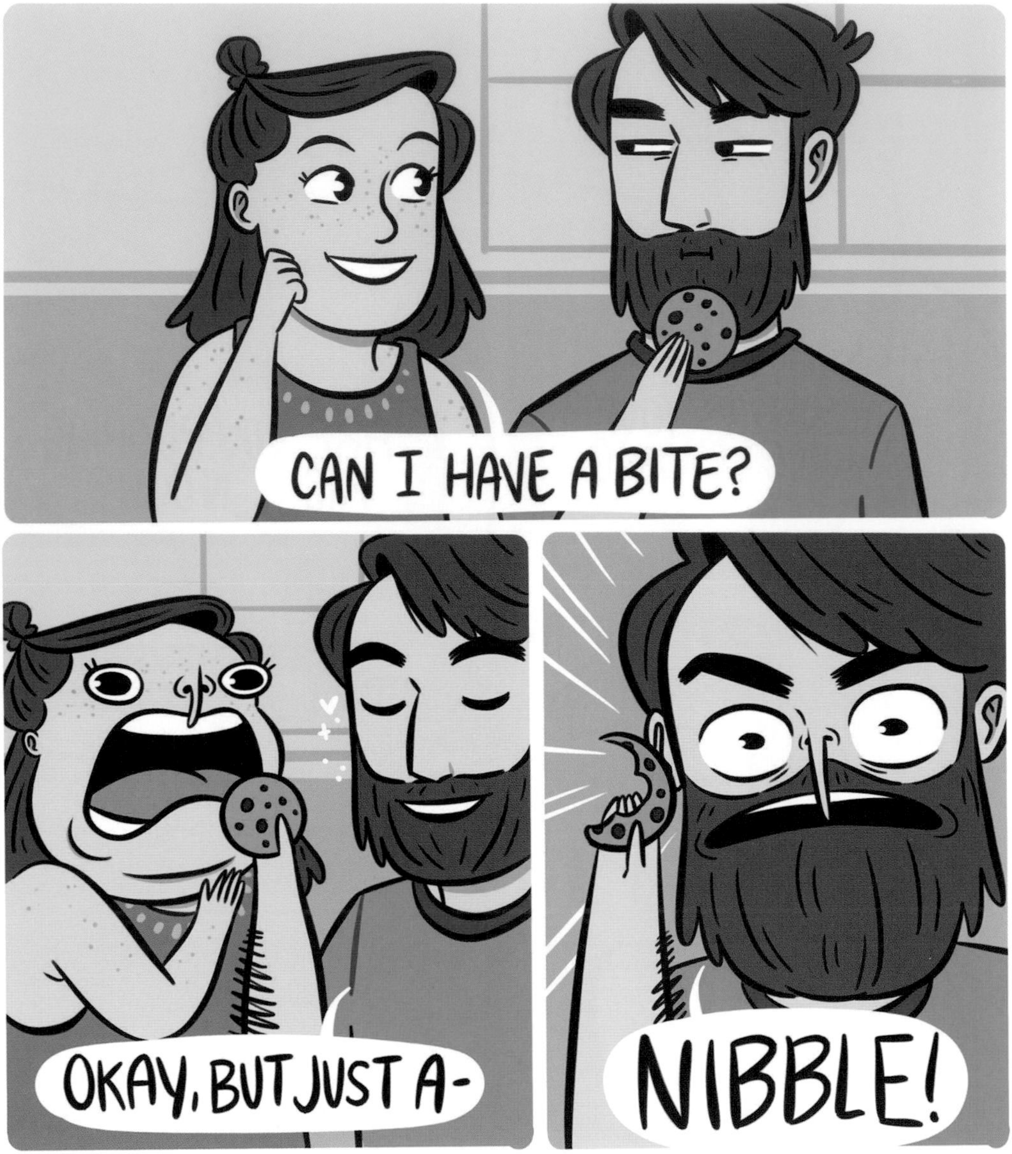
CAN I HAVE A BITE?
OKAY, BUT JUST A-
NIBBLE!

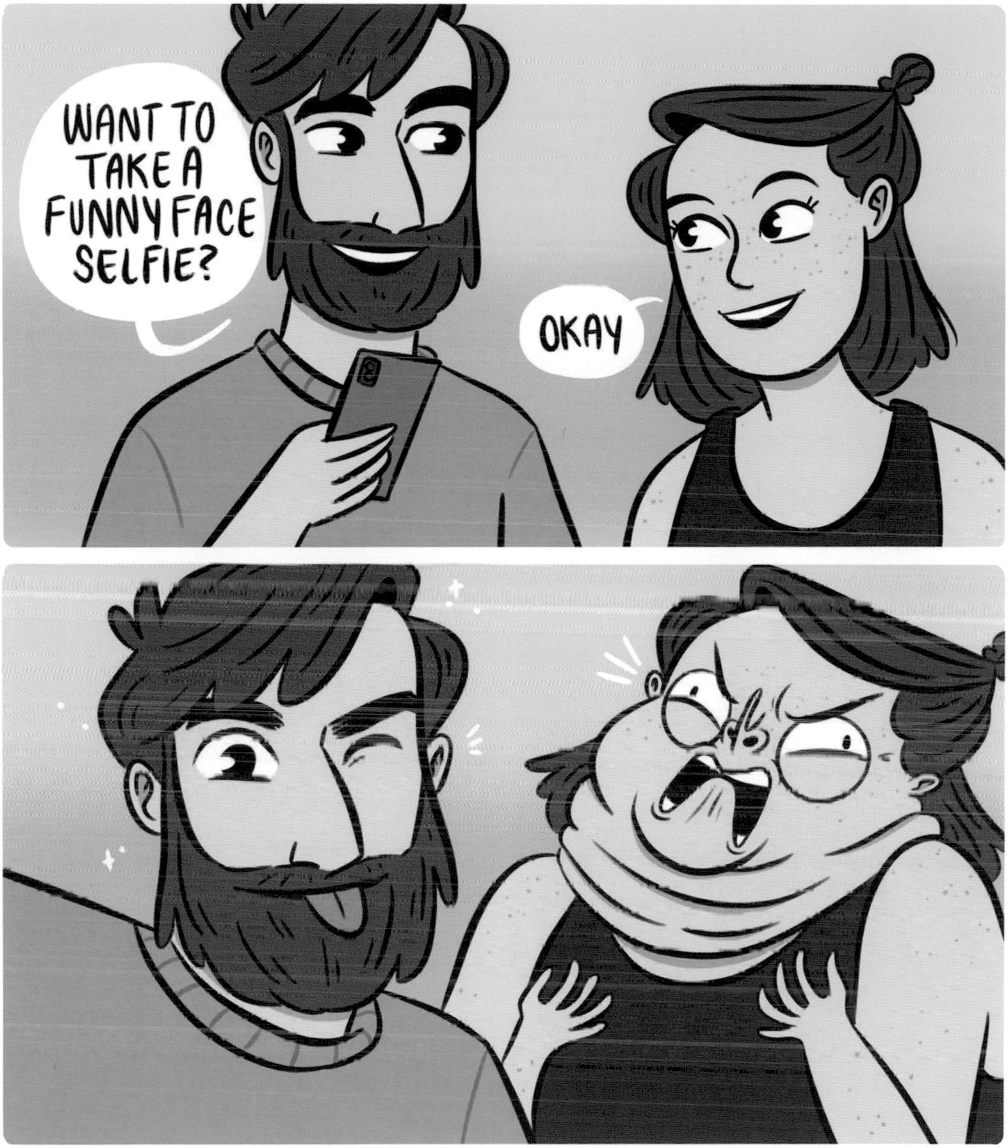
WANT TO TAKE A FUNNY FACE SELFIE?
OKAY

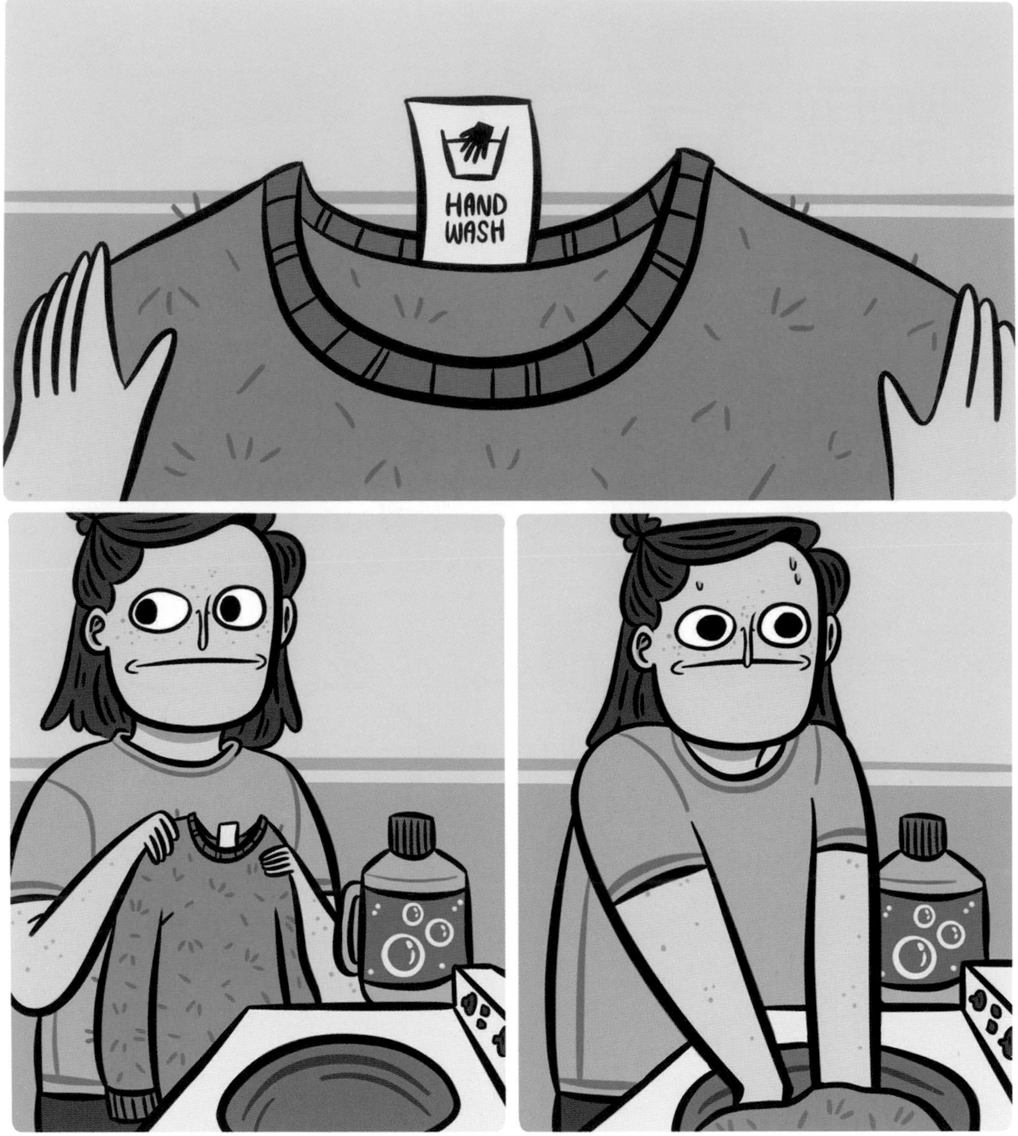
HAND
WASH

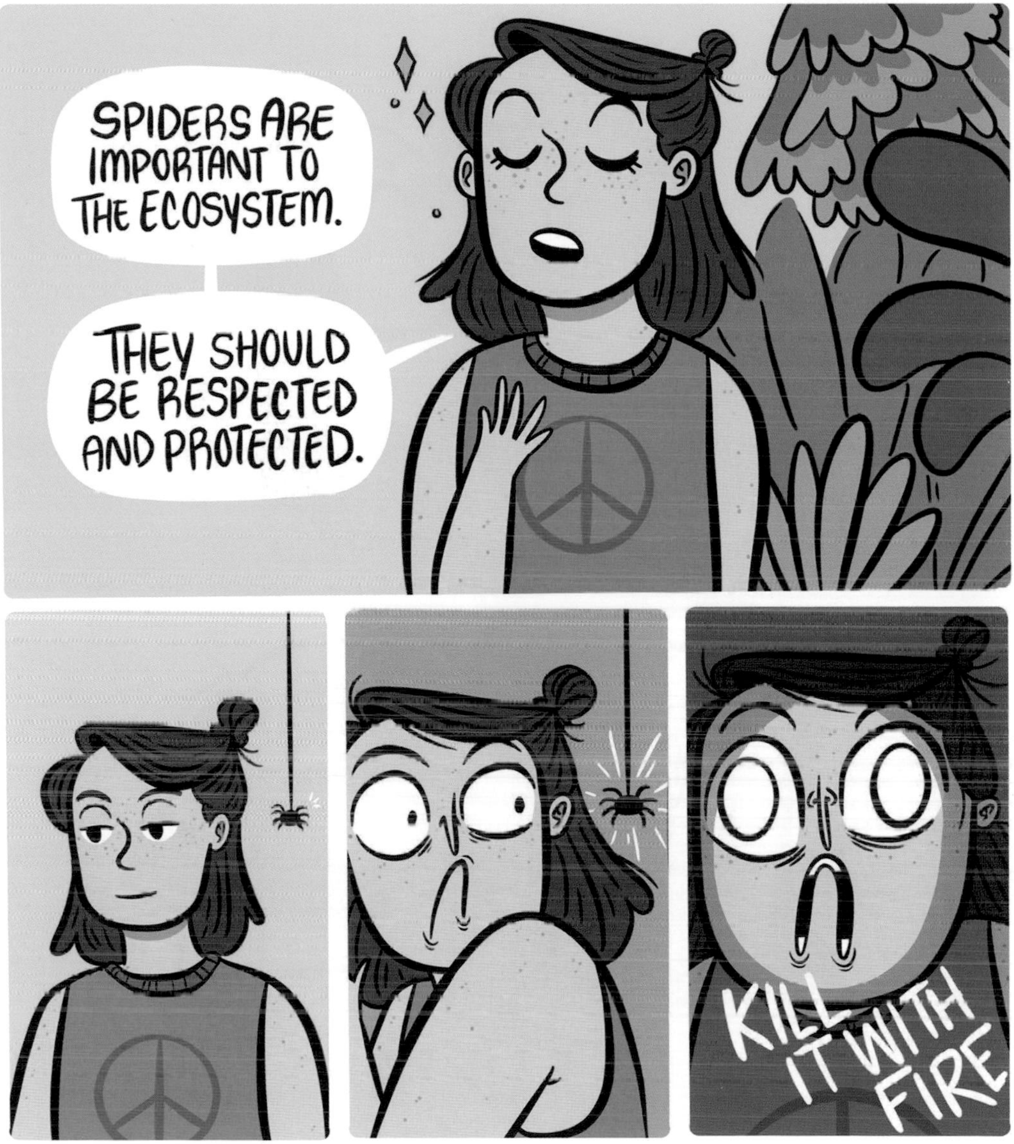
SPIDERS ARE IMPORTANT TO THE ECOSYSTEM.
THEY SHOULD BE RESPECTED AND PROTECTED.
KILL IT WITH FIRE

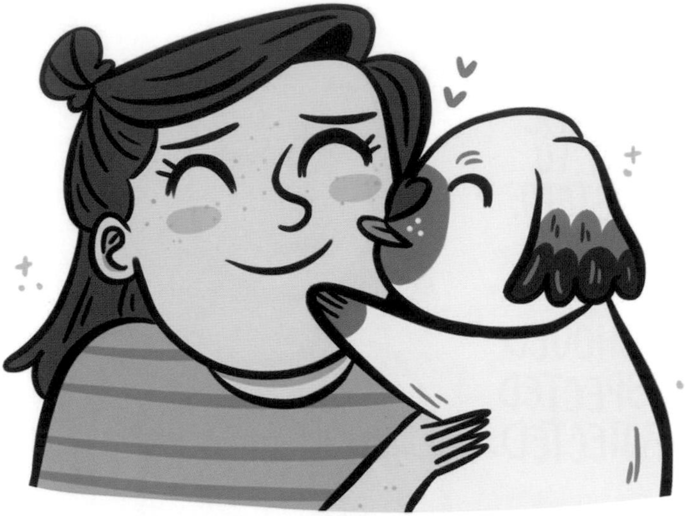

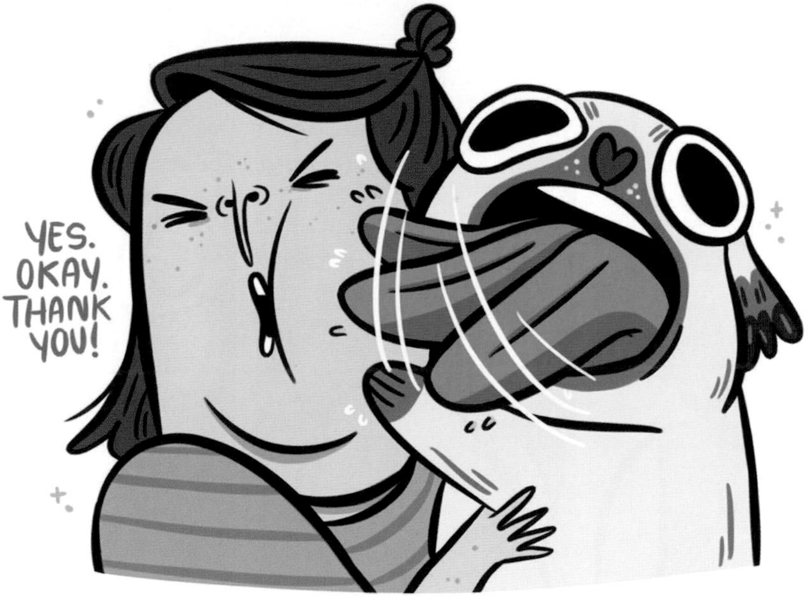
YES.
OKAY.
THANK
YOU!

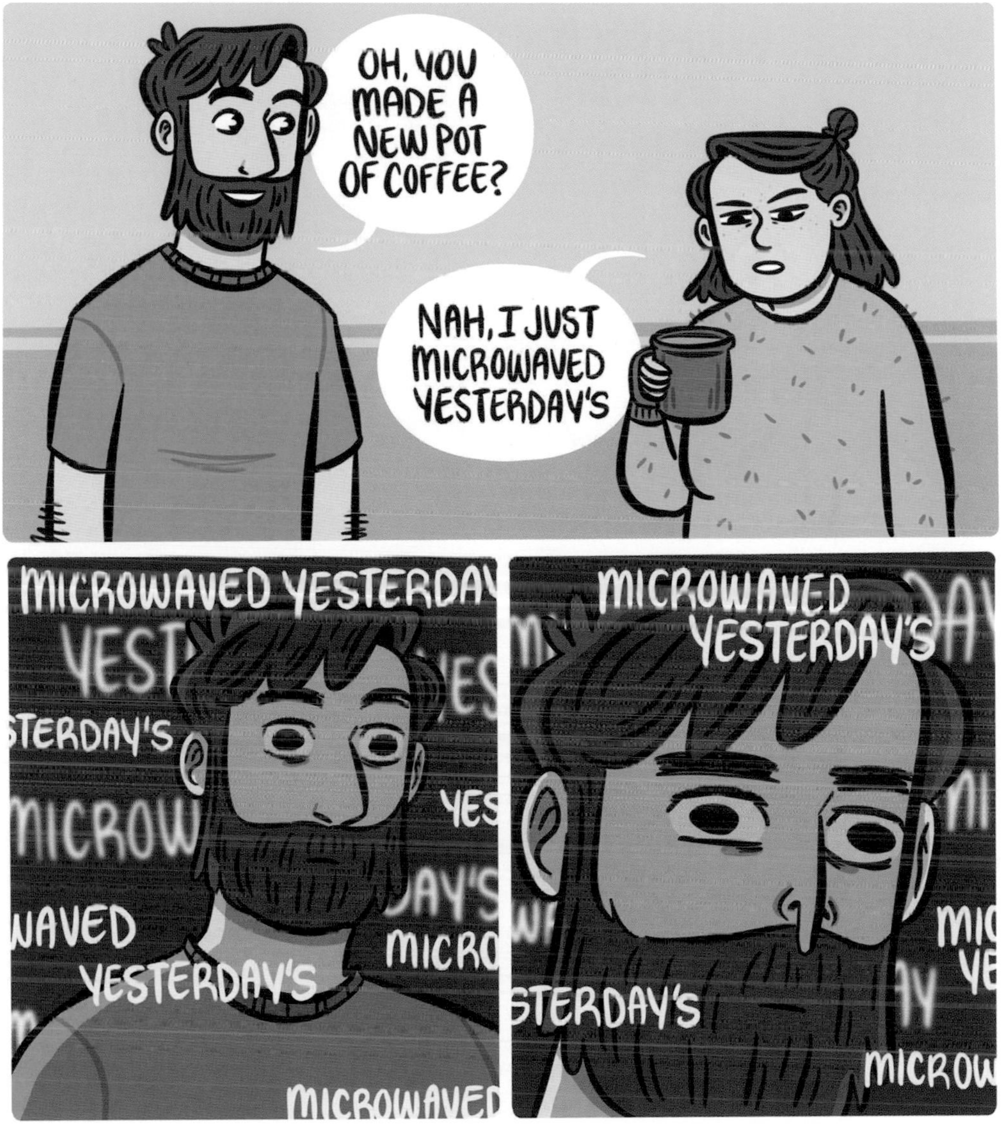
OH, YOU MADE A NEW POT OF COFFEE?
NAH, I JUST MICROWAVED YESTERDAY'S
MICROWAVED YESTERDAY'S
MICROWAVED YESTERDAY'S

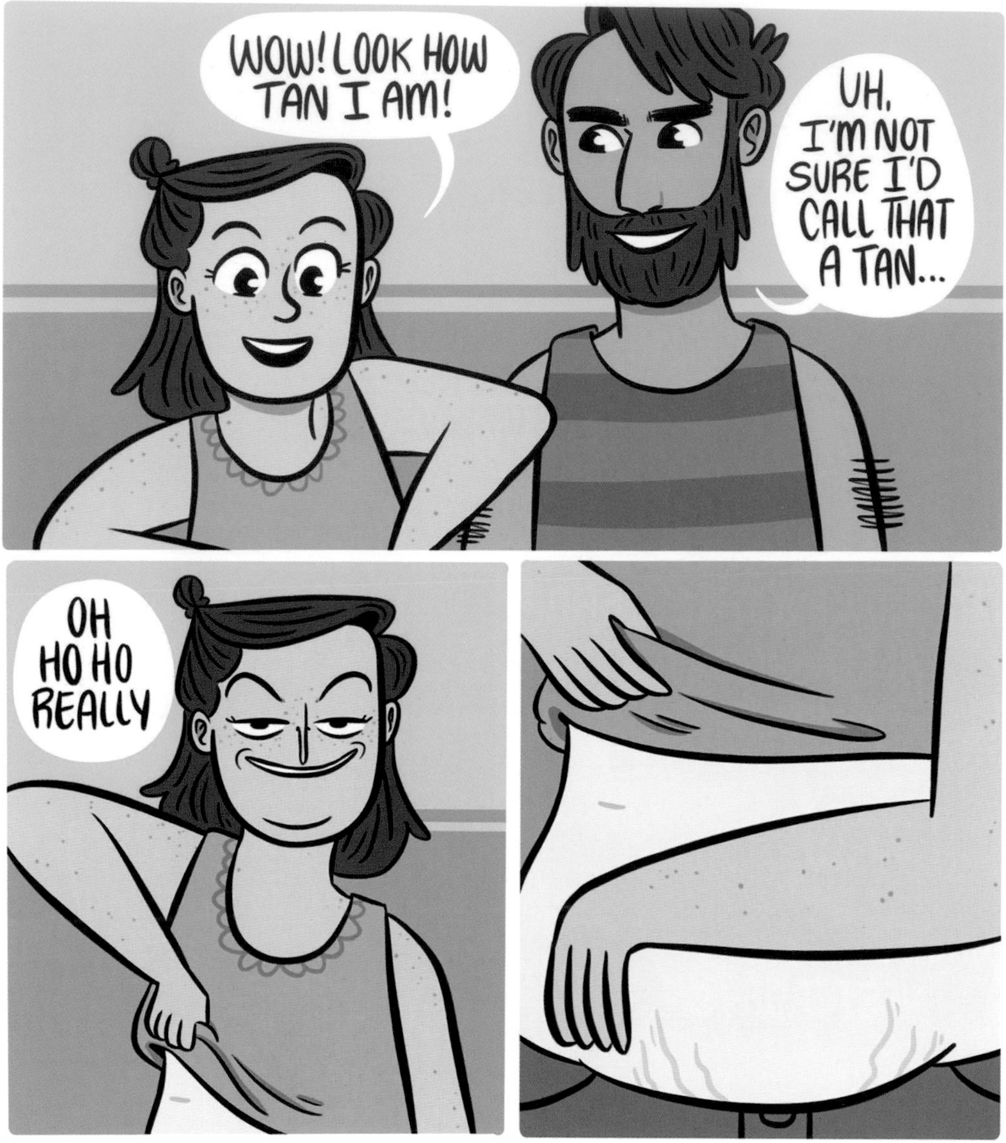
WOW! LOOK HOW TAN I AM!
UH, I'M NOT SURE I'D CALL THAT A TAN...
OH HO HO REALLY

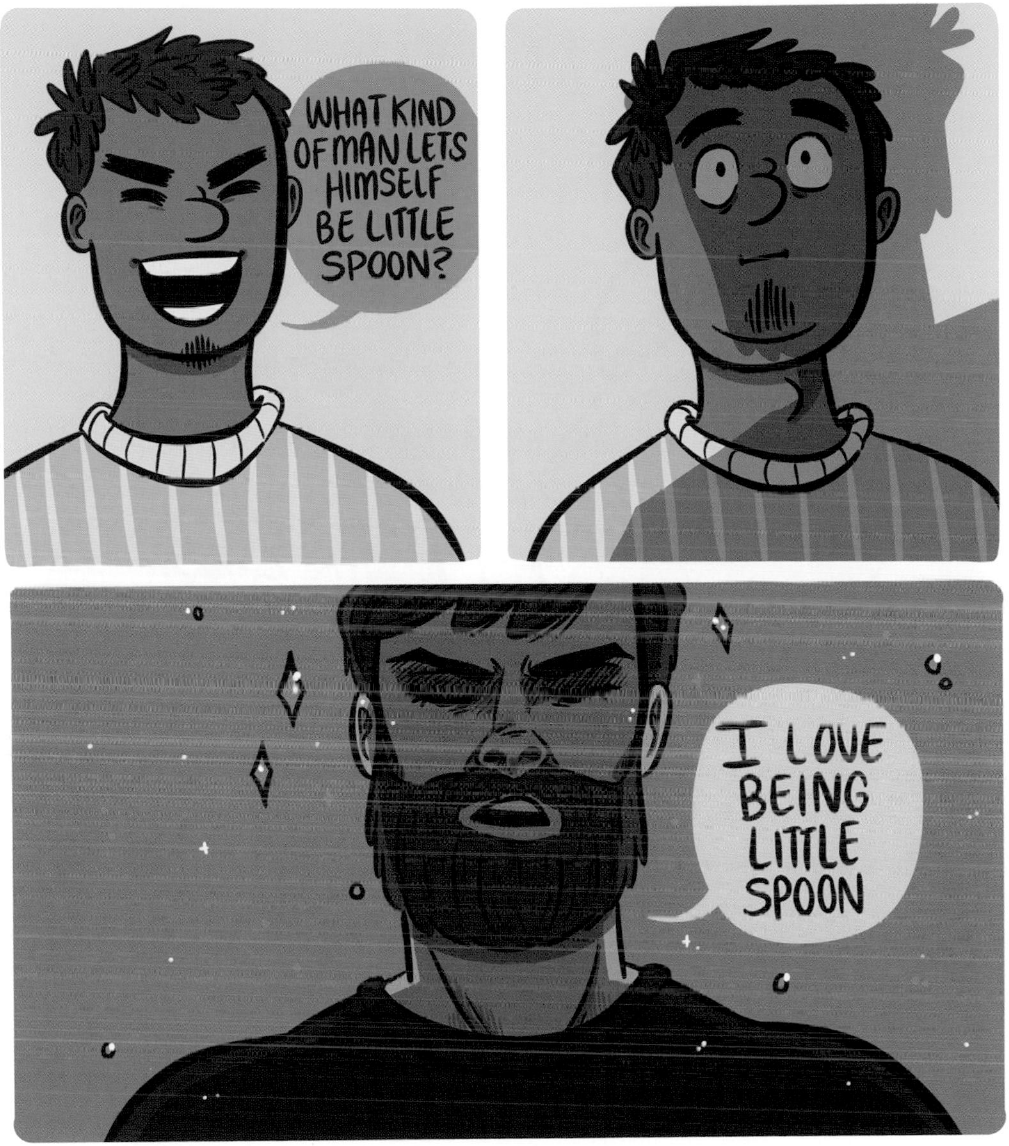
WHAT KIND OF MAN LETS HIMSELF BE LITTLE SPOON?
I LOVE BEING LITTLE SPOON

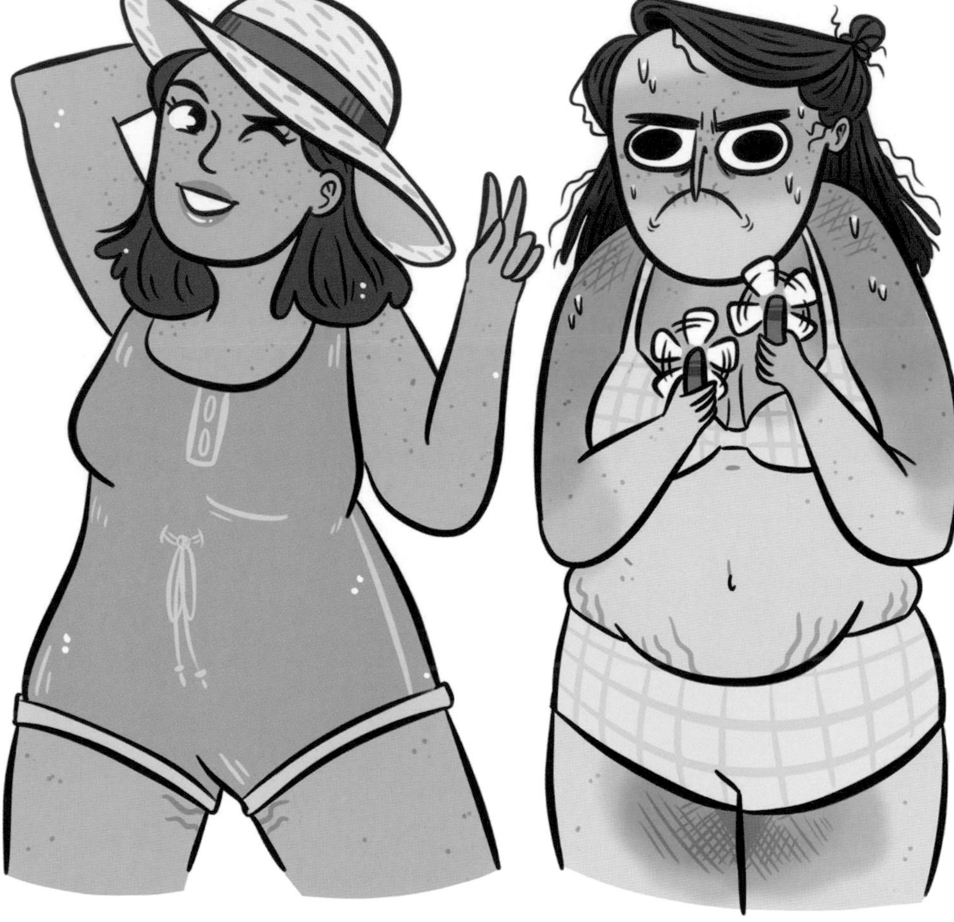
SUMMER
EXPECTATION:
REALITY:

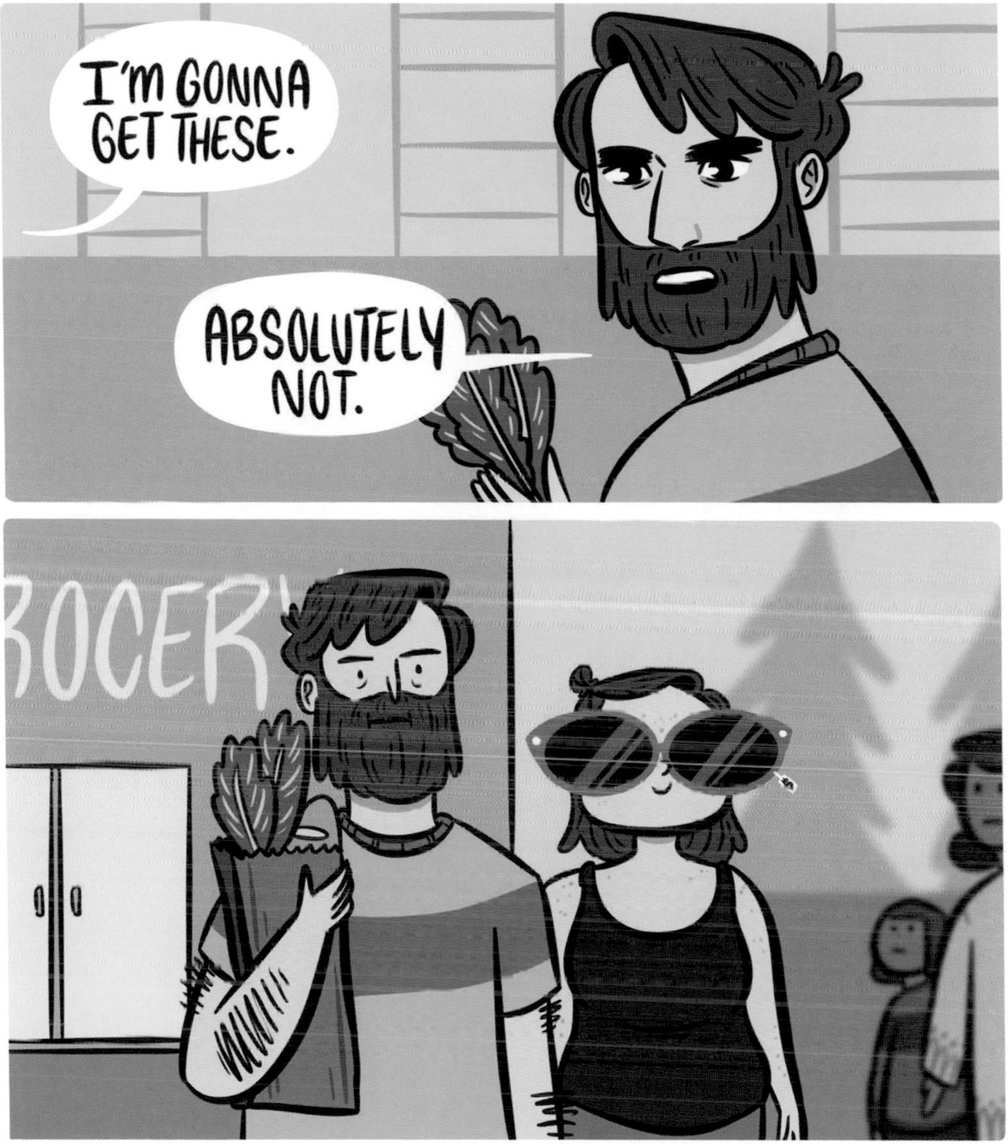
I'M GONNA GET THESE.
ABSOLUTELY NOT.

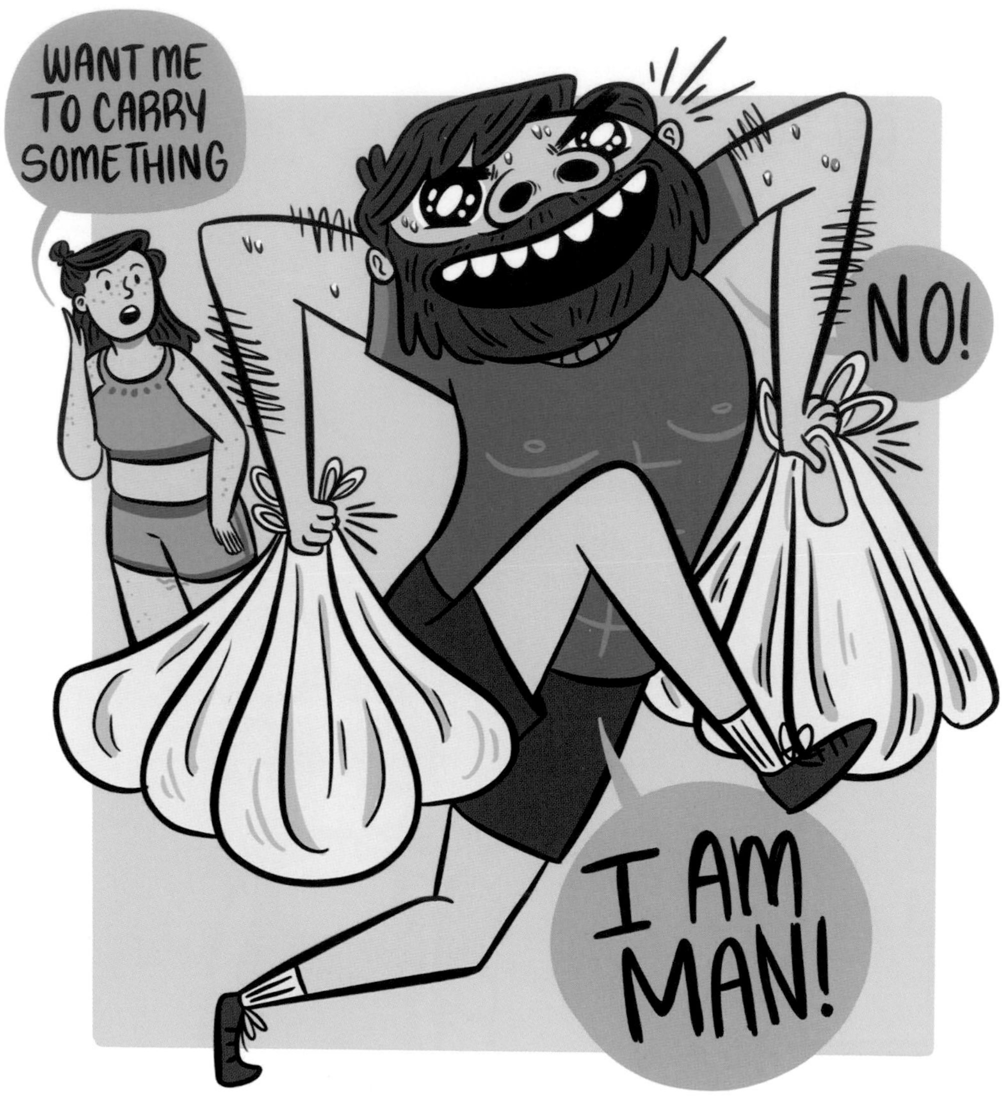
WANT ME TO CARRY SOMETHING
NO!
I AM MAN!

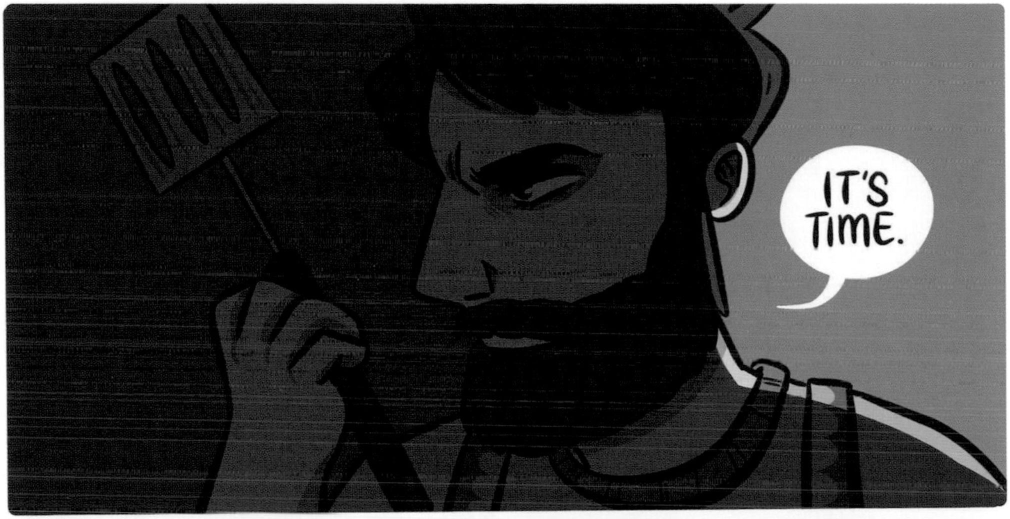
IT'S TIME.

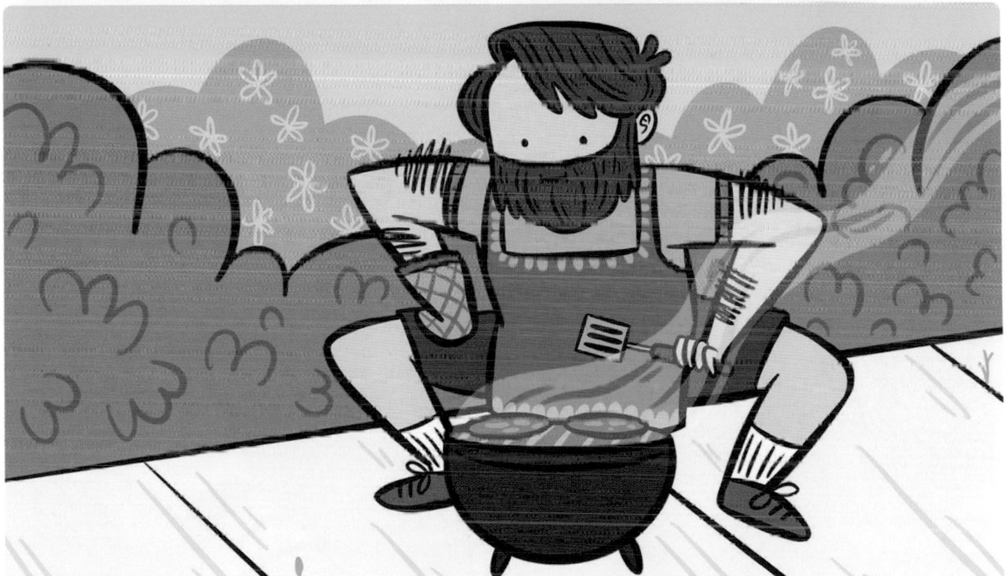

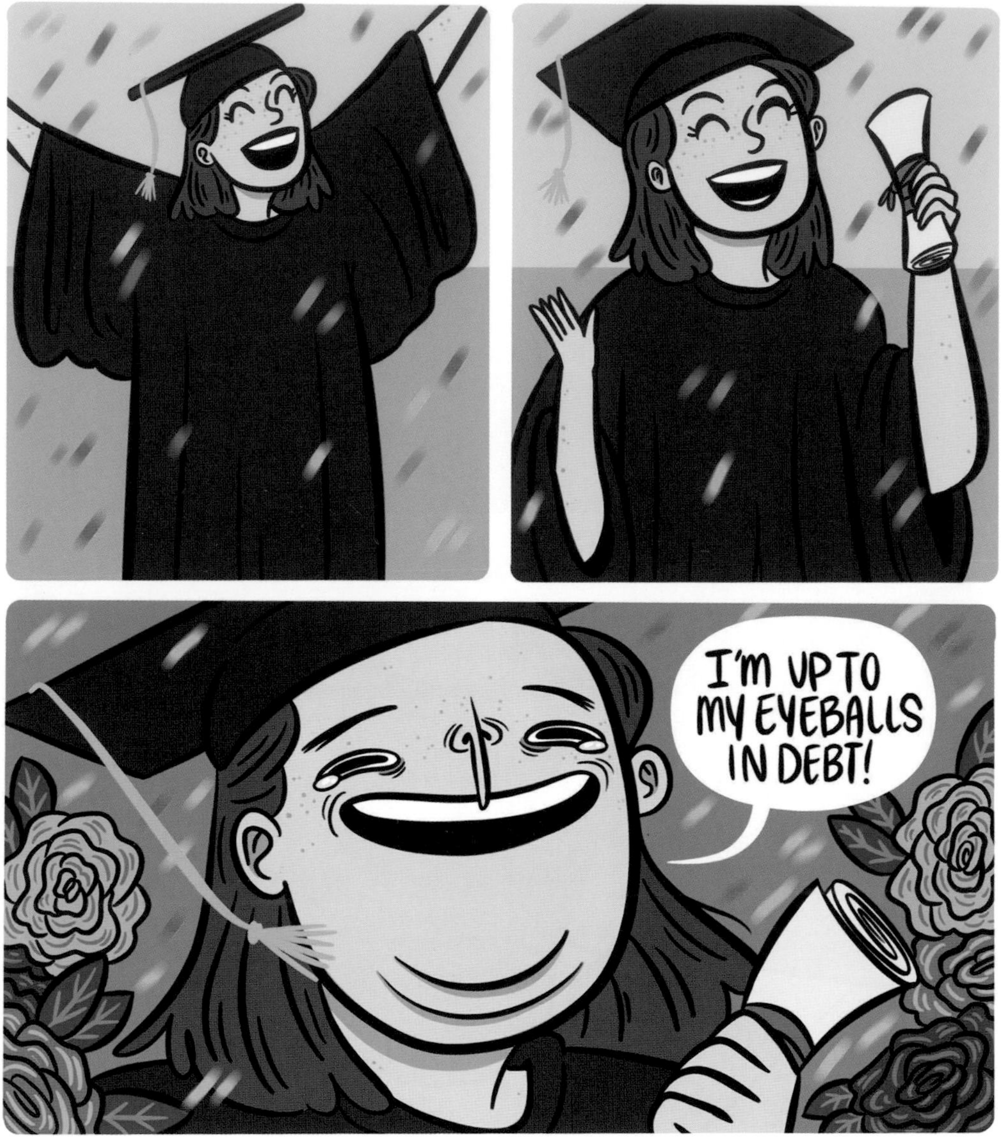
I'M UP TO MY EYEBALLS IN DEBT!

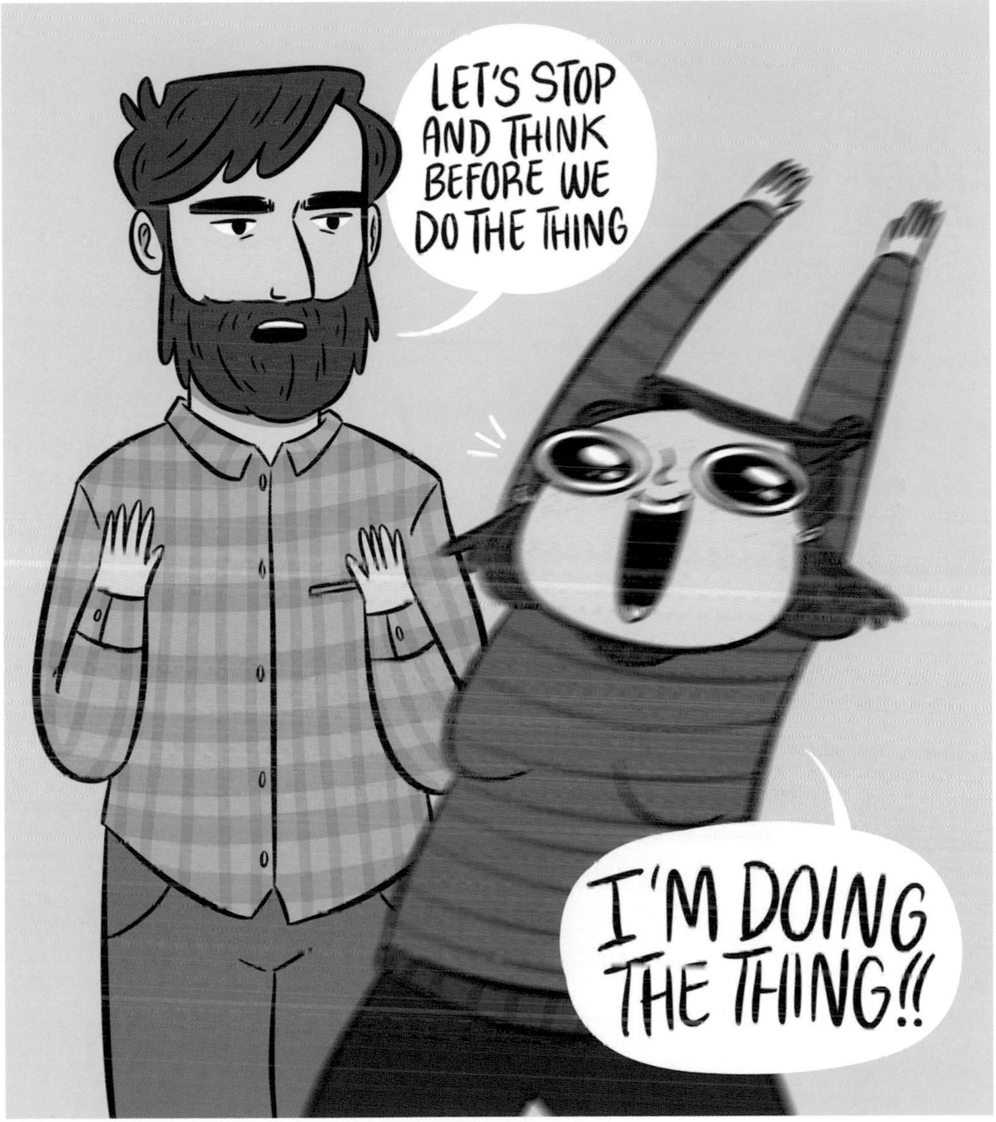
LET'S STOP AND THINK BEFORE WE DO THE THING
I'M DOING THE THING!!

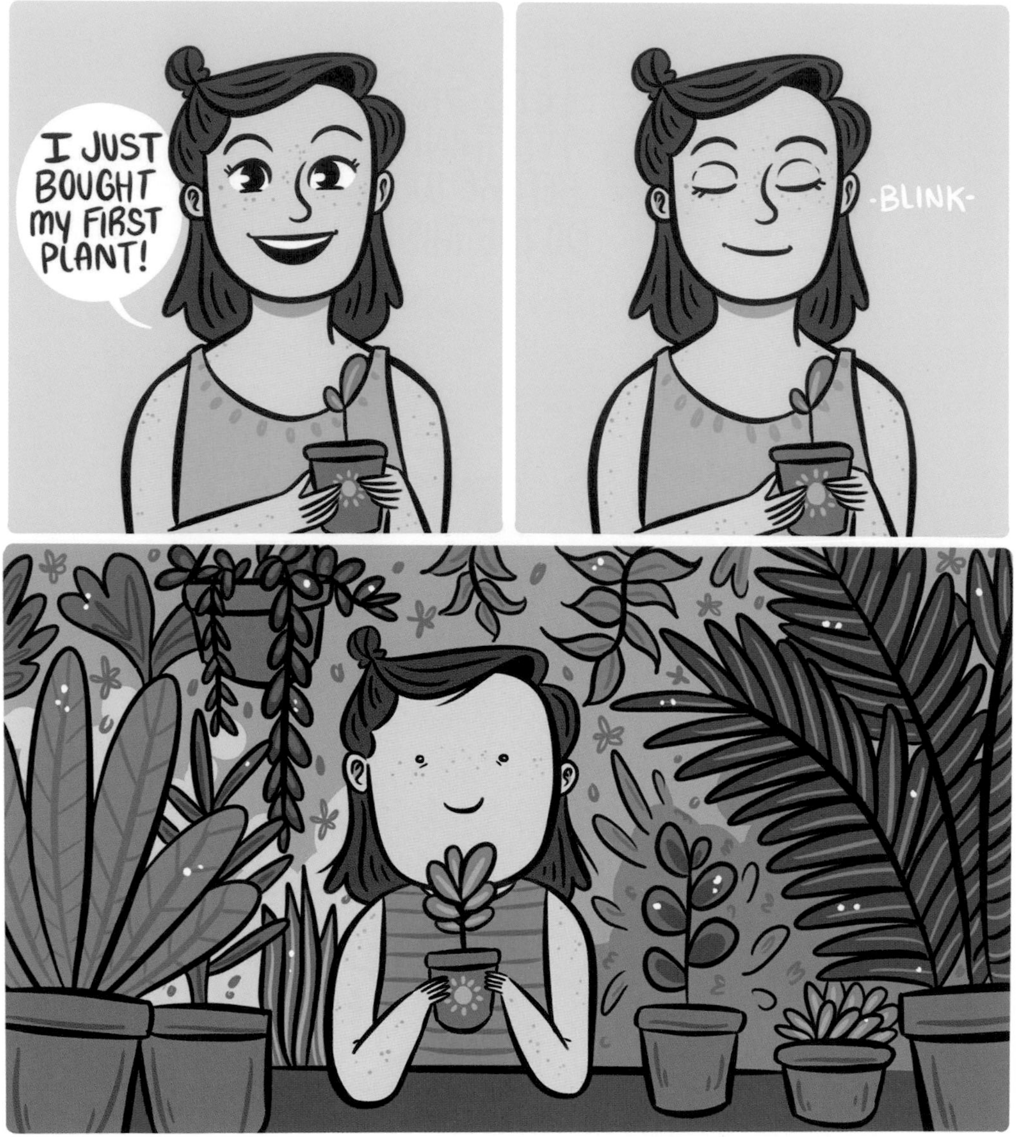
I JUST BOUGHT my FIRST PLANT!
-BLINK-

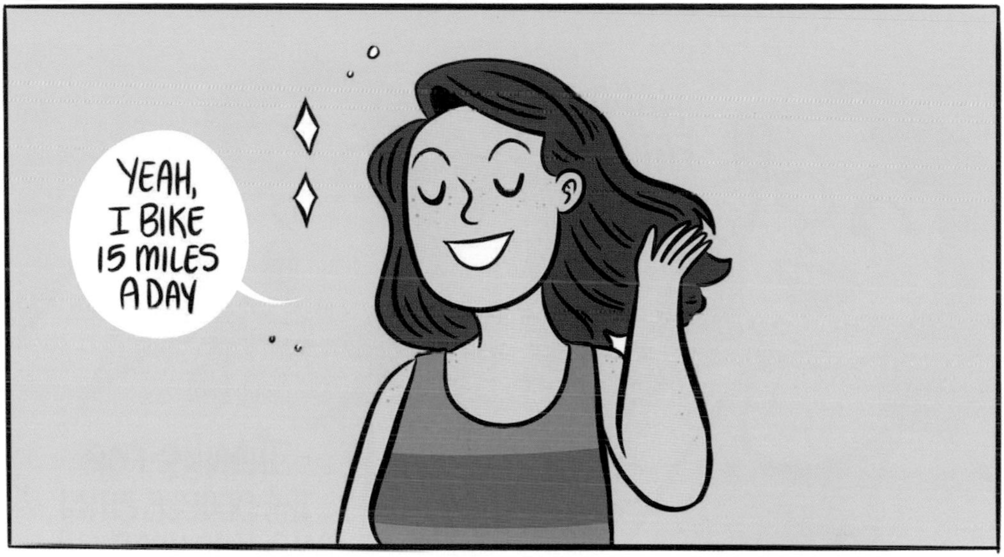
YEAH, I BIKE 15 MILES A DAY

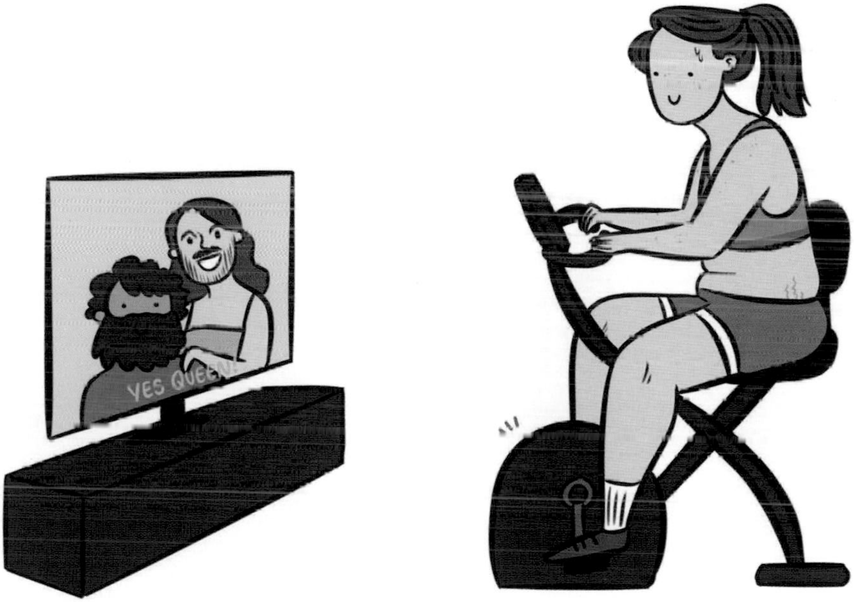
YES QUEEN!

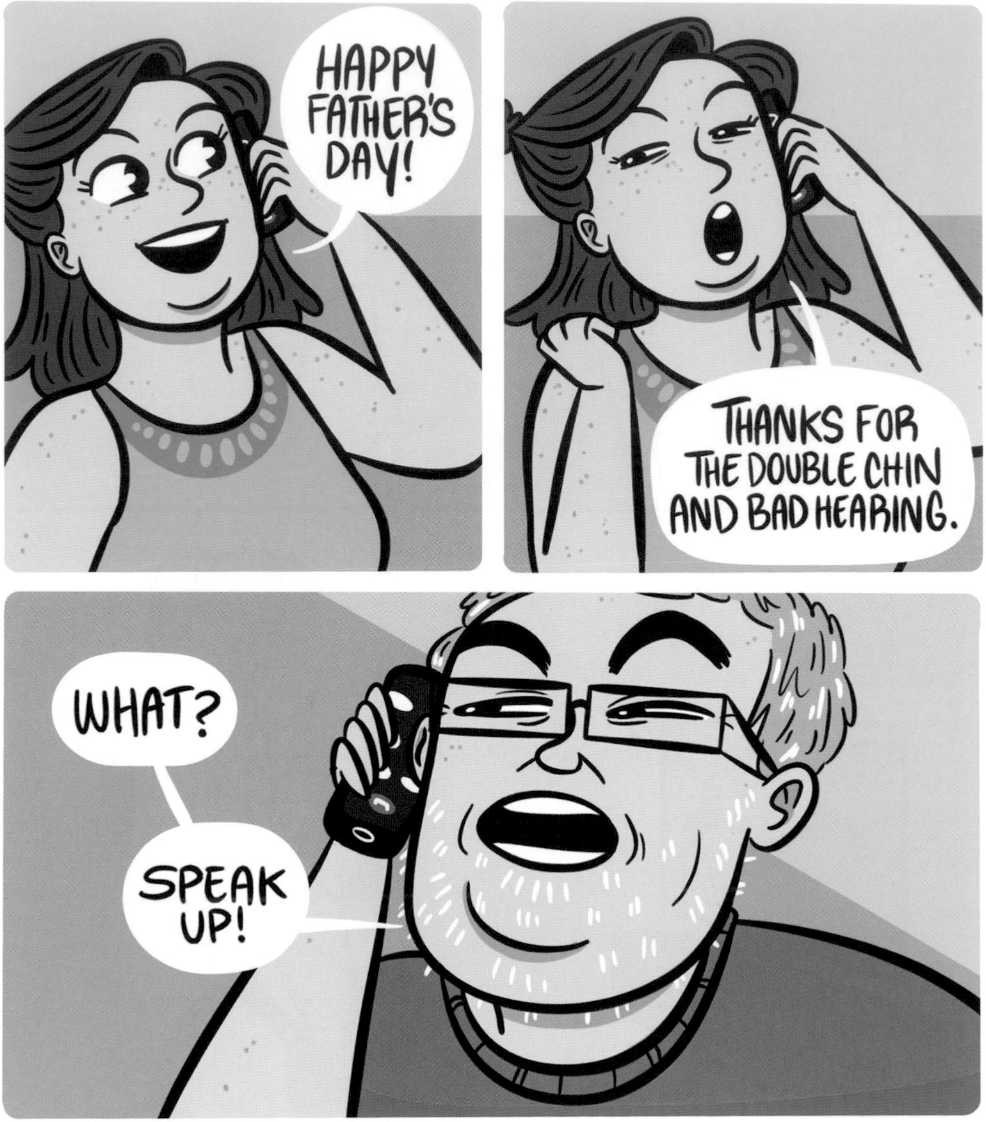
HAPPY FATHER'S DAY!
THANKS FOR THE DOUBLE CHIN AND BAD HEARING.
WHAT?
SPEAK UP!

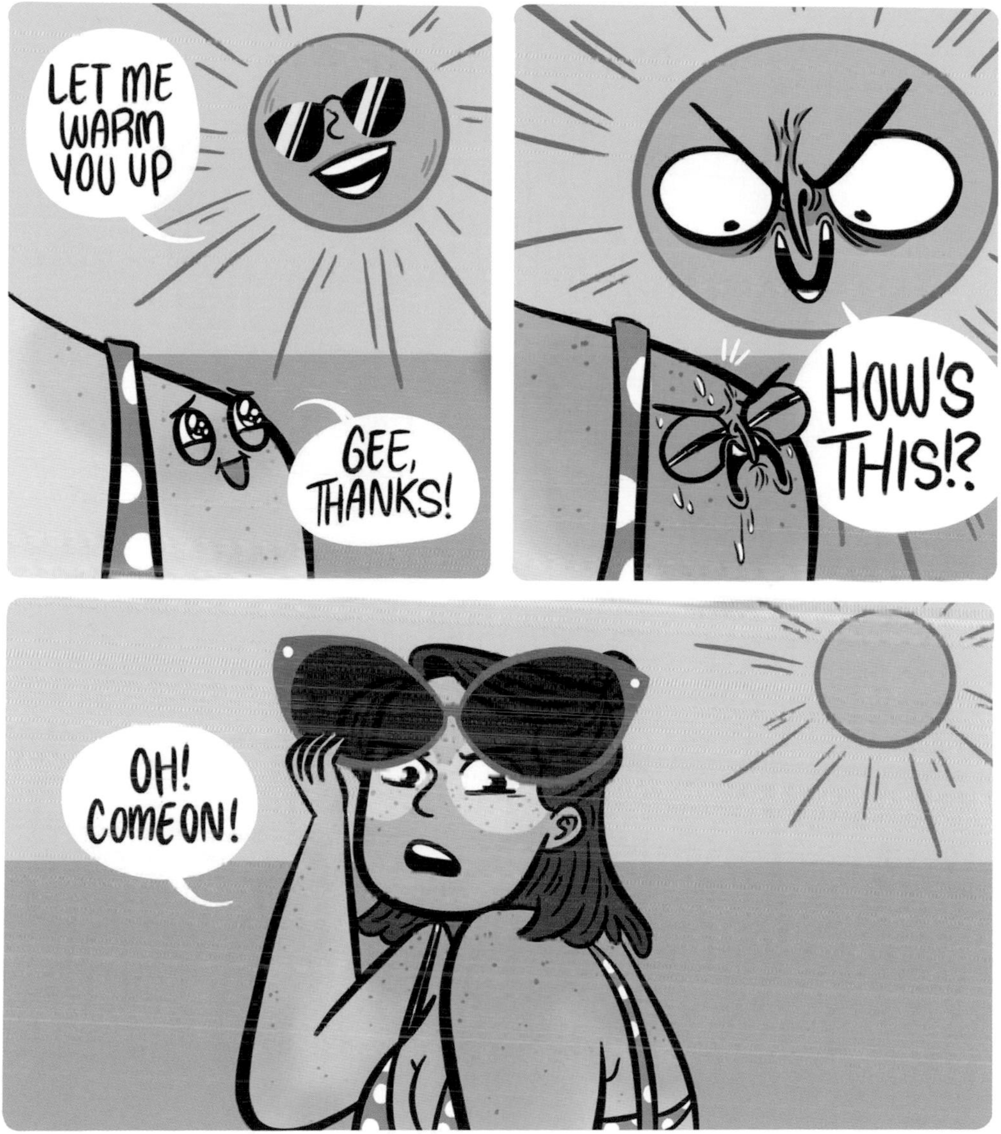

LET ME WARM YOU UP
GEE, THANKS!
HOW'S THIS!?
OH! COMEON!

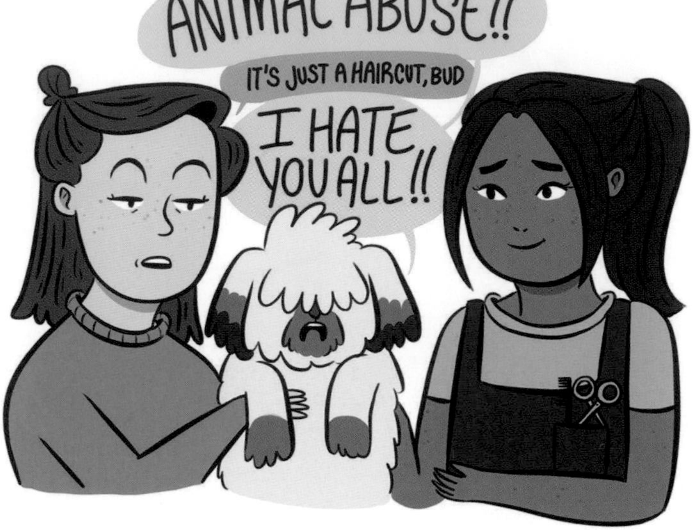
ANIMAL ABUSE!!
IT'S JUST A HAIRCUT, BUD
I HATE YOU ALL!!

2 HOURS LATER:

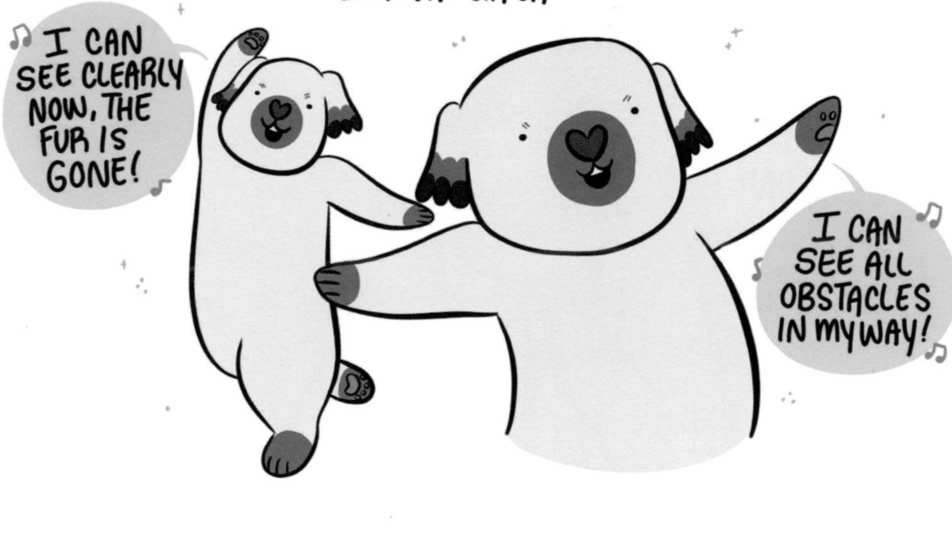
I CAN SEE CLEARLY NOW, THE FUR IS GONE!
I CAN SEE ALL OBSTACLES IN MY WAY!

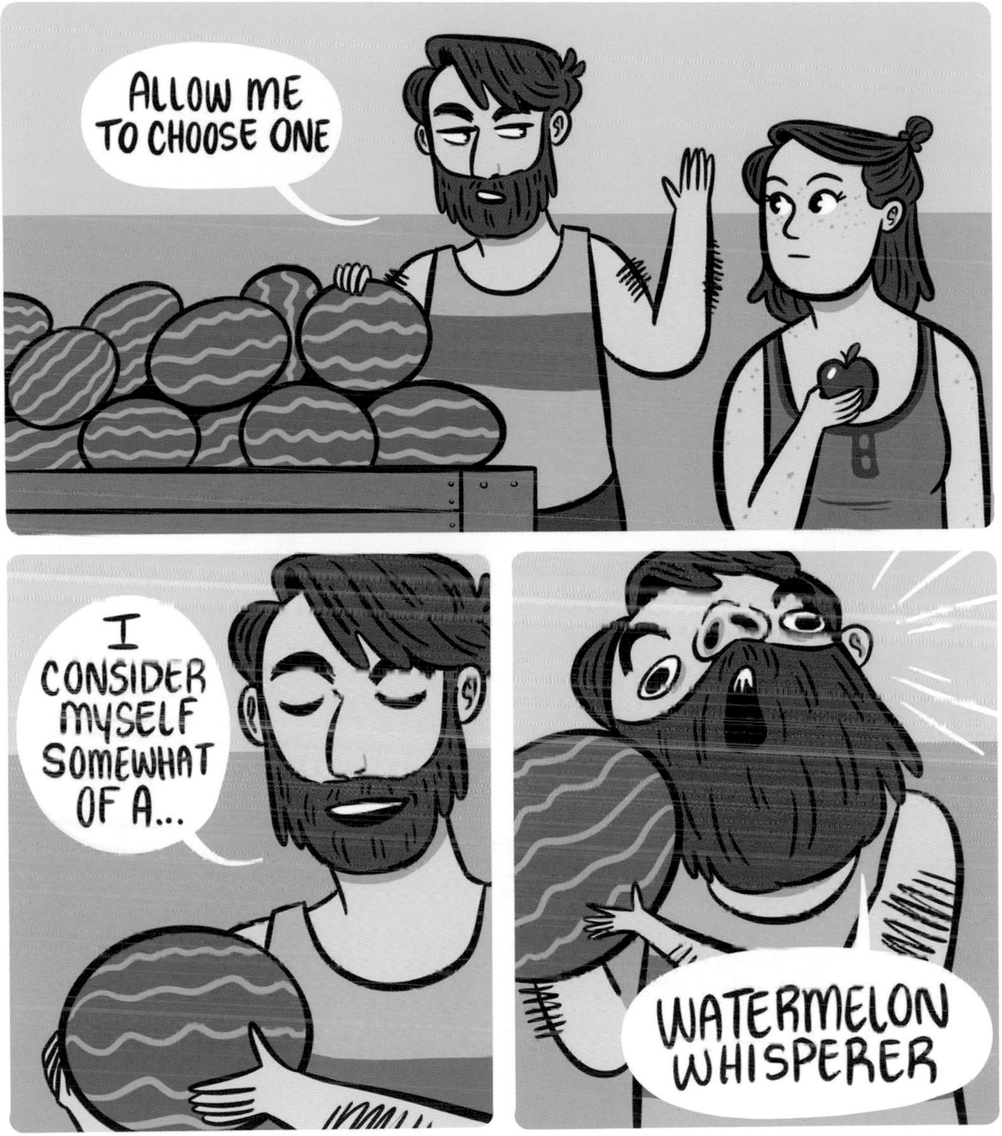
ALLOW ME TO CHOOSE ONE
I CONSIDER MYSELF SOMEWHAT OF A...
WATERMELON WHISPERER

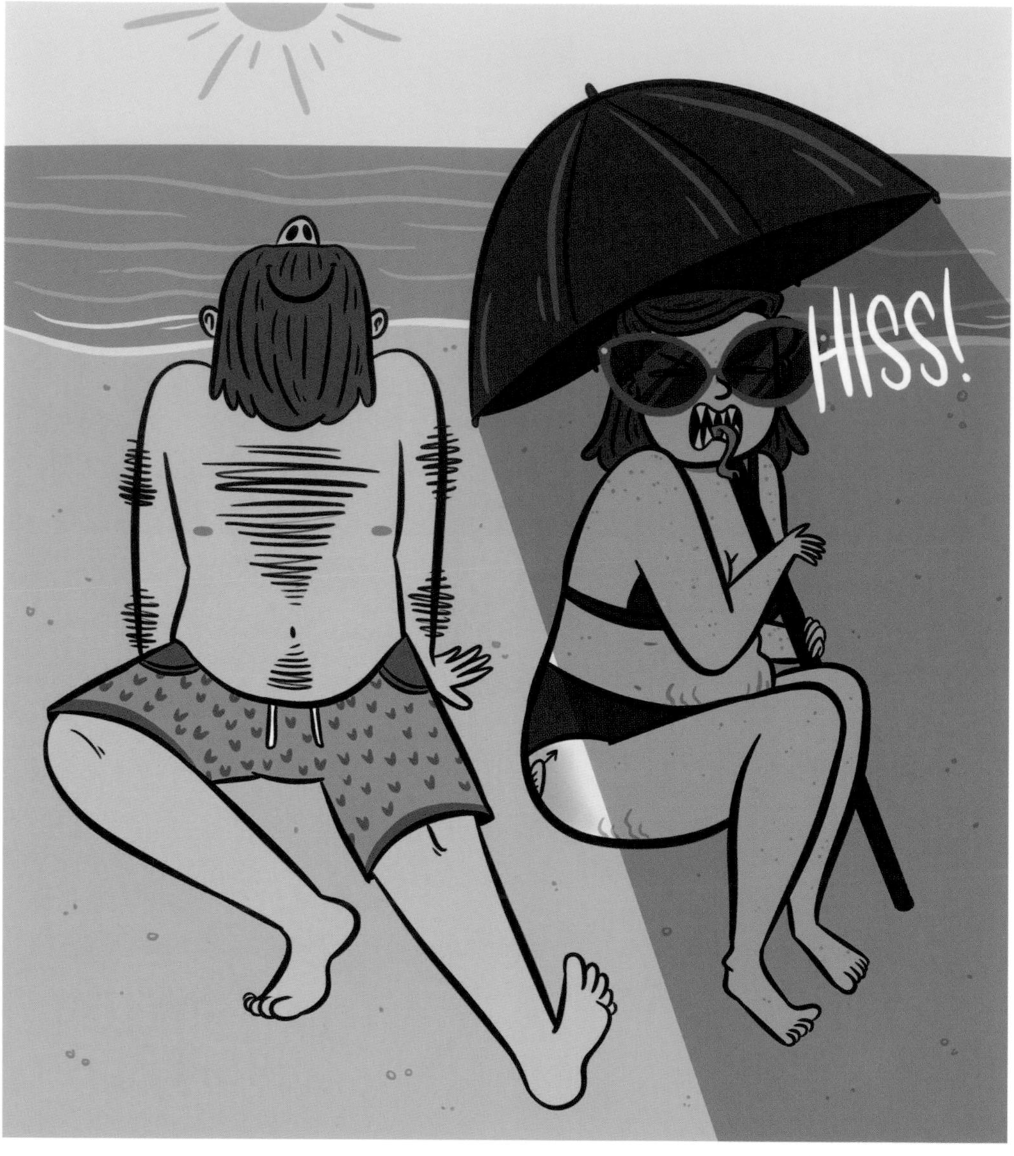
HISS!

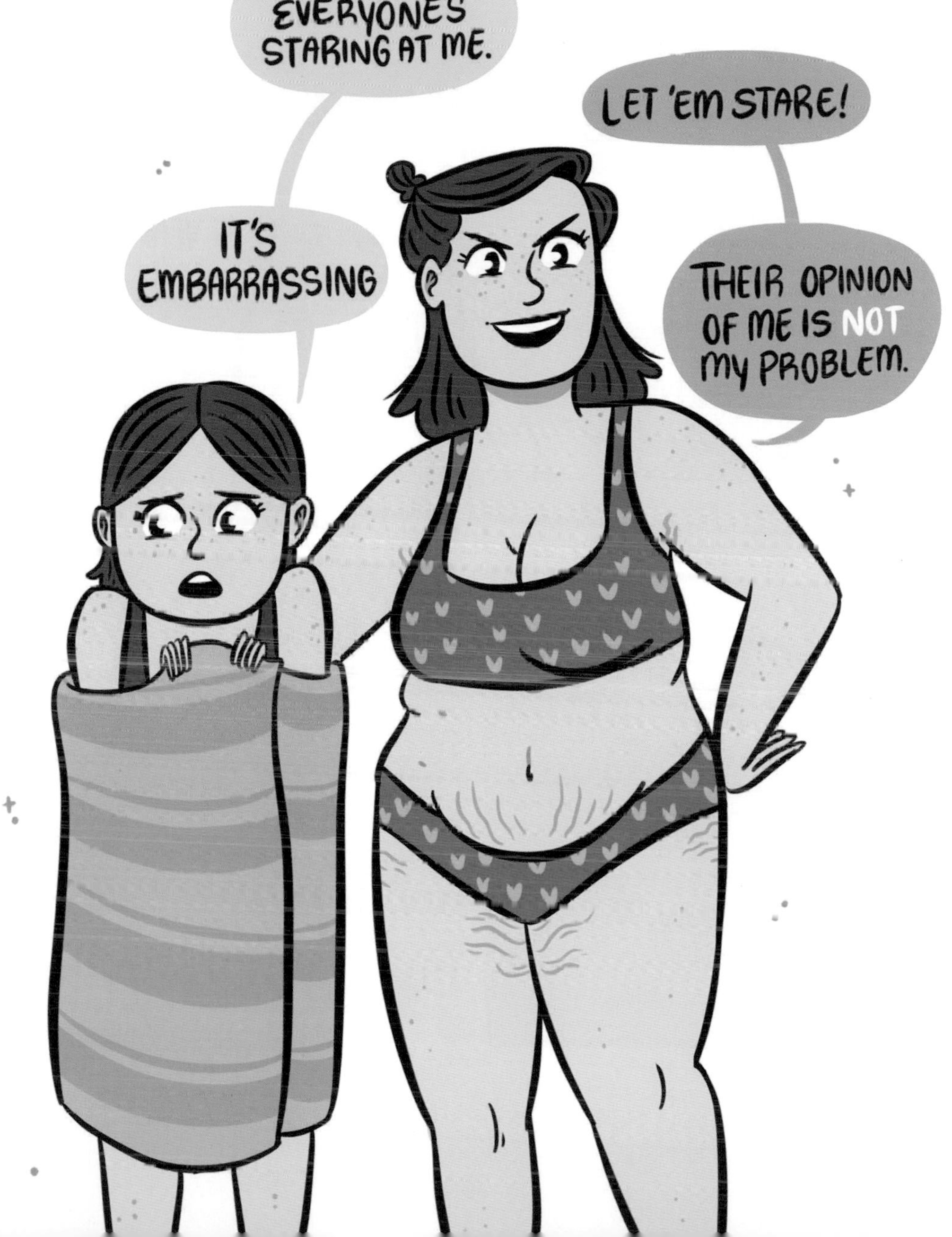
I'M SO FAT. EVERYONE'S STARING AT ME.
IT'S EMBARRASSING
LET 'EM STARE!
THEIR OPINION OF ME IS NOT MY PROBLEM.

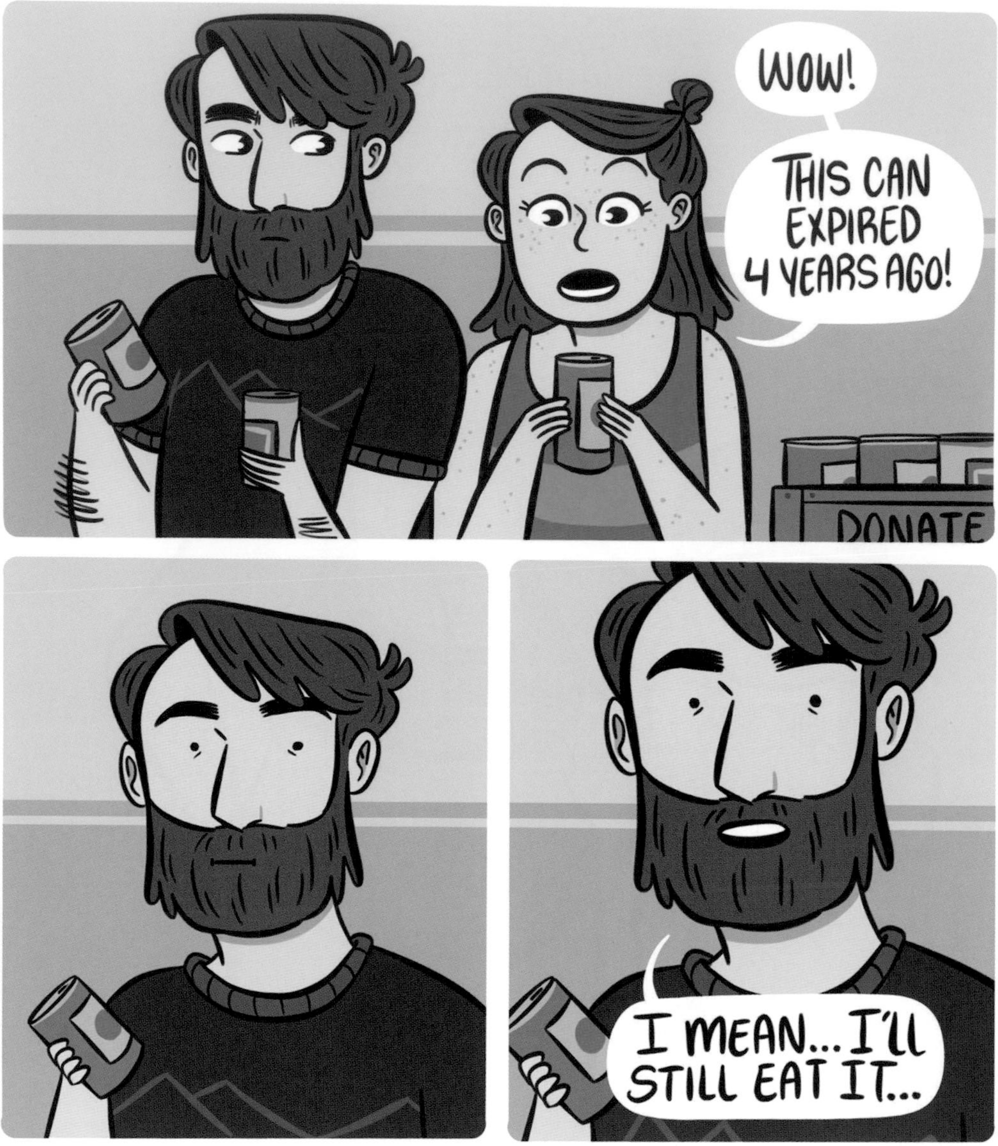
WOW!
THIS CAN EXPIRED 4 YEARS AGO!
DONATE
I MEAN... I'LL STILL EAT IT...

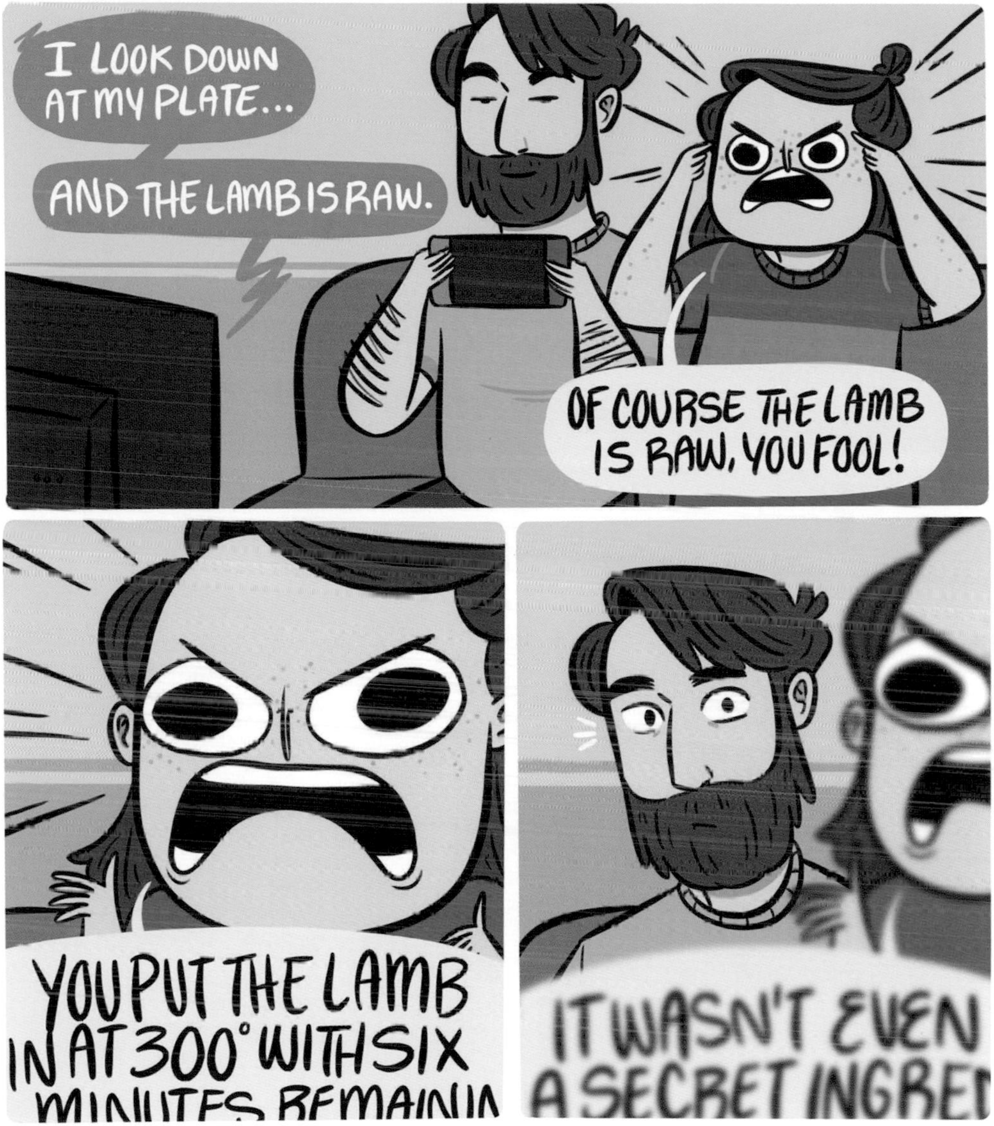
I LOOK DOWN AT MY PLATE...
AND THE LAMB IS RAW.
OF COURSE THE LAMB IS RAW, YOU FOOL!
YOU PUT THE LAMB IN AT 300° WITH SIX
IT WASN'T EVEN
A SECRET INGRE

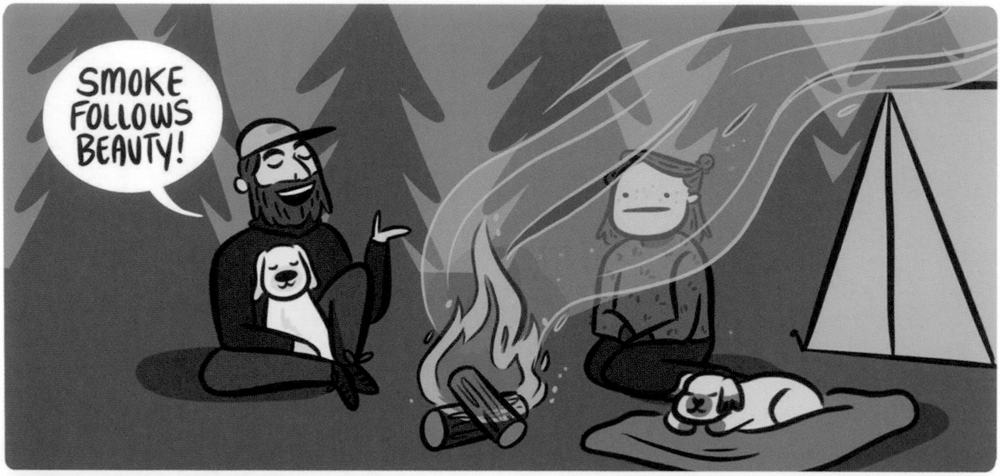
SMOKE FOLLOWS BEAUTY!

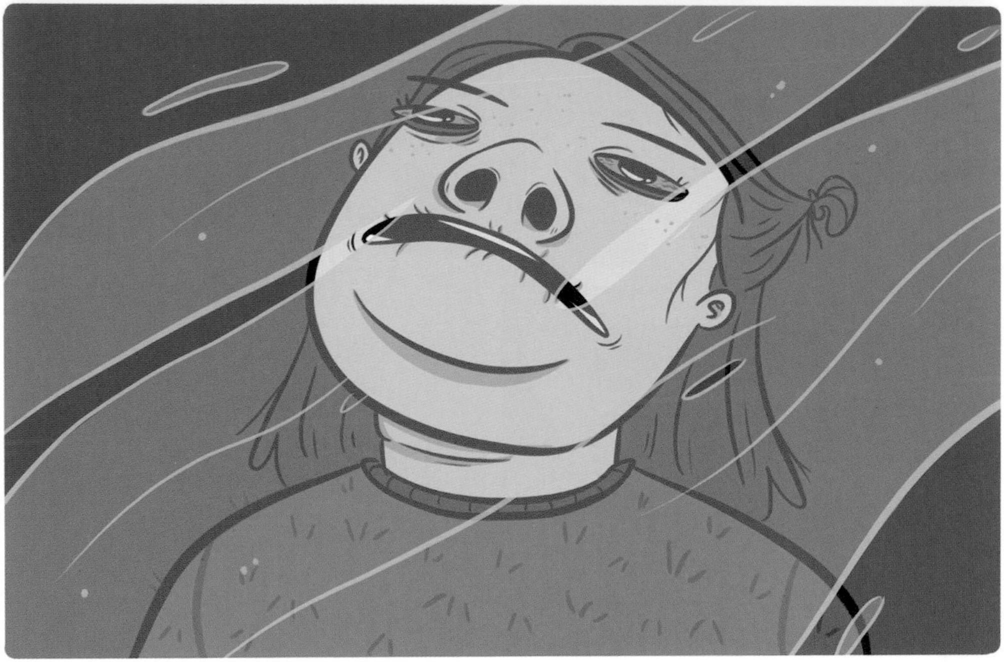

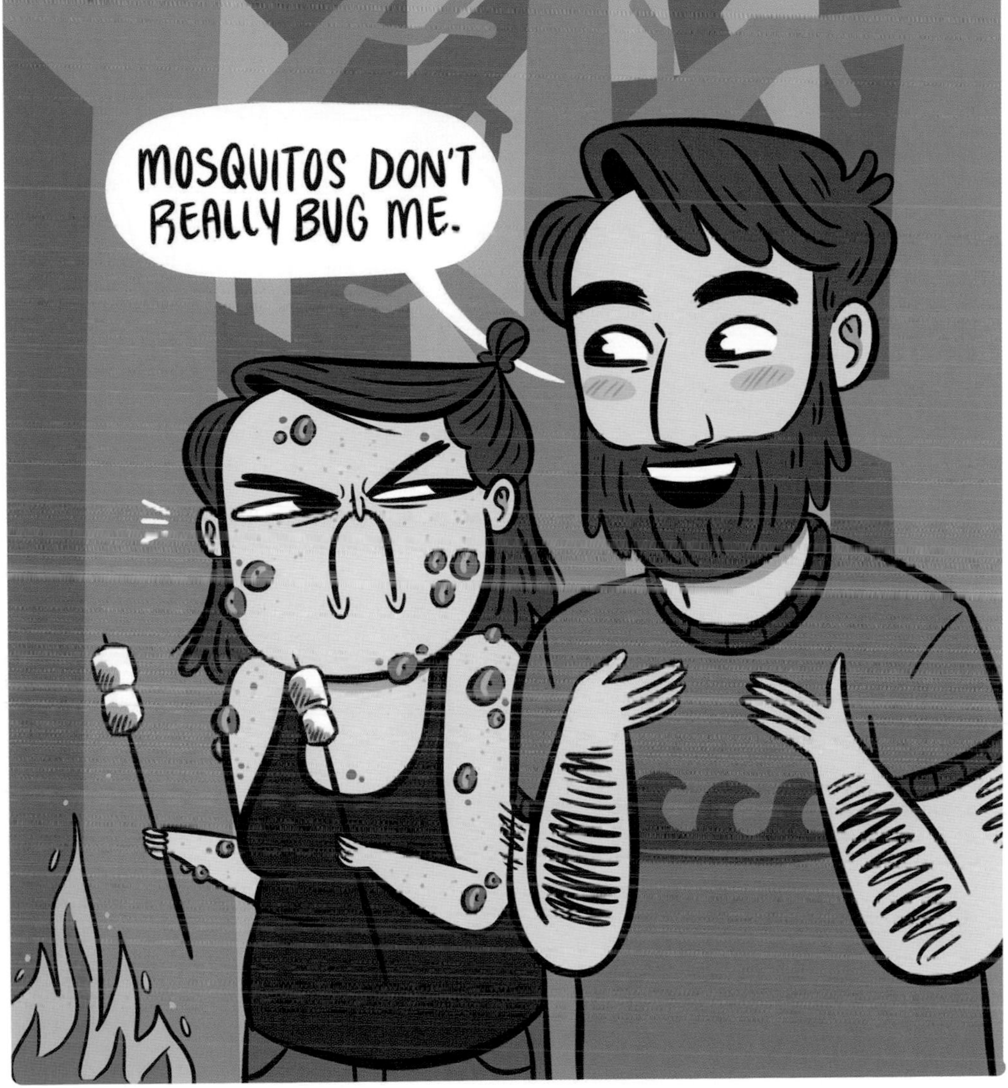
MOSQUITOS DON'T REALLY BUG ME.

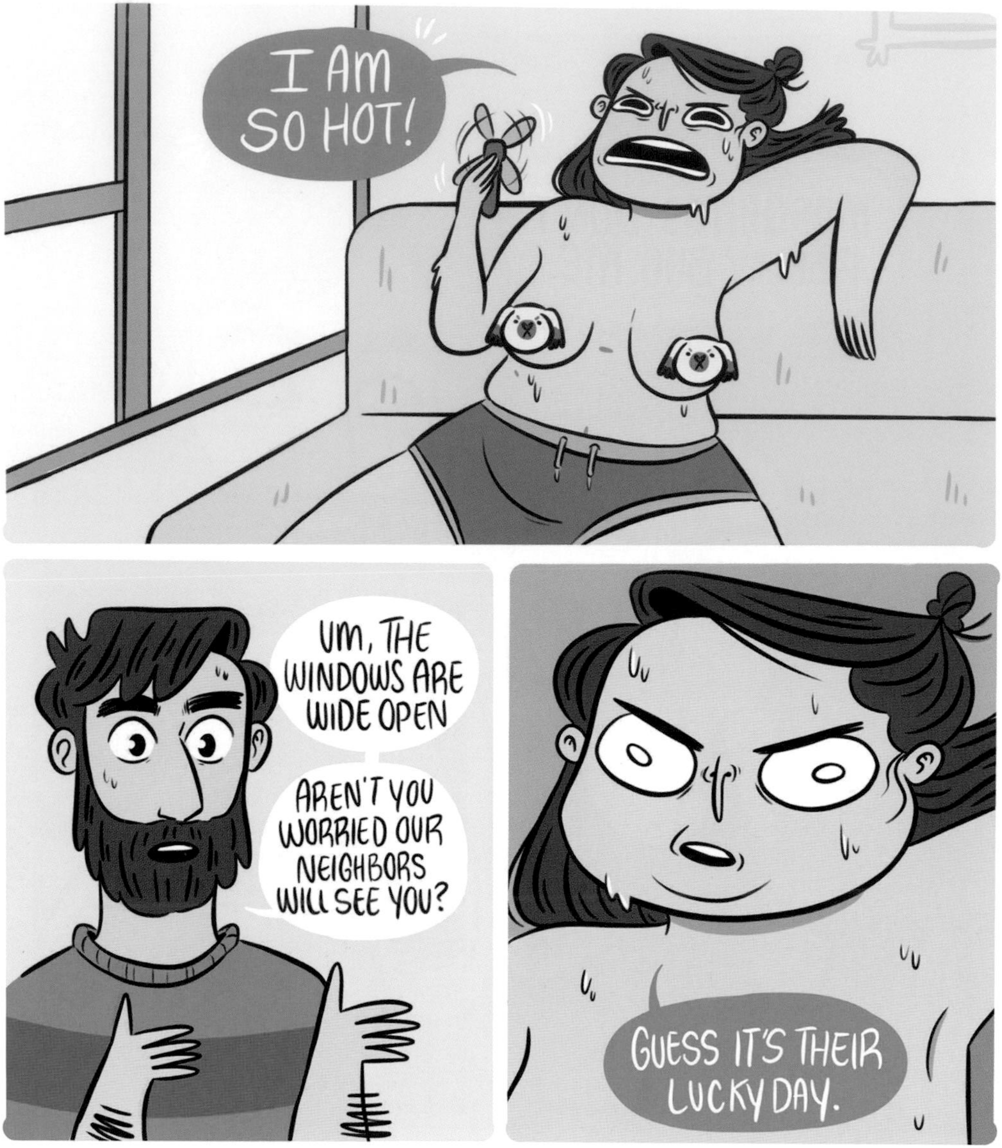
I AM SO HOT!
UM, THE WINDOWS ARE WIDE OPEN
AREN'T YOU WORRIED OUR NEIGHBORS WILL SEE YOU?
GUESS IT'S THEIR LUCKY DAY.

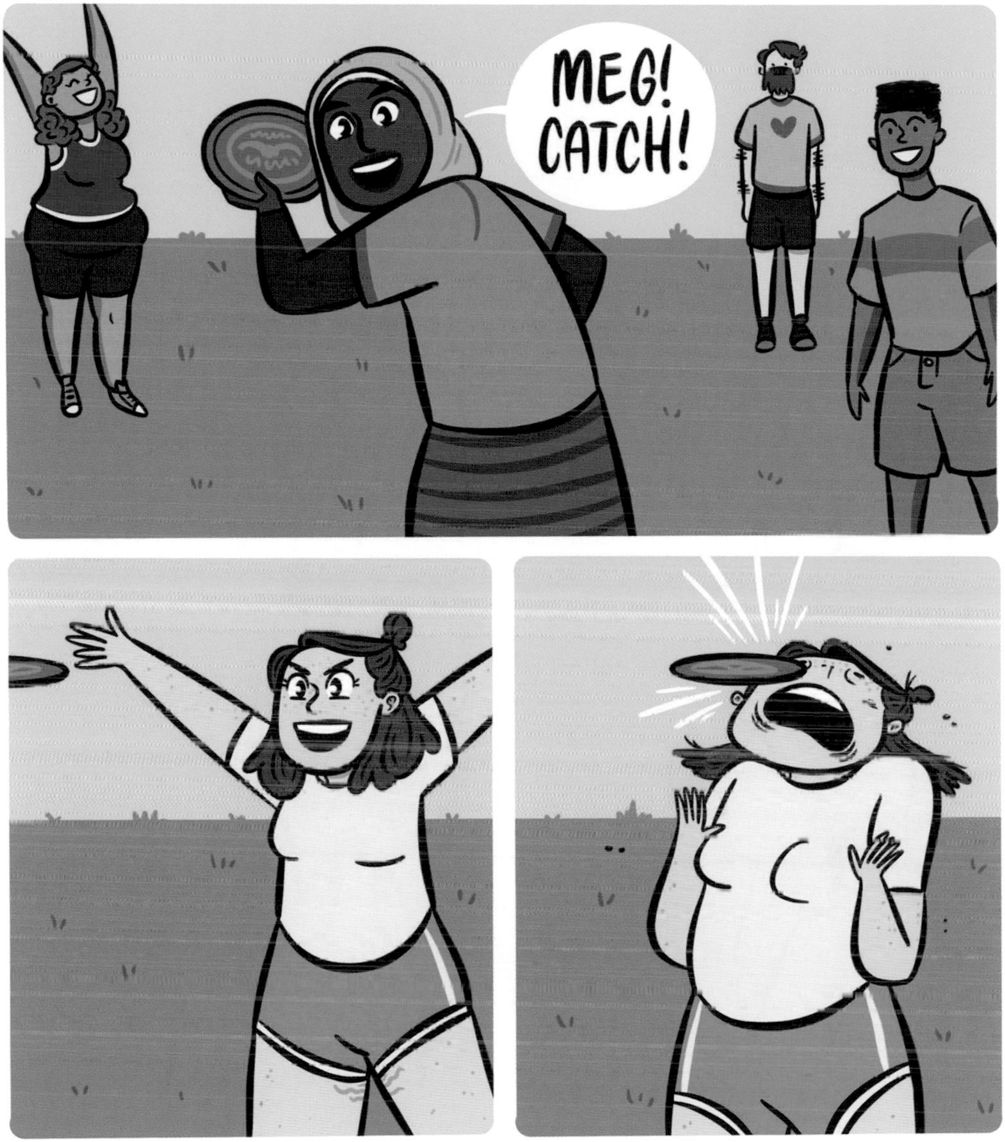
MEG!
CATCH!

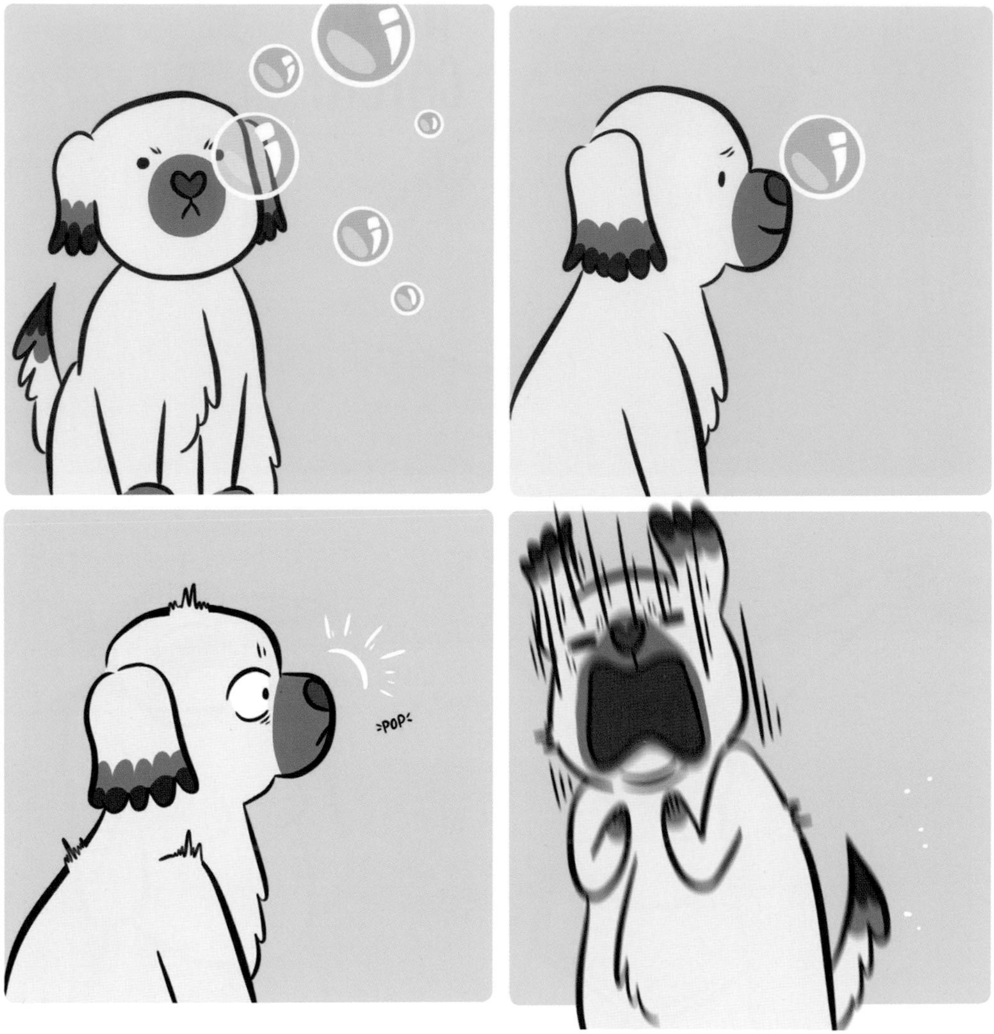
POP

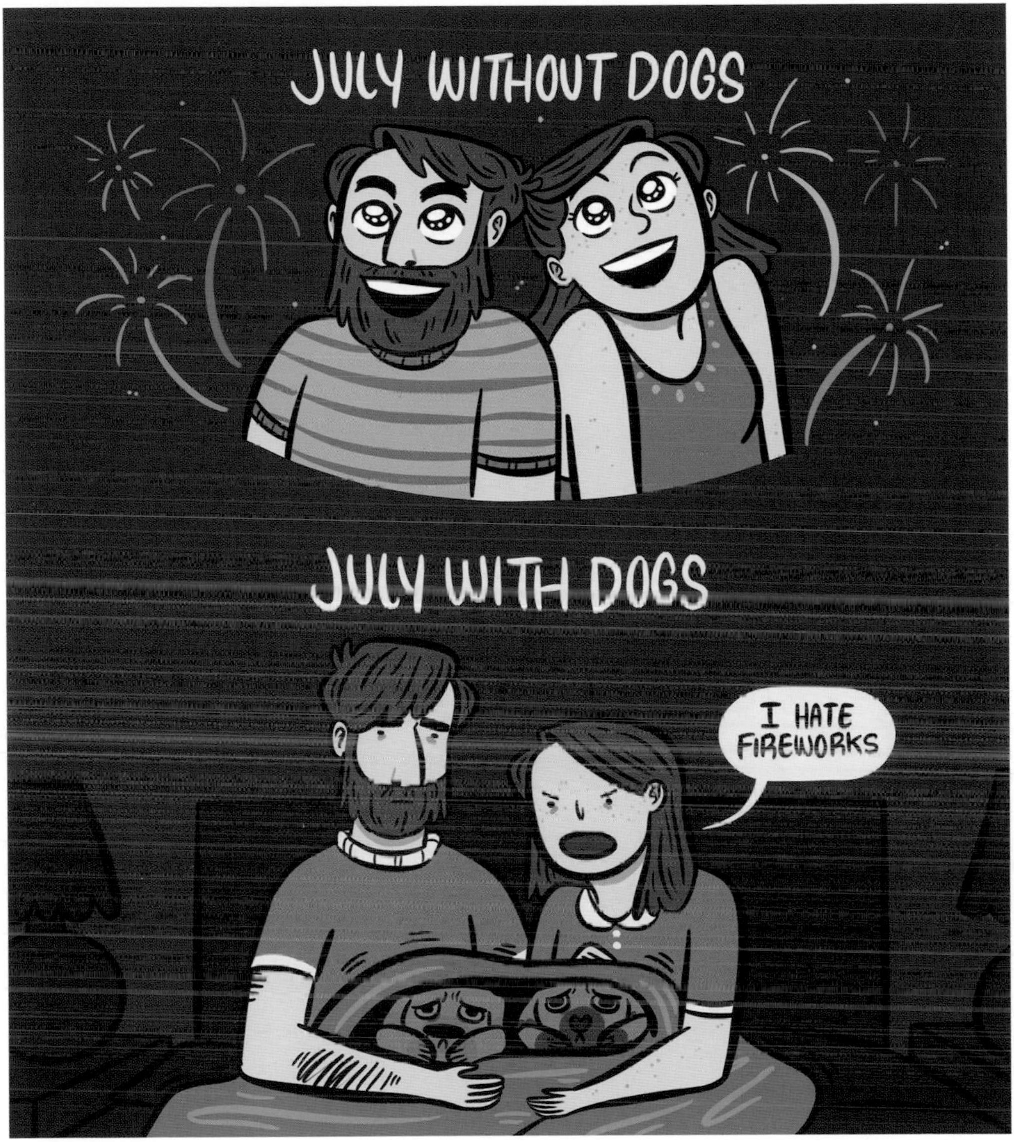
JULY WITHOUT DOGS
JULY WITH DOGS
I HATE FIREWORKS

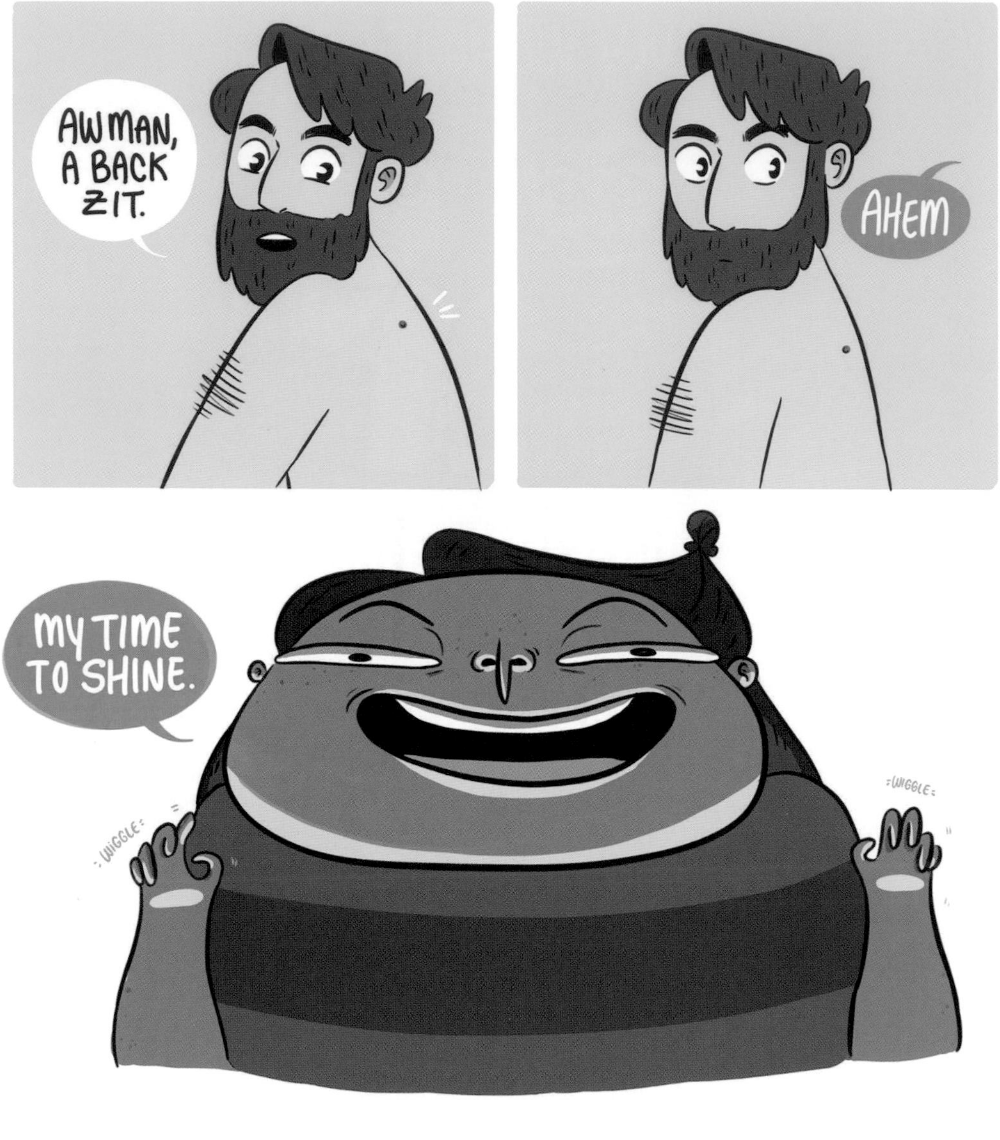
AW MAN, A BACK ZIT.
AHEM
MY TIME TO SHINE.
WIGGLE
WIGGLE

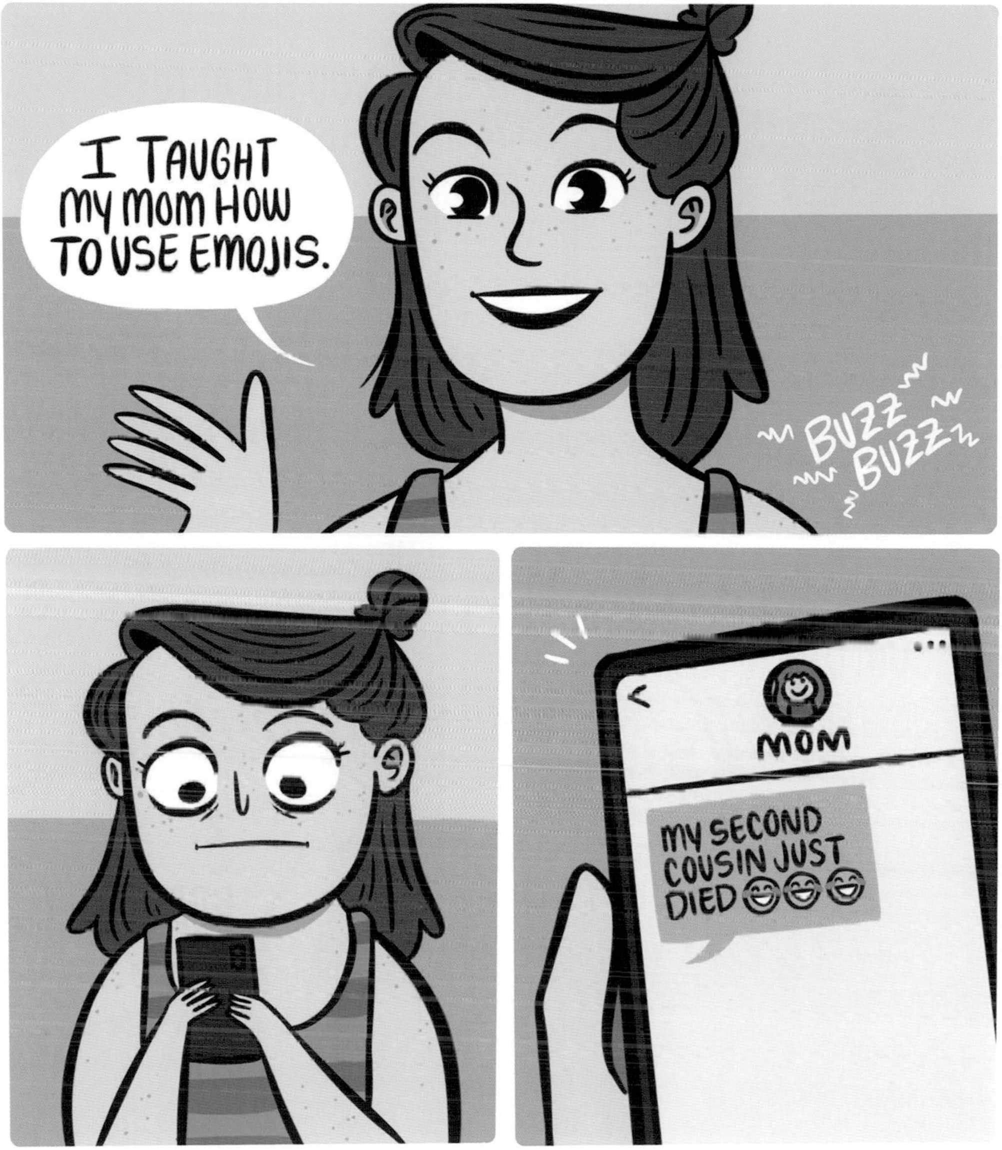
I TAUGHT MY MOM HOW TO USE EMOJIS.
BUZZ BUZZ
MOM
MY SECOND COUSIN JUST DIED 😂😂😂

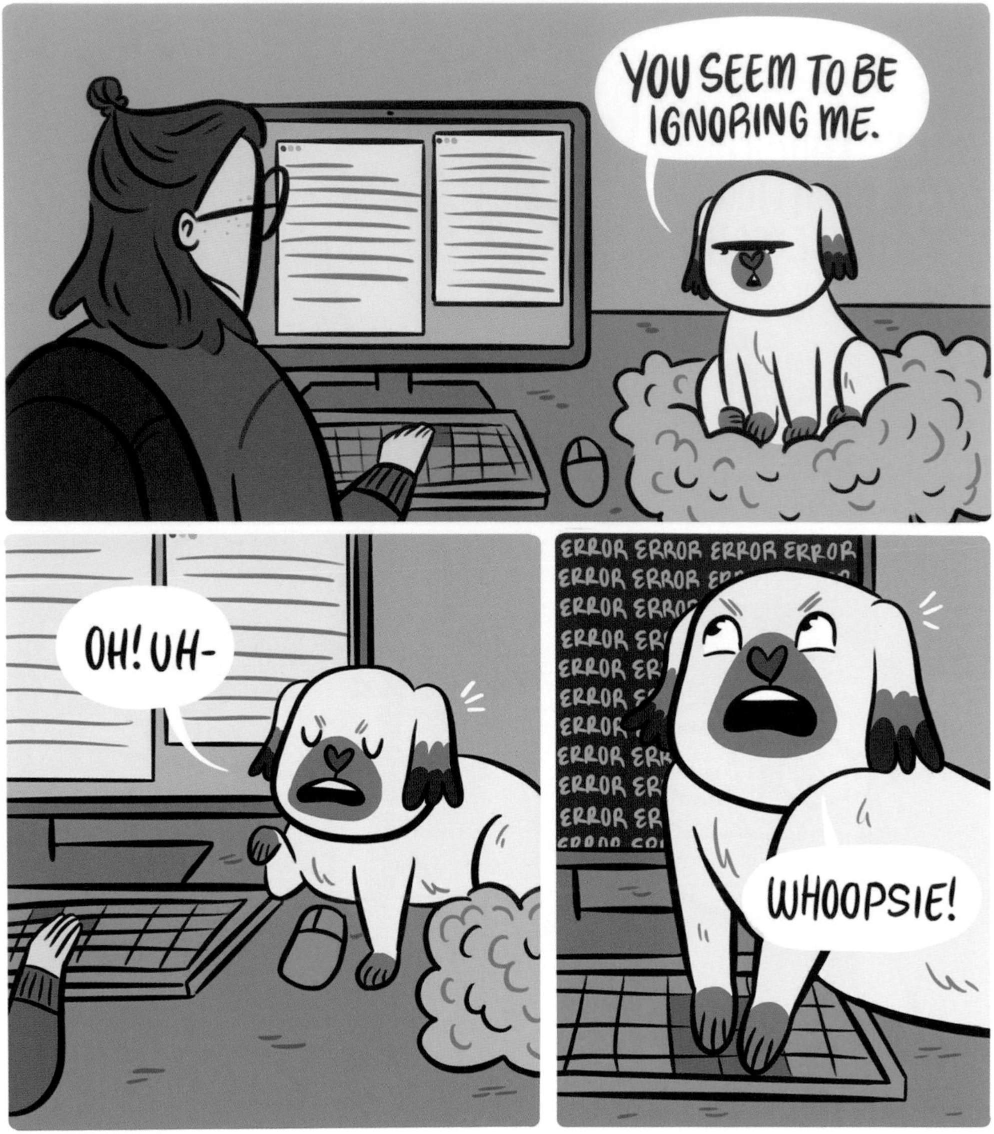
YOU SEEM TO BE IGNORING ME.
OH! UH-
ERROR ERROR ERROR ERROR
WHOOPSIE!

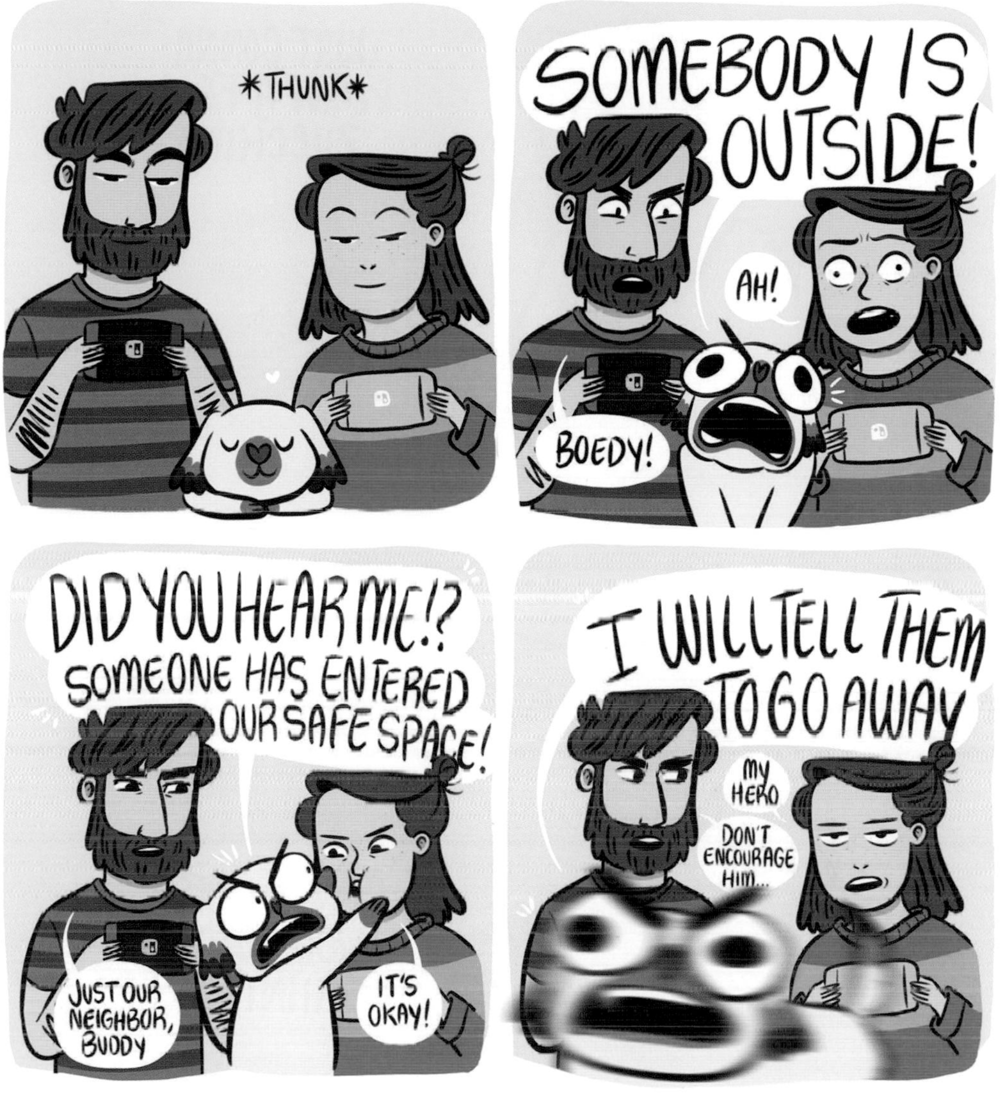
THUNK
SOMEBODY IS OUTSIDE!
AH!
BOEDY!
DID YOU HEAR ME!? SOMEONE HAS ENTERED OUR SAFE SPACE!
JUST OUR NEIGHBOR, BUDDY
IT'S OKAY!
I WILL TELL THEM TO GO AWAY
MY HERO
DON'T ENCOURAGE HIM...

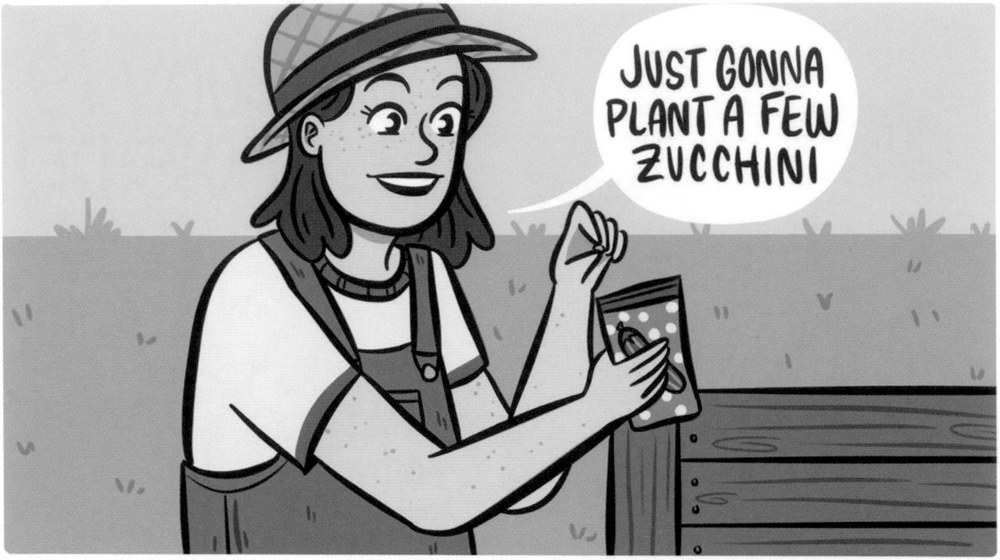
JUST GONNA PLANT A FEW ZUCCHINI

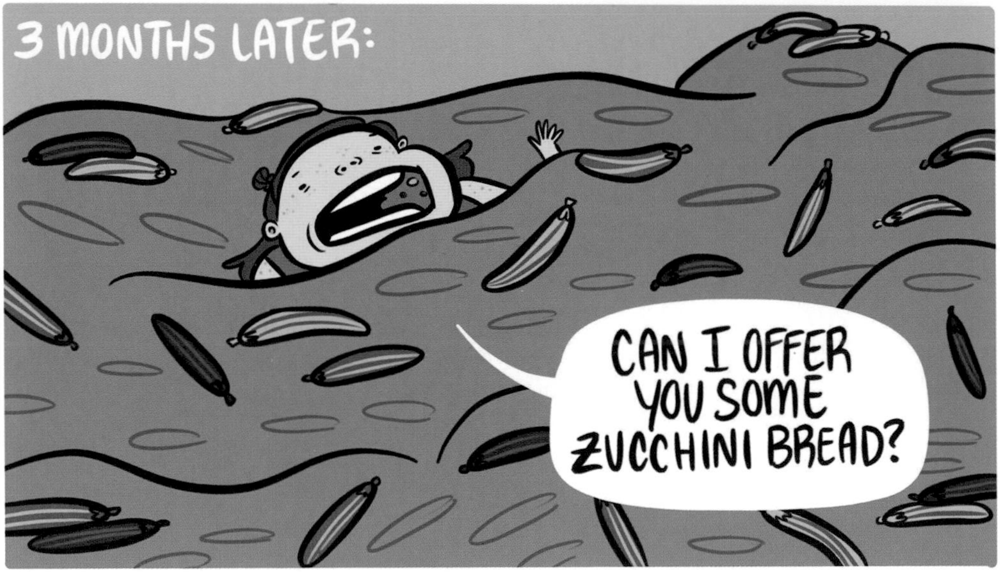
3 MONTHS LATER:
CAN I OFFER YOU SOME ZUCCHINI BREAD?

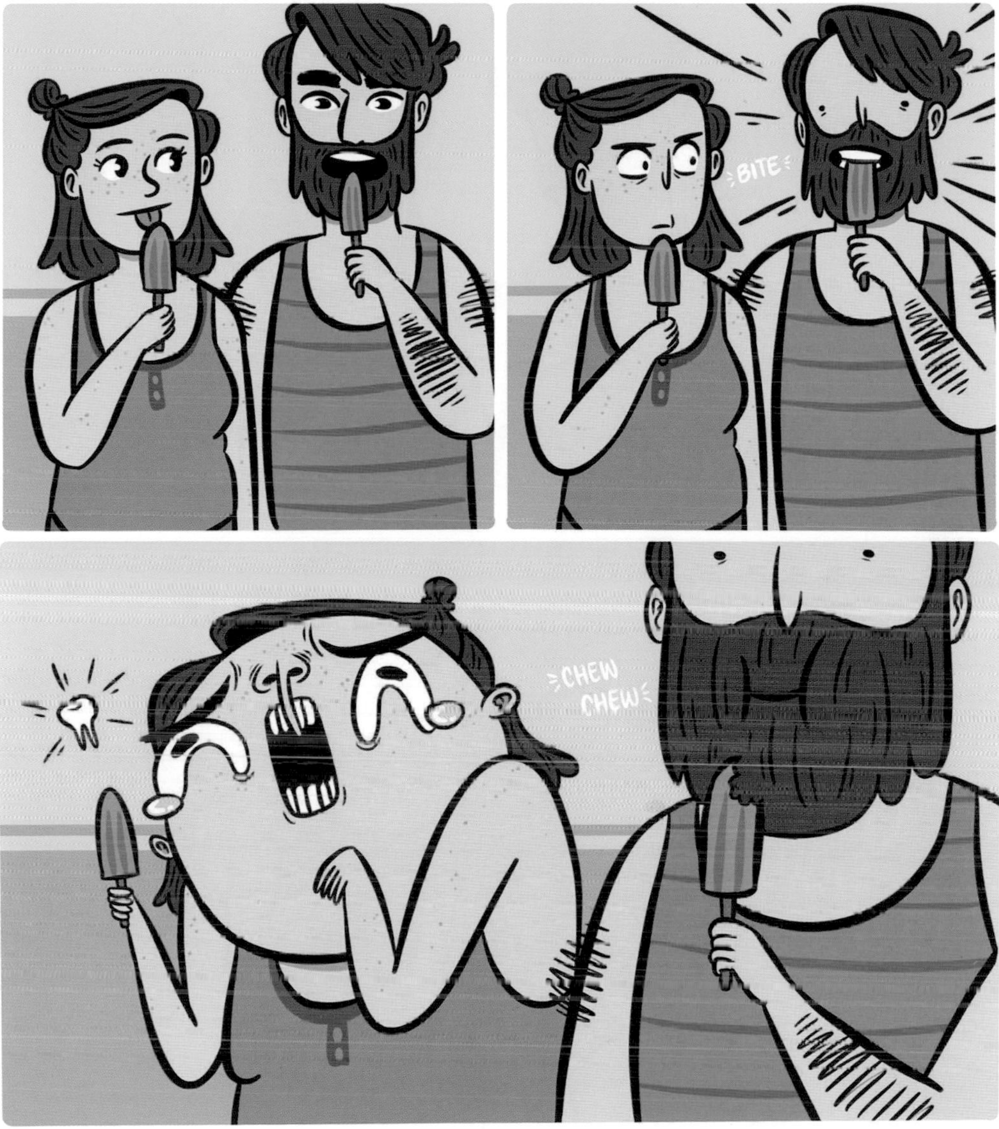
BITE
CHEW
CHEW

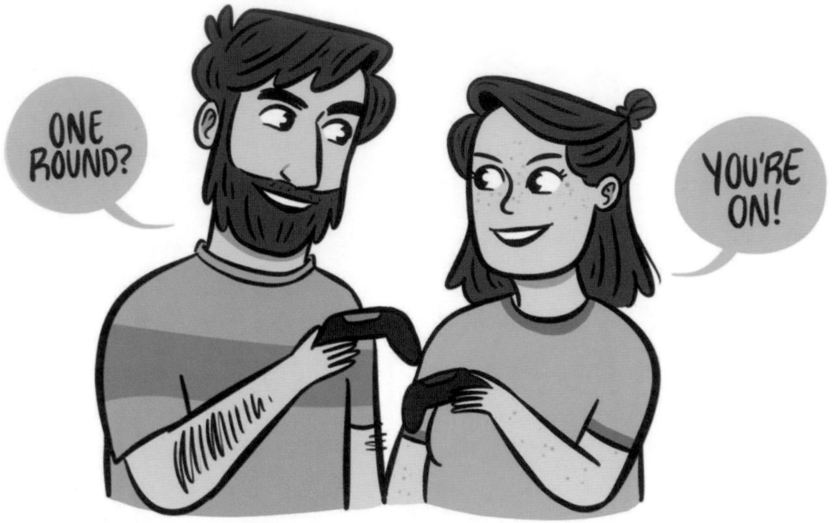
ONE ROUND?
YOU'RE ON!

5 MINUTES LATER:

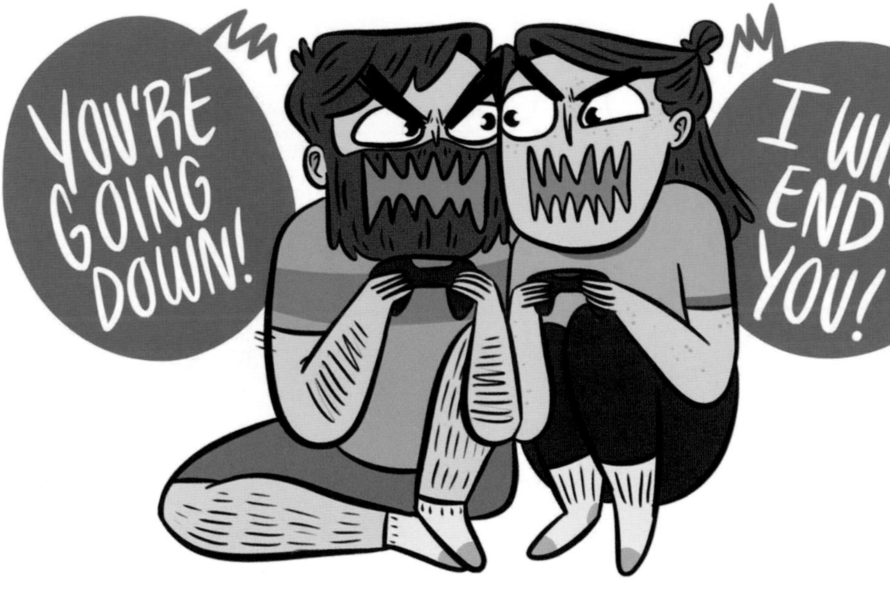
YOU'RE GOING DOWN!
I WILL END YOU!

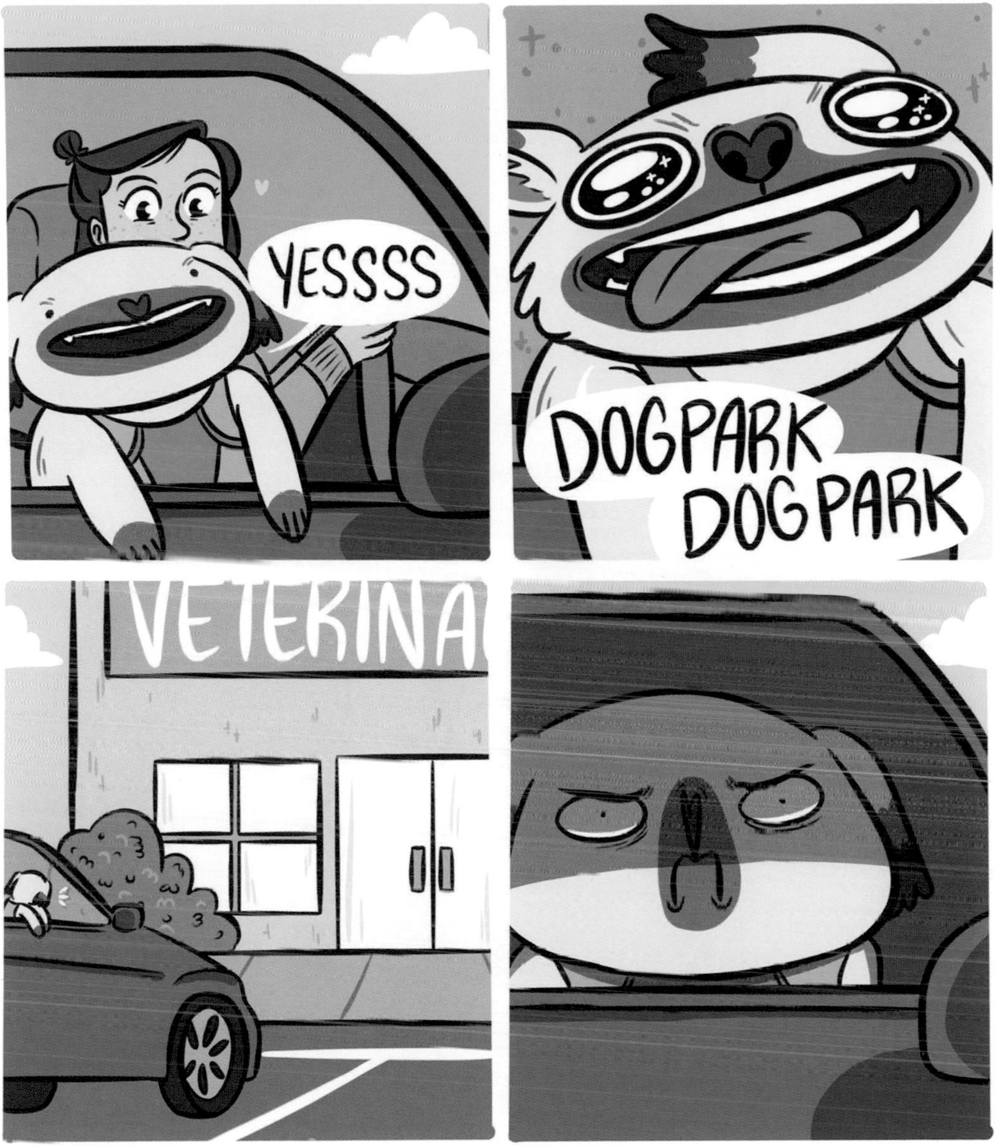
YESSSS
DOGPARK DOGPARK
VETERINA

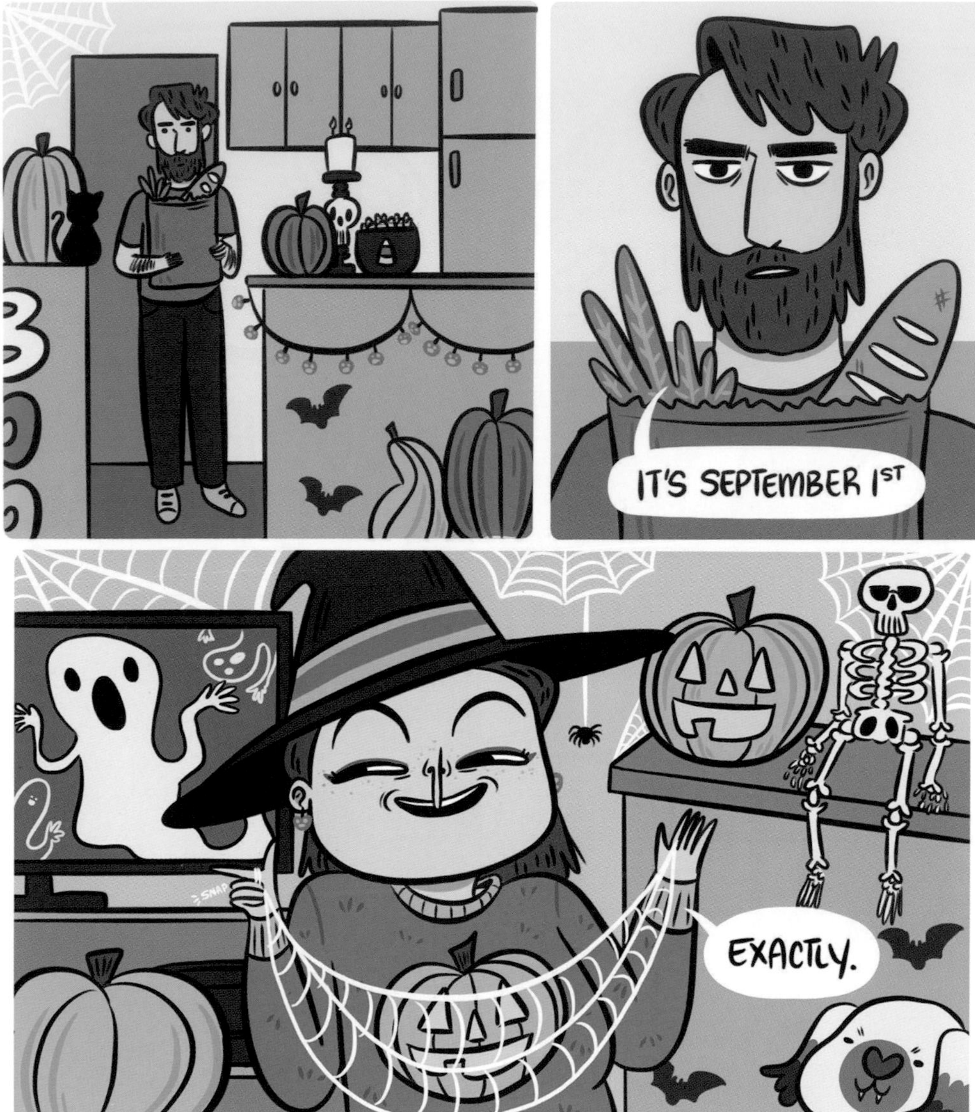
IT'S SEPTEMBER 1ST
SNAP
EXACTLY.

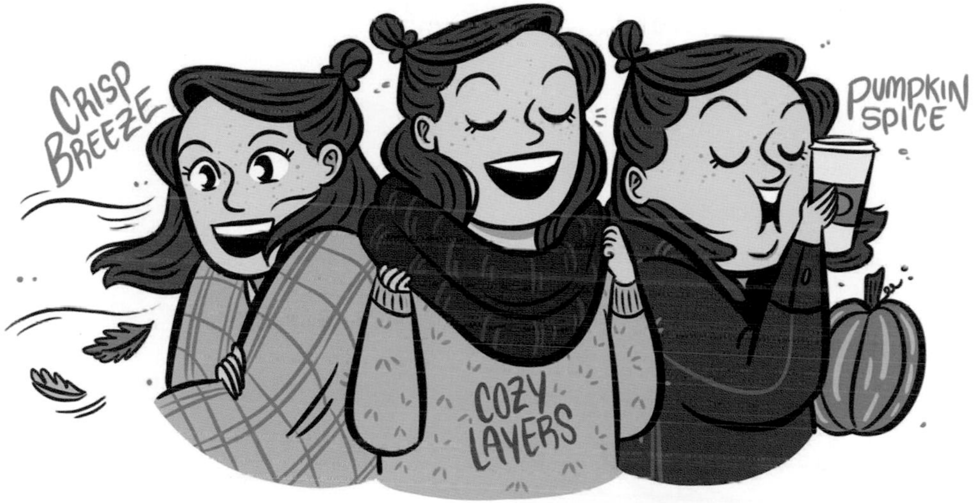
CRISP BREEZE
COZY LAYERS
PUMPKIN SPICE

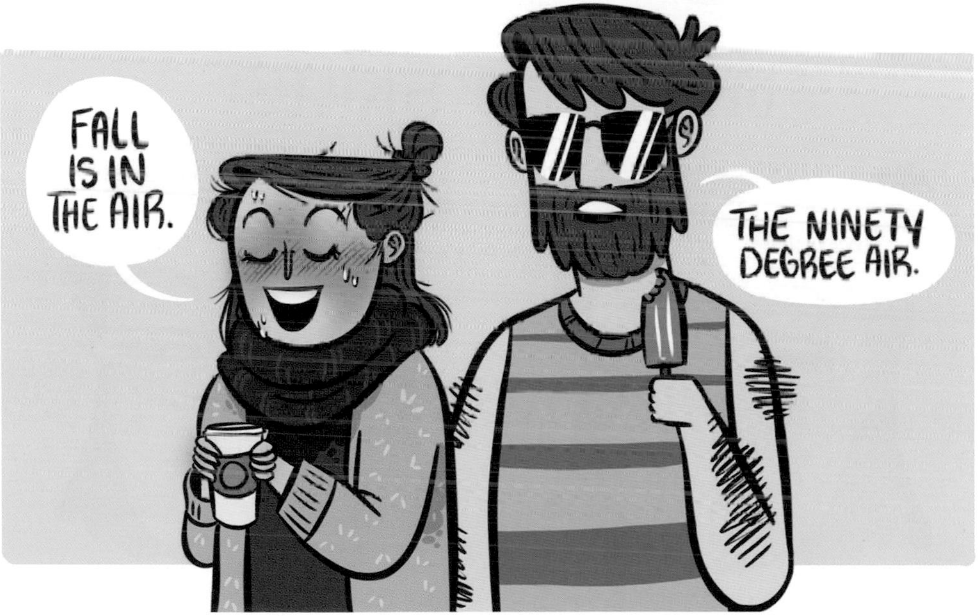
FALL IS IN THE AIR.
THE NINETY DEGREE AIR.

MY FRIEND'S MAKEUP SKILLS:

MY MAKEUP SKILLS:

NAILED IT.

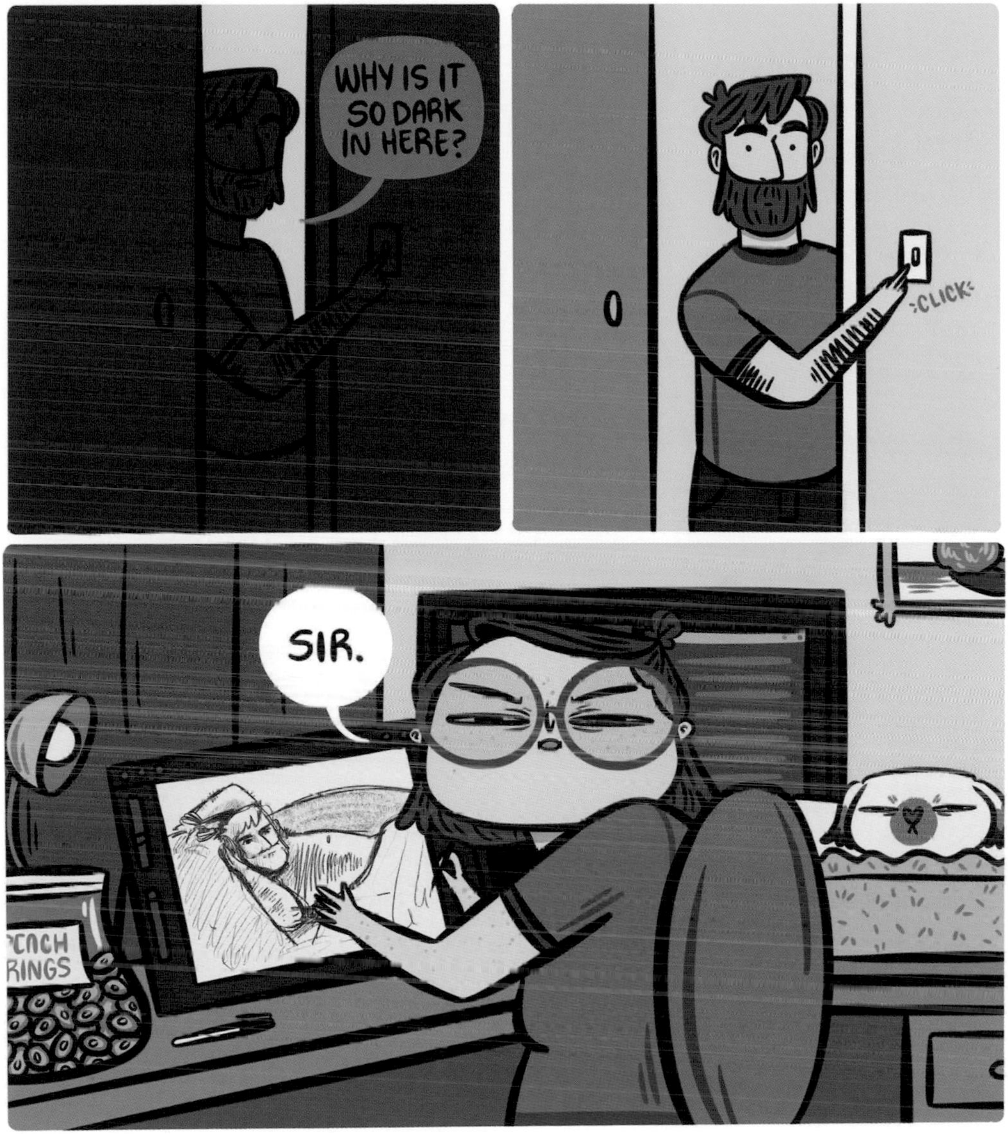
WHY IS IT SO DARK IN HERE?
CLICK
SIR.
PEACH RINGS

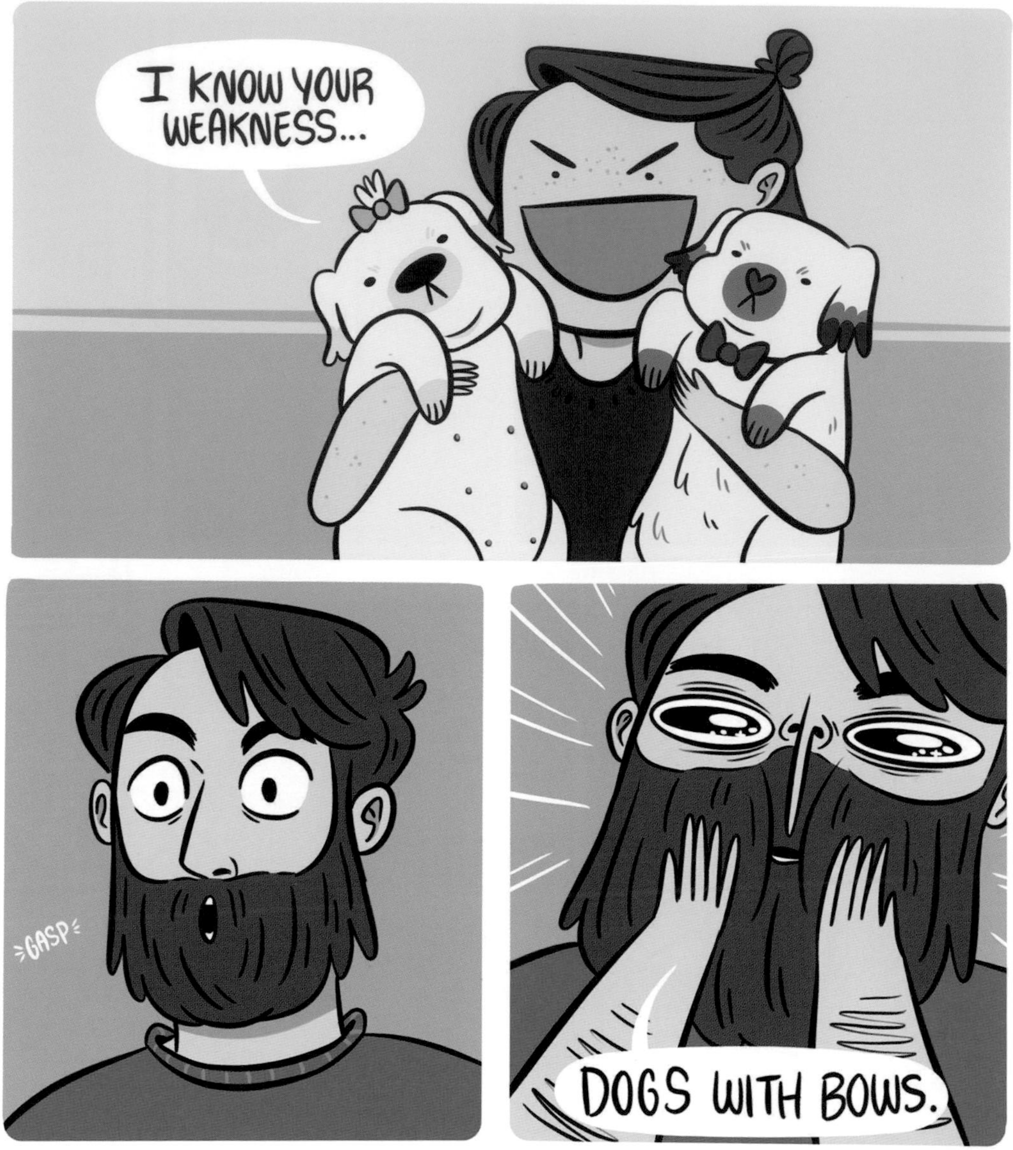
I KNOW YOUR WEAKNESS...
GASP
DOGS WITH BOWS.

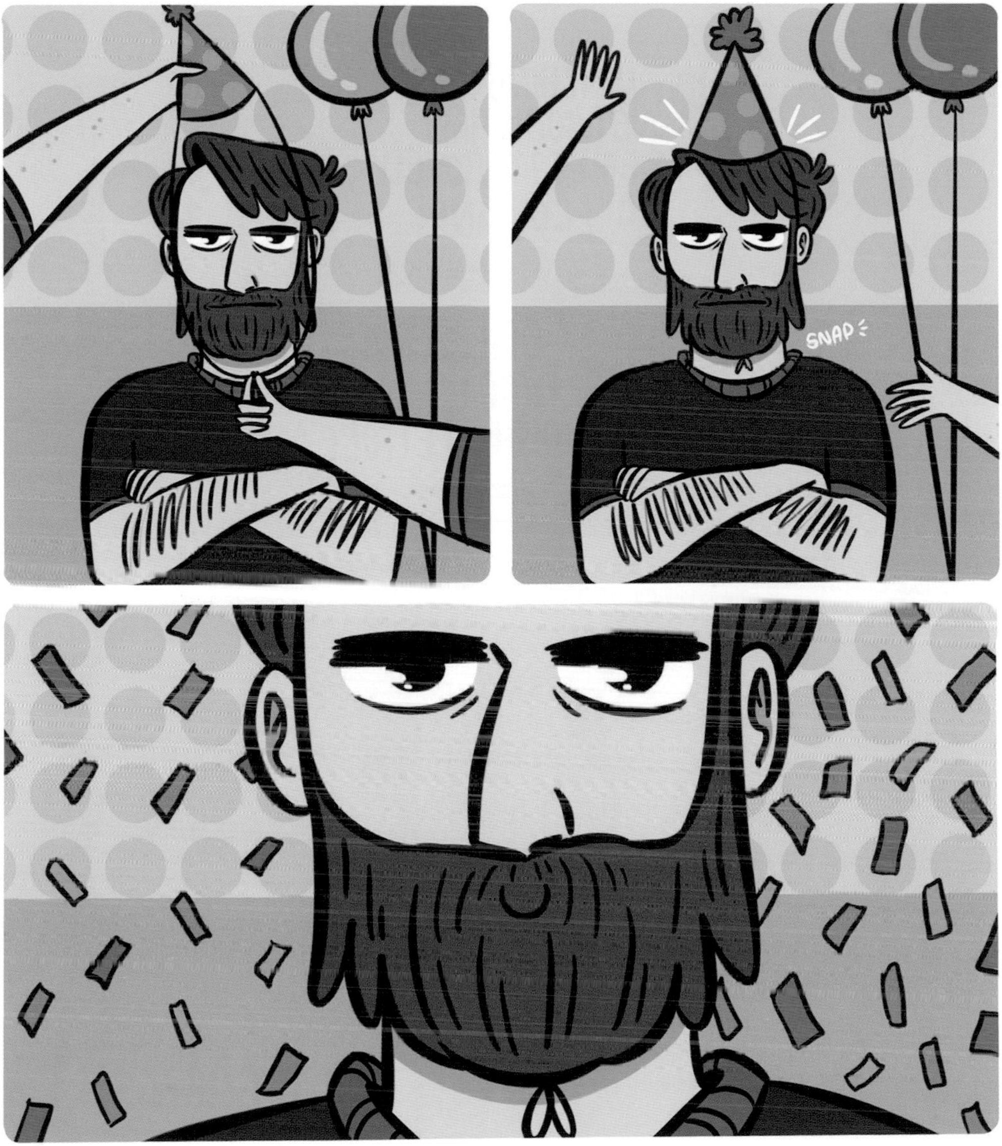
SNAP

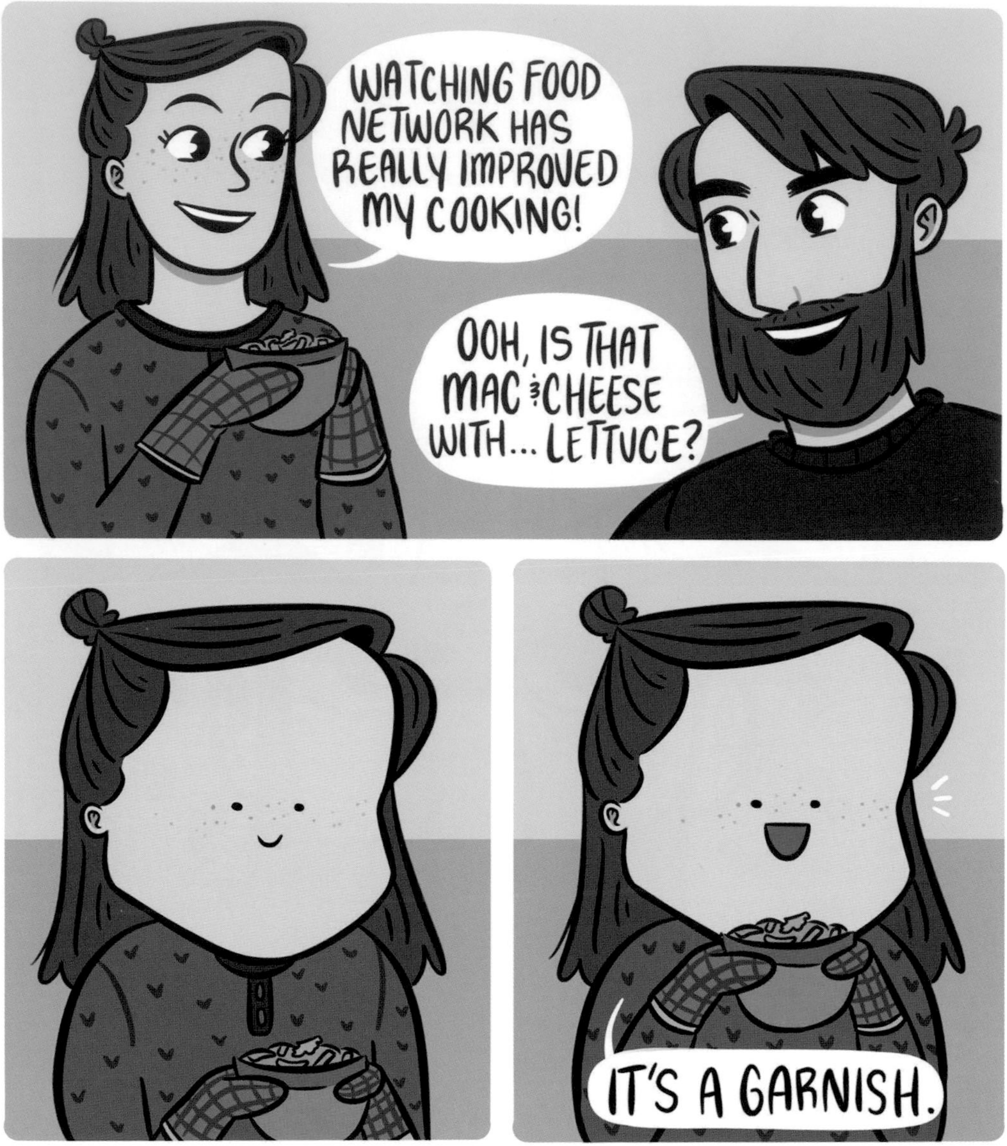
WATCHING FOOD NETWORK HAS REALLY IMPROVED MY COOKING!
OOH, IS THAT MAC & CHEESE WITH... LETTUCE?
IT'S A GARNISH.

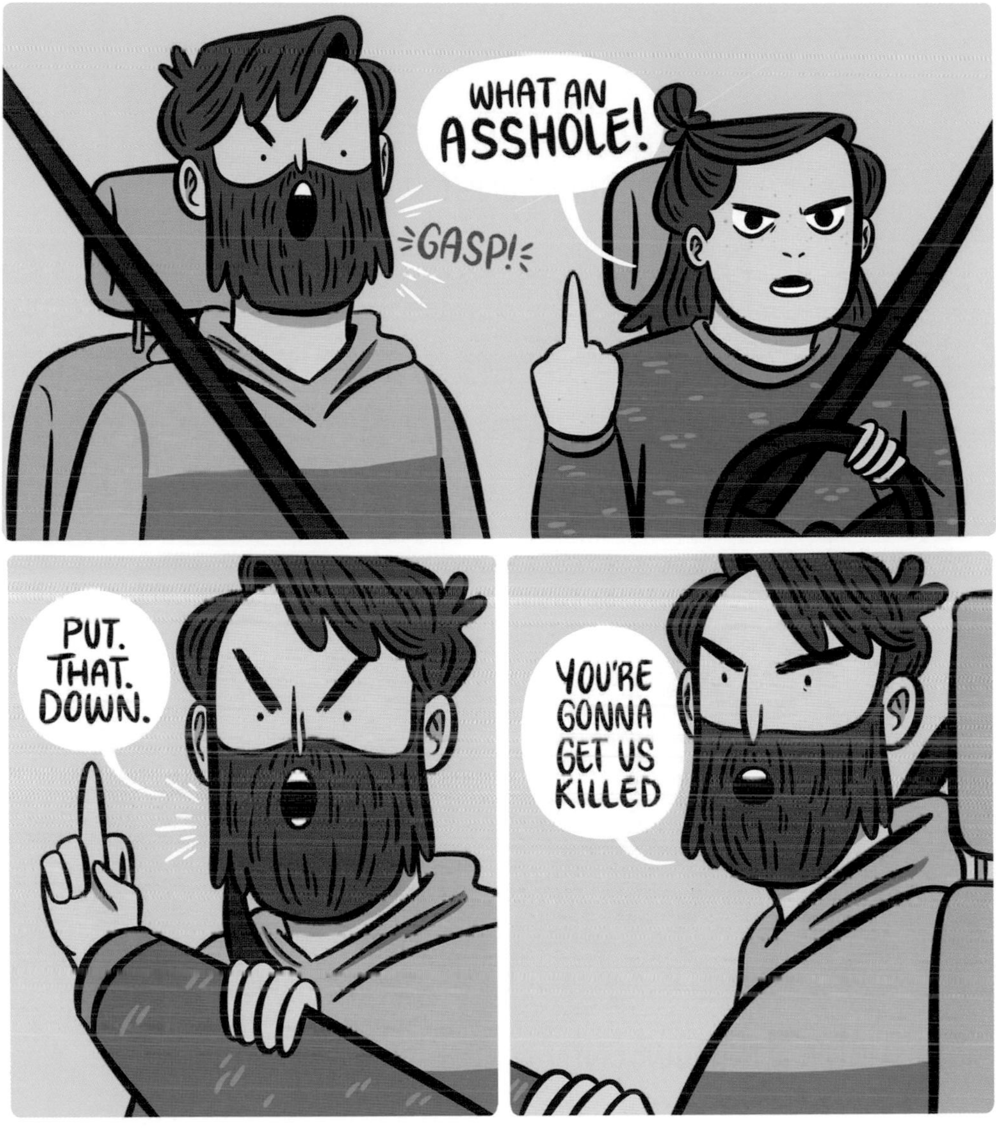
GASP!
WHAT AN ASSHOLE!
PUT. THAT. DOWN.
YOU'RE GONNA GET US KILLED

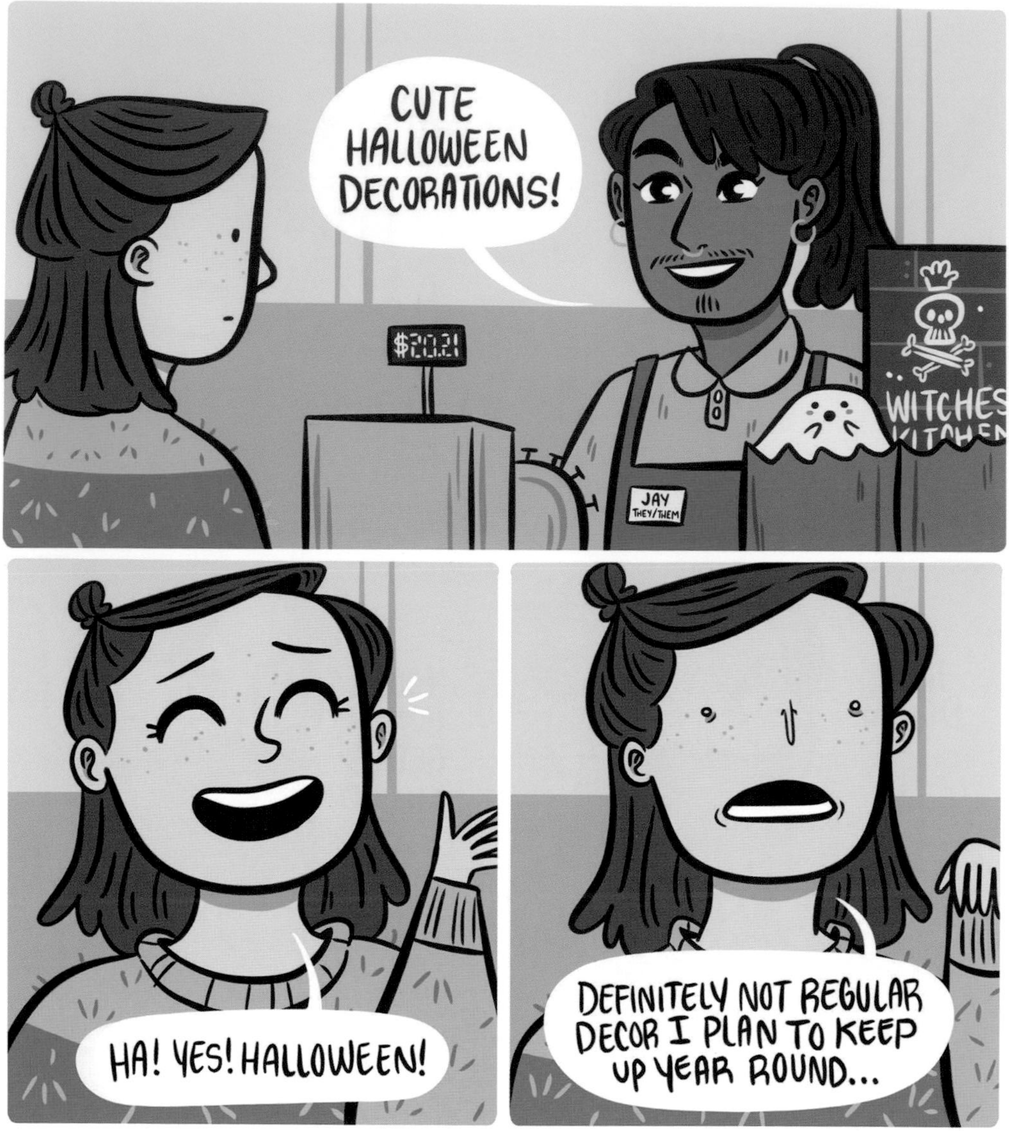
CUTE HALLOWEEN DECORATIONS!
$20.21
JAY THEY/THEM
WITCHES
HA! YES! HALLOWEEN!
DEFINITELY NOT REGULAR DECOR I PLAN TO KEEP UP YEAR ROUND...

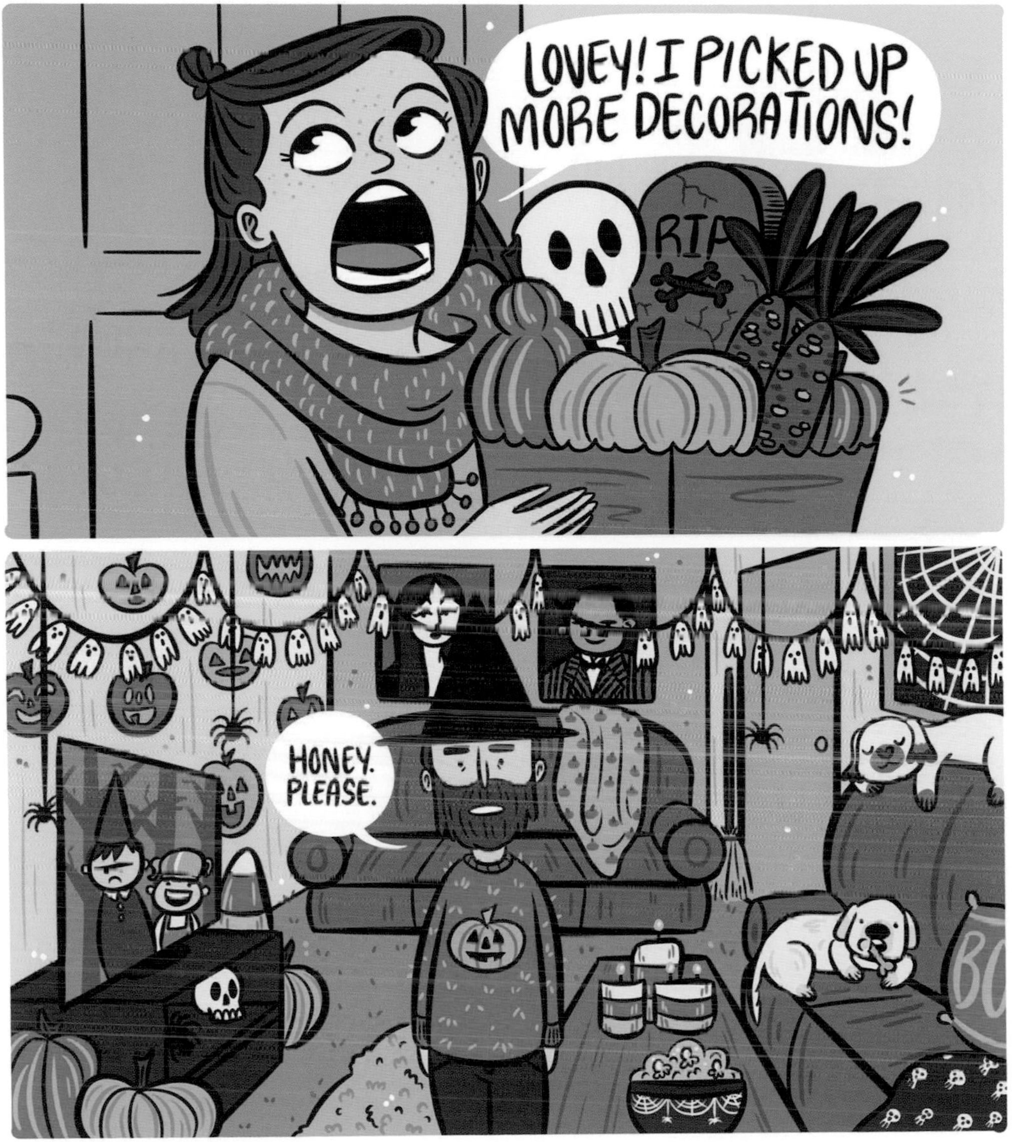
LOVEY! I PICKED UP MORE DECORATIONS!
RIP
HONEY. PLEASE.

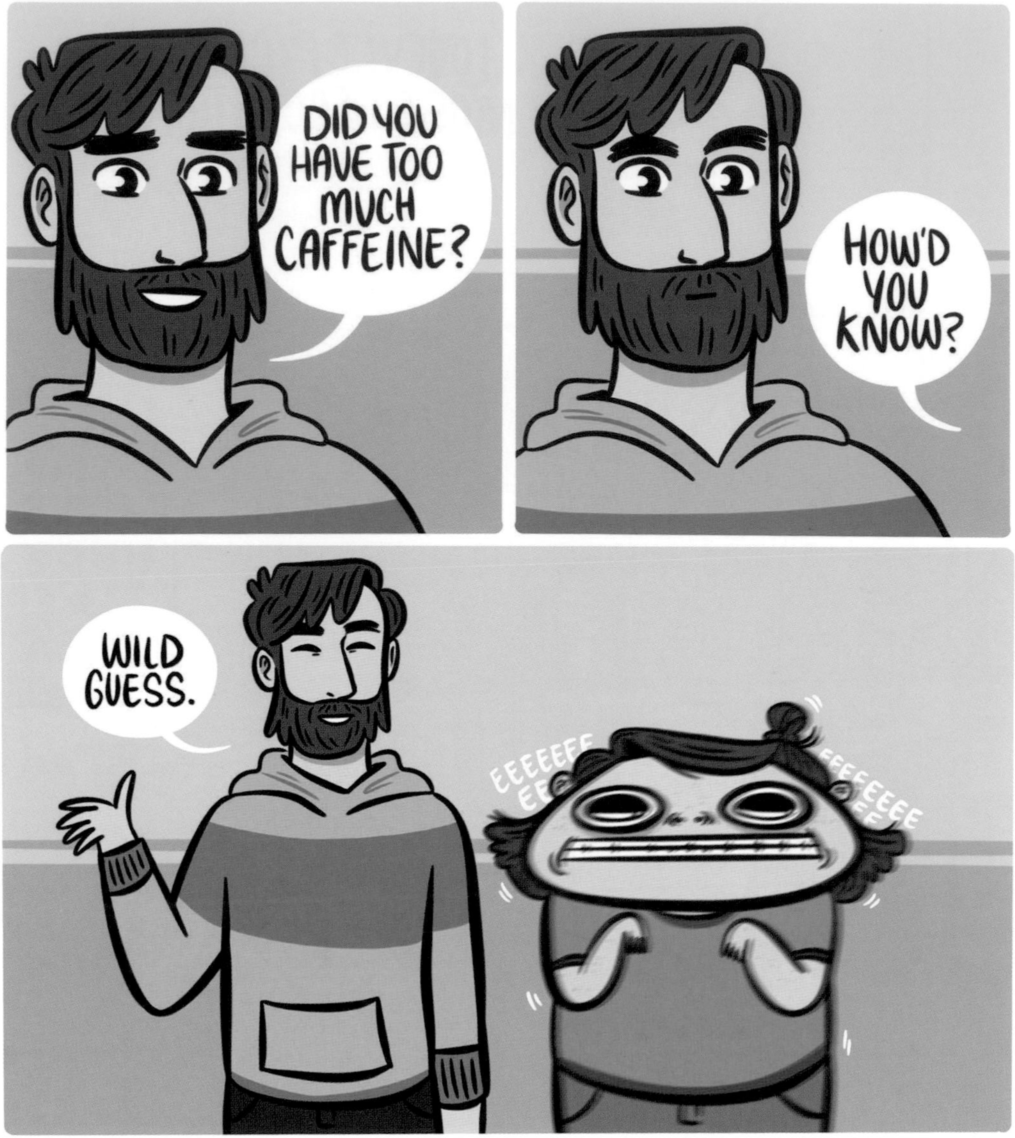
DID YOU HAVE TOO MUCH CAFFEINE?
HOW'D YOU KNOW?
WILD GUESS.
EEEEEEE EE
EEEEEEE EE

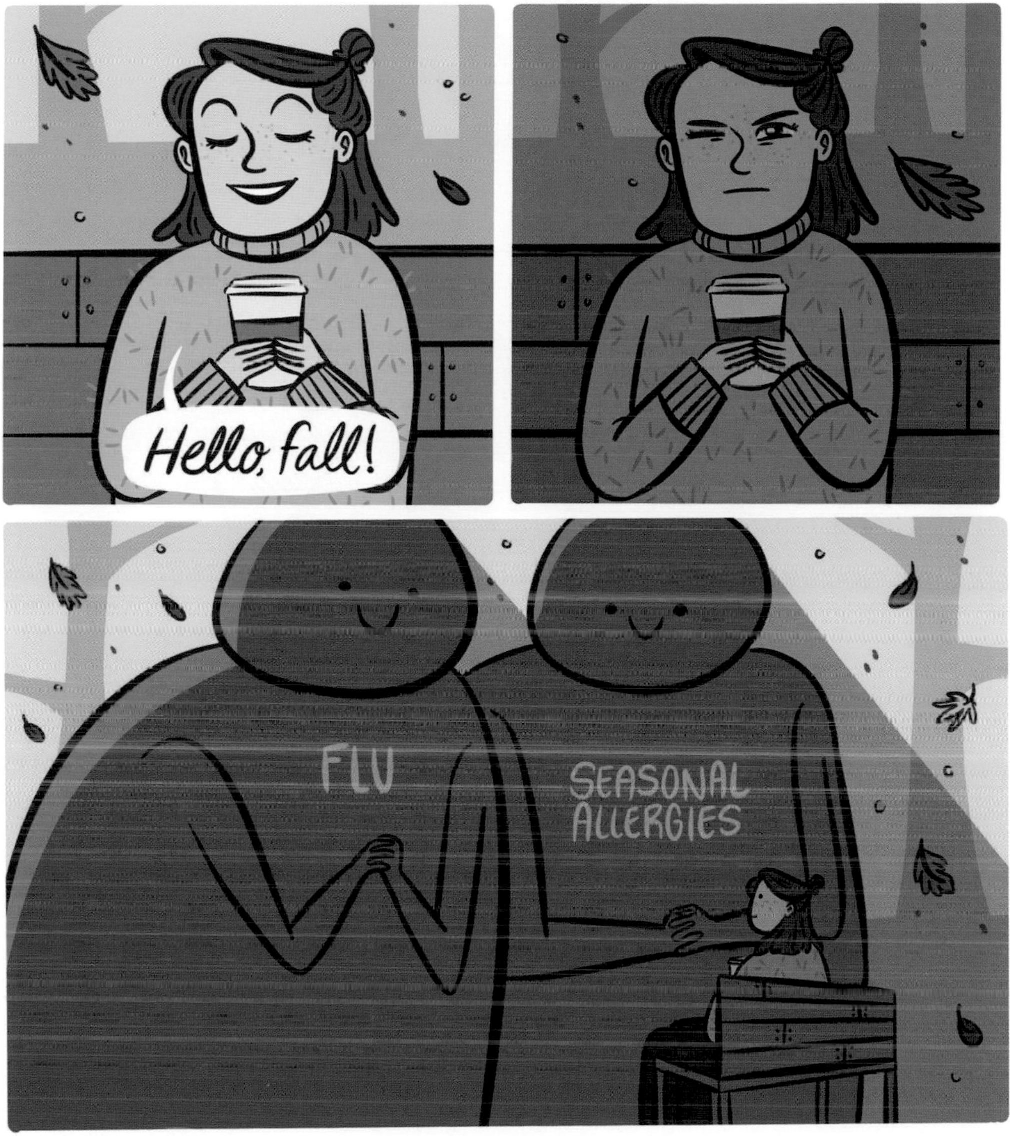
Hello, fall!
FLU
SEASONAL ALLERGIES

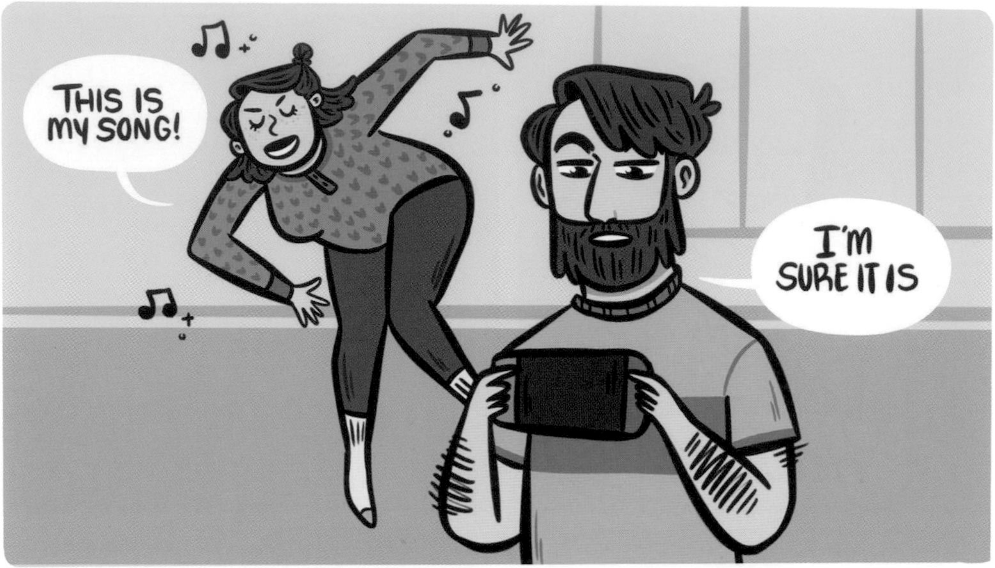
THIS IS MY SONG!
I'M SURE IT IS

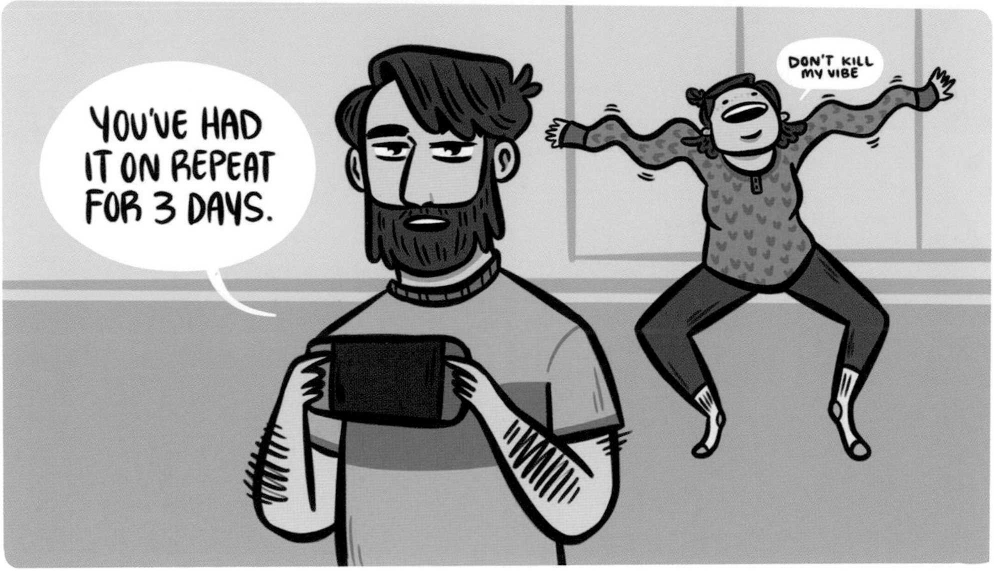
YOU'VE HAD IT ON REPEAT FOR 3 DAYS.
DON'T KILL MY VIBE

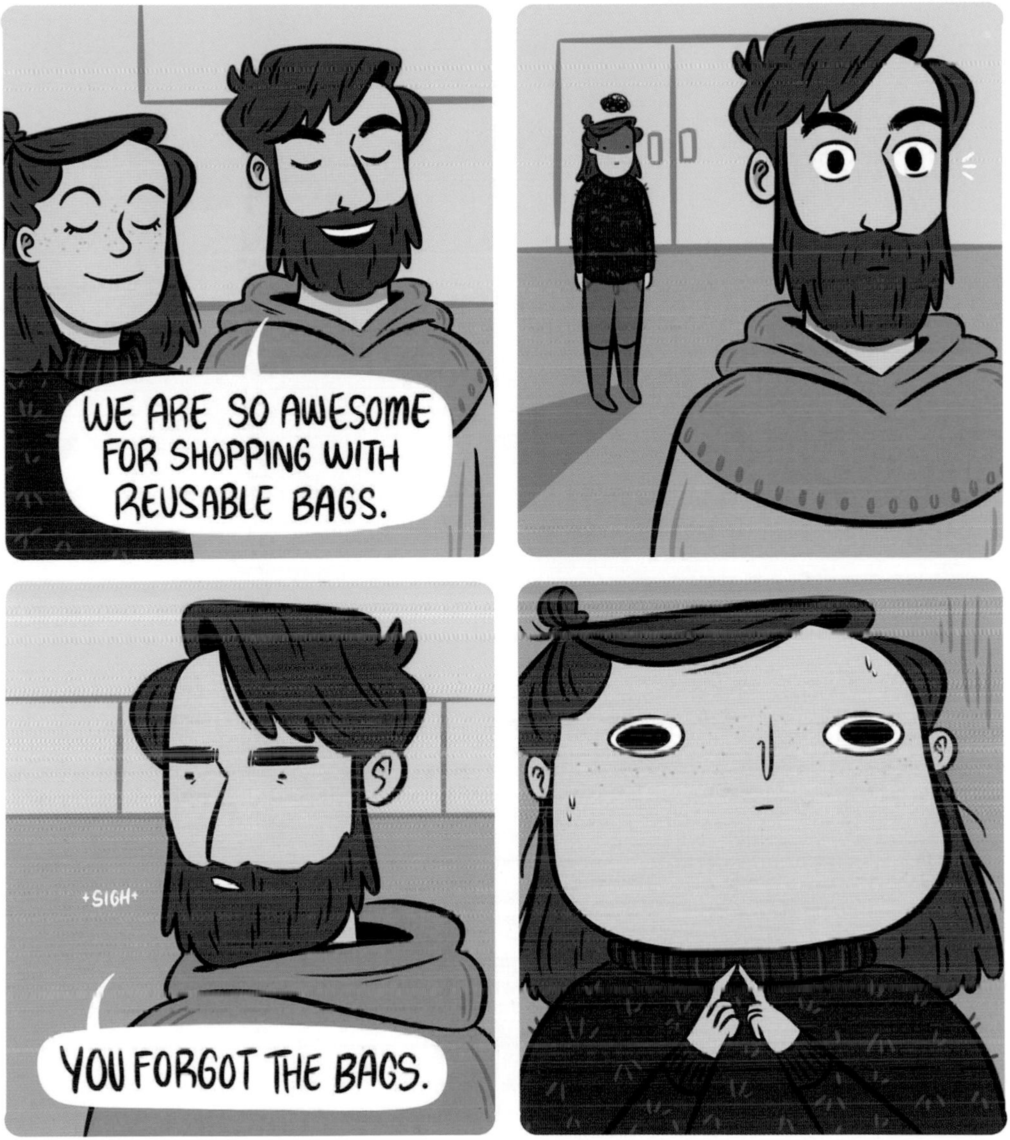
WE ARE SO AWESOME FOR SHOPPING WITH REUSABLE BAGS.
+SIGH+
YOU FORGOT THE BAGS.

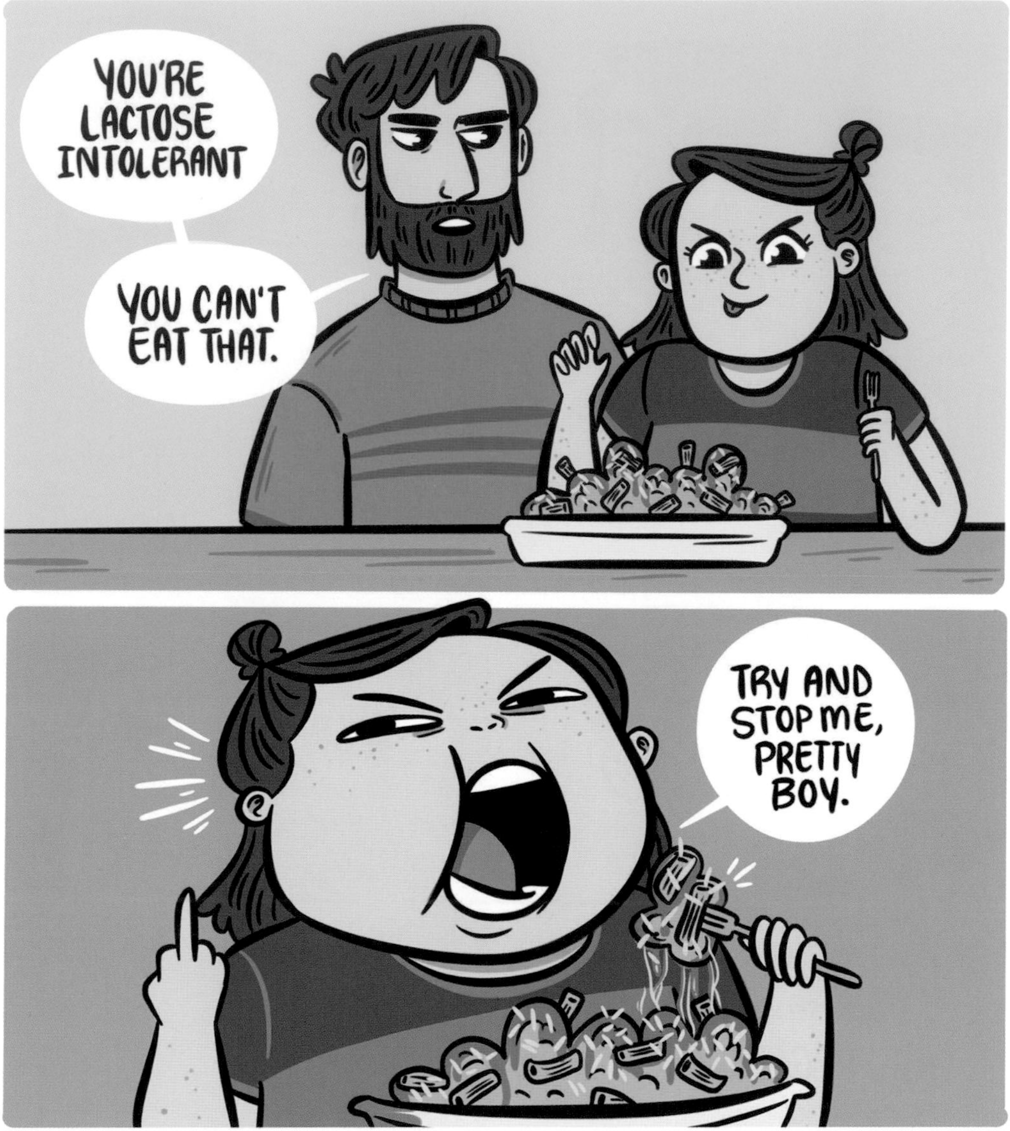
YOU'RE LACTOSE INTOLERANT
YOU CAN'T EAT THAT.
TRY AND STOP ME, PRETTY BOY.

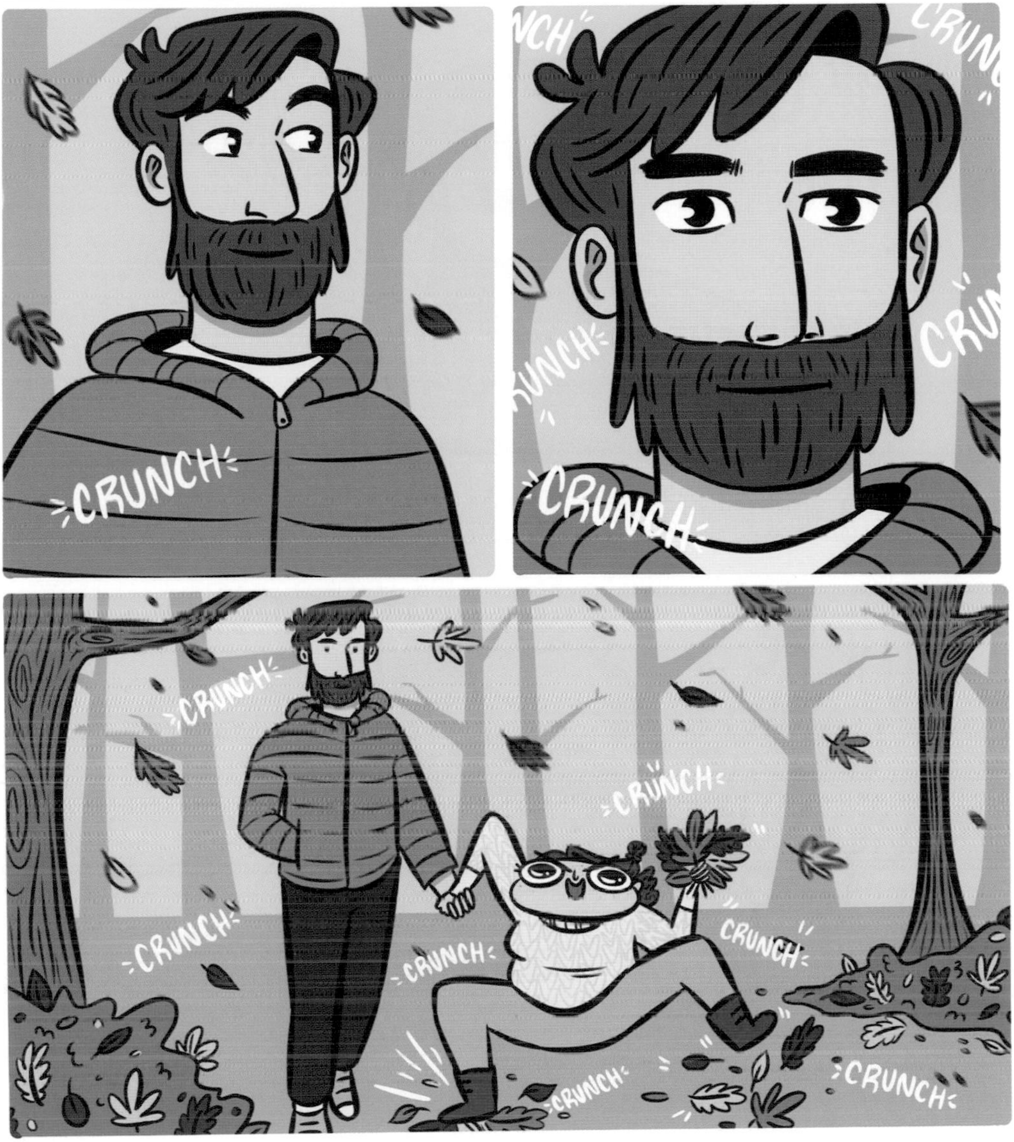
CRUNCH
CRUNCH
CRUNCH
CRUNCH
CRUNCH
CRUNCH
CRUNCH
CRUNCH
CRUNCH

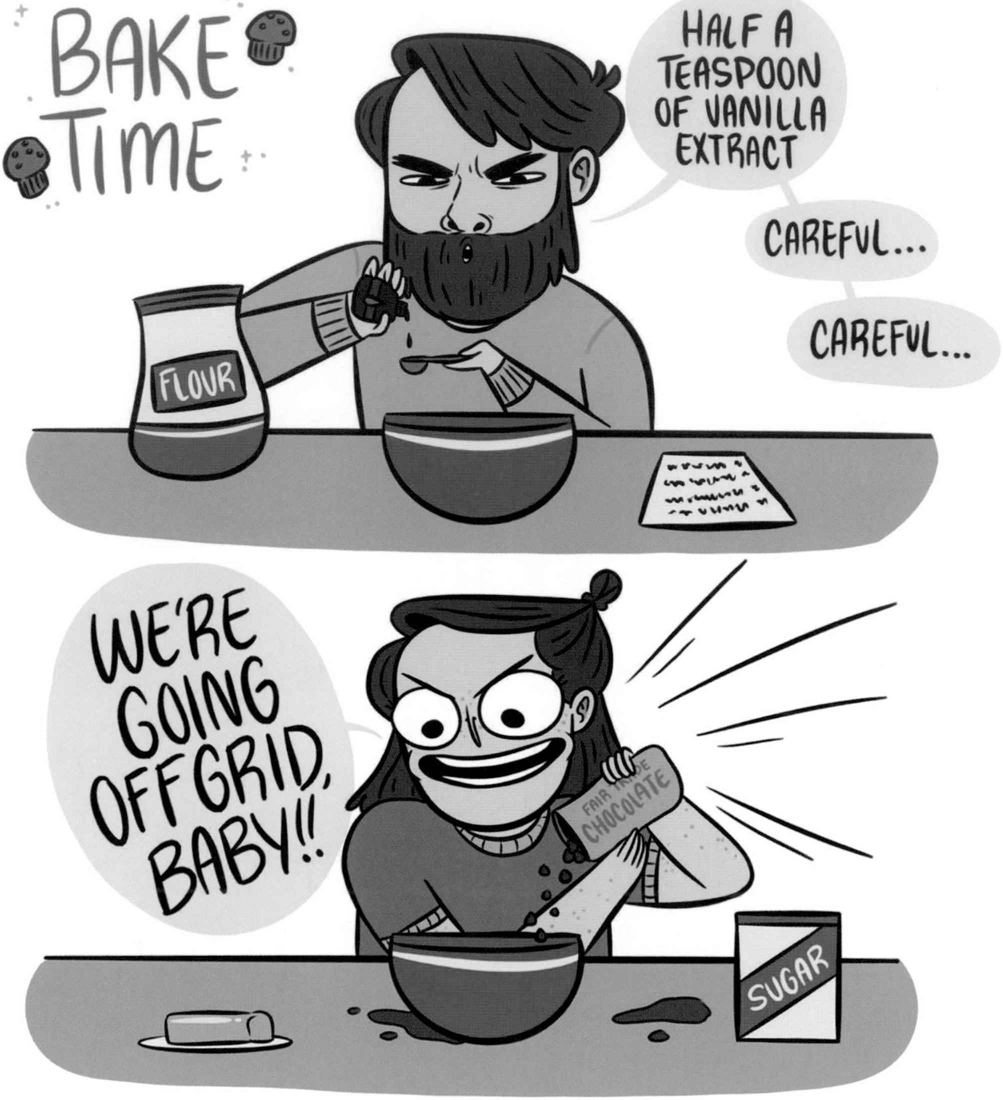
BAKE TIME
HALF A TEASPOON OF VANILLA EXTRACT
CAREFUL...
CAREFUL...
FLOUR
WE'RE GOING OFFGRID, BABY!!
CHOCOLATE
SUGAR

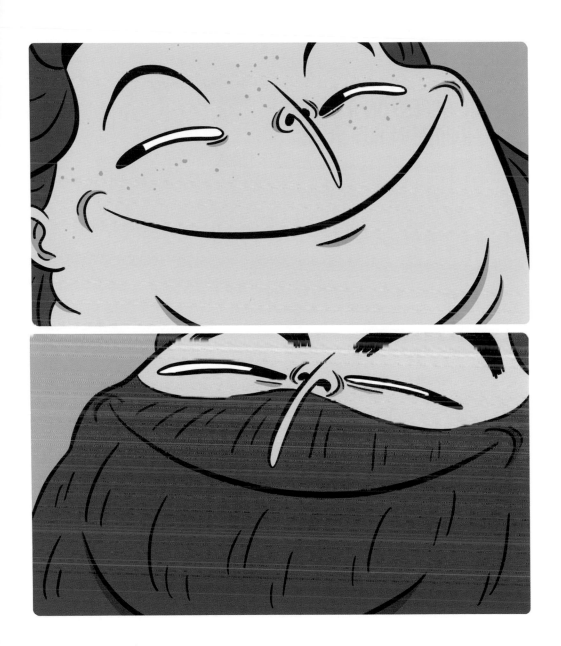

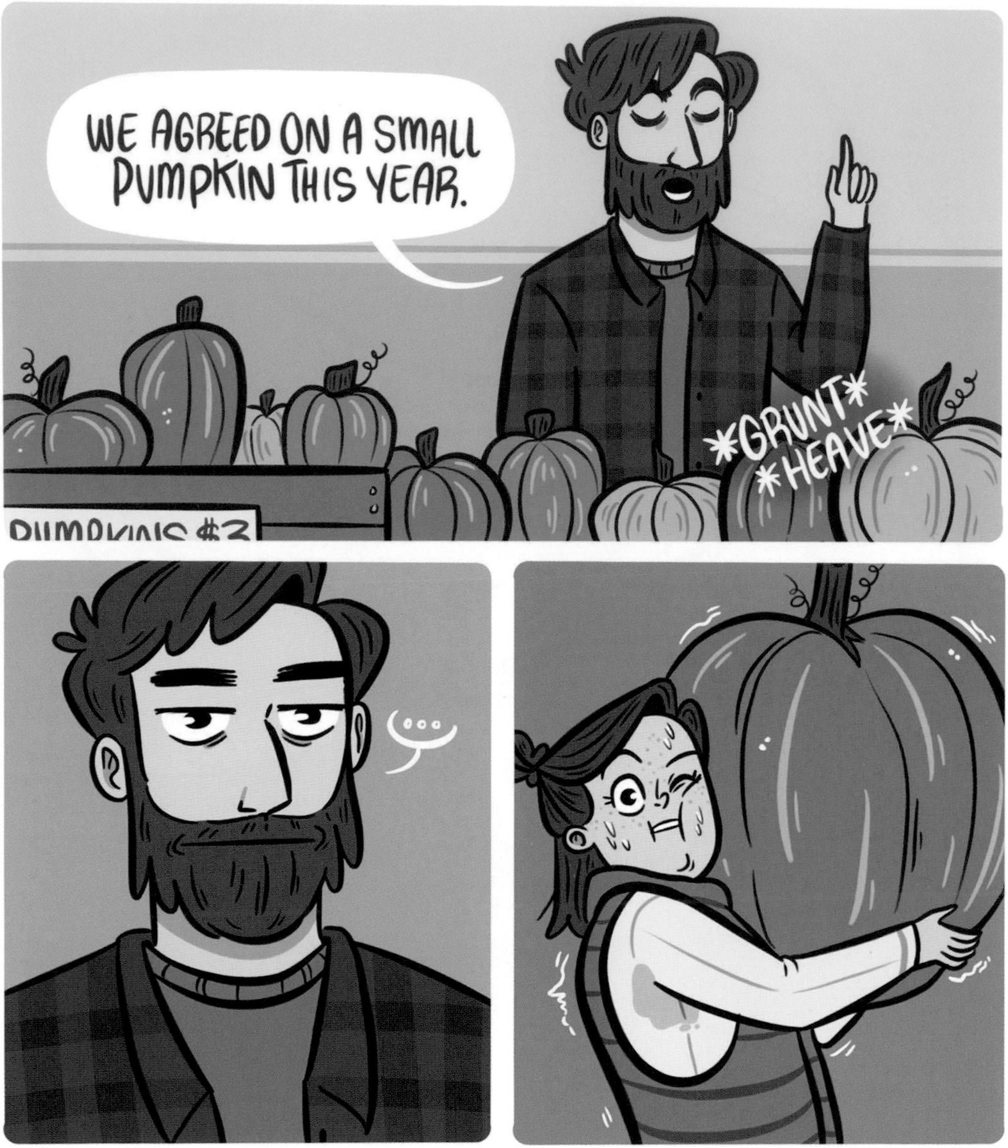
WE AGREED ON A SMALL PUMPKIN THIS YEAR.
GRUNT *HEAVE*
...

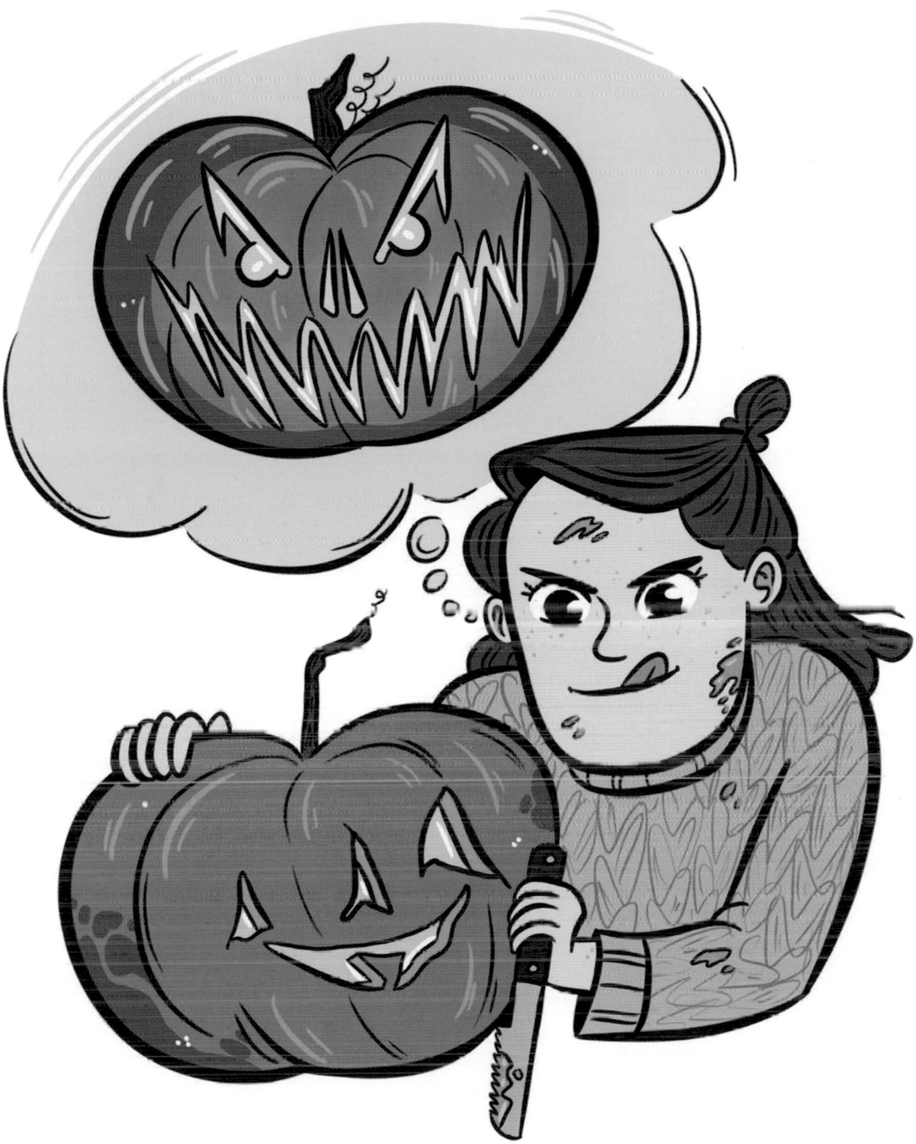

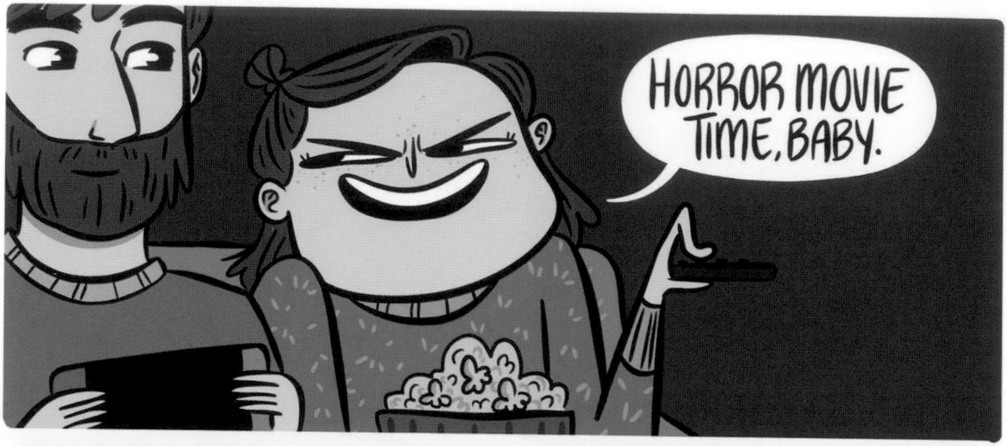
HORROR MOVIE TIME, BABY.

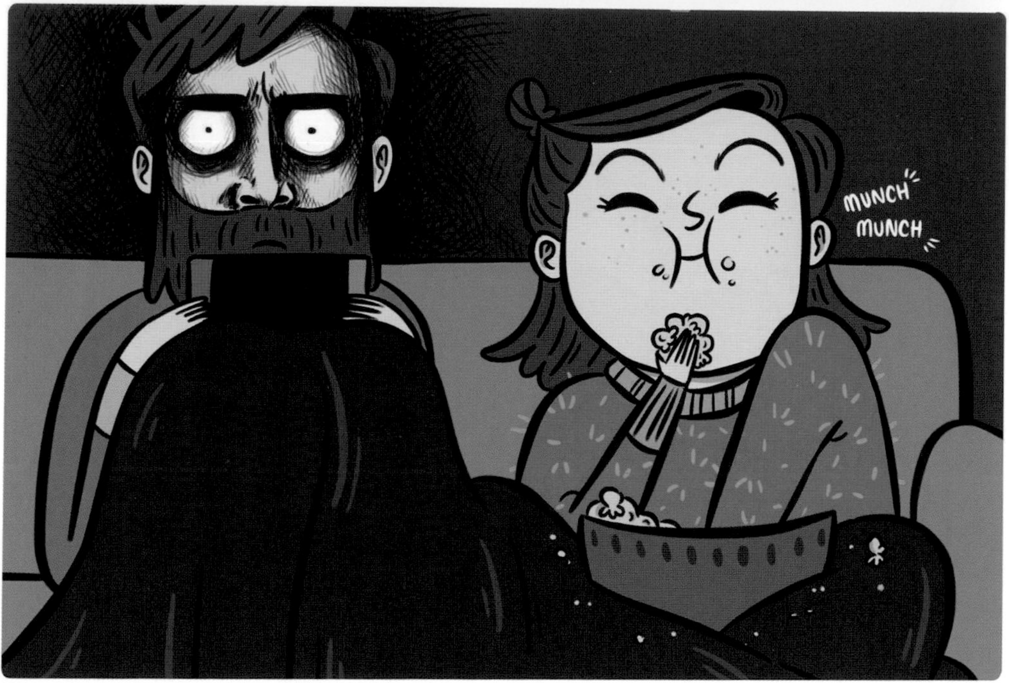
MUNCH
MUNCH

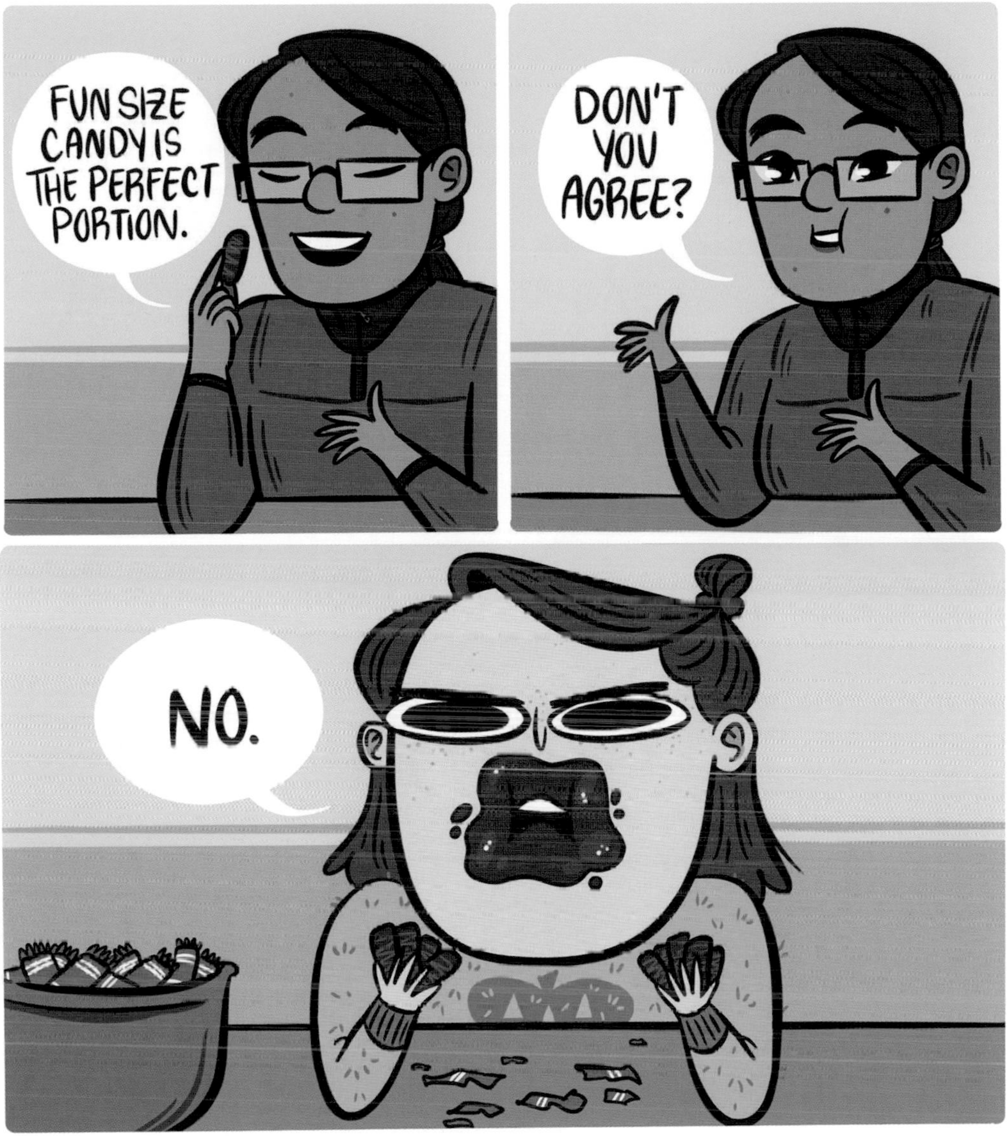
FUN SIZE CANDY IS THE PERFECT PORTION.
DON'T YOU AGREE?
NO.

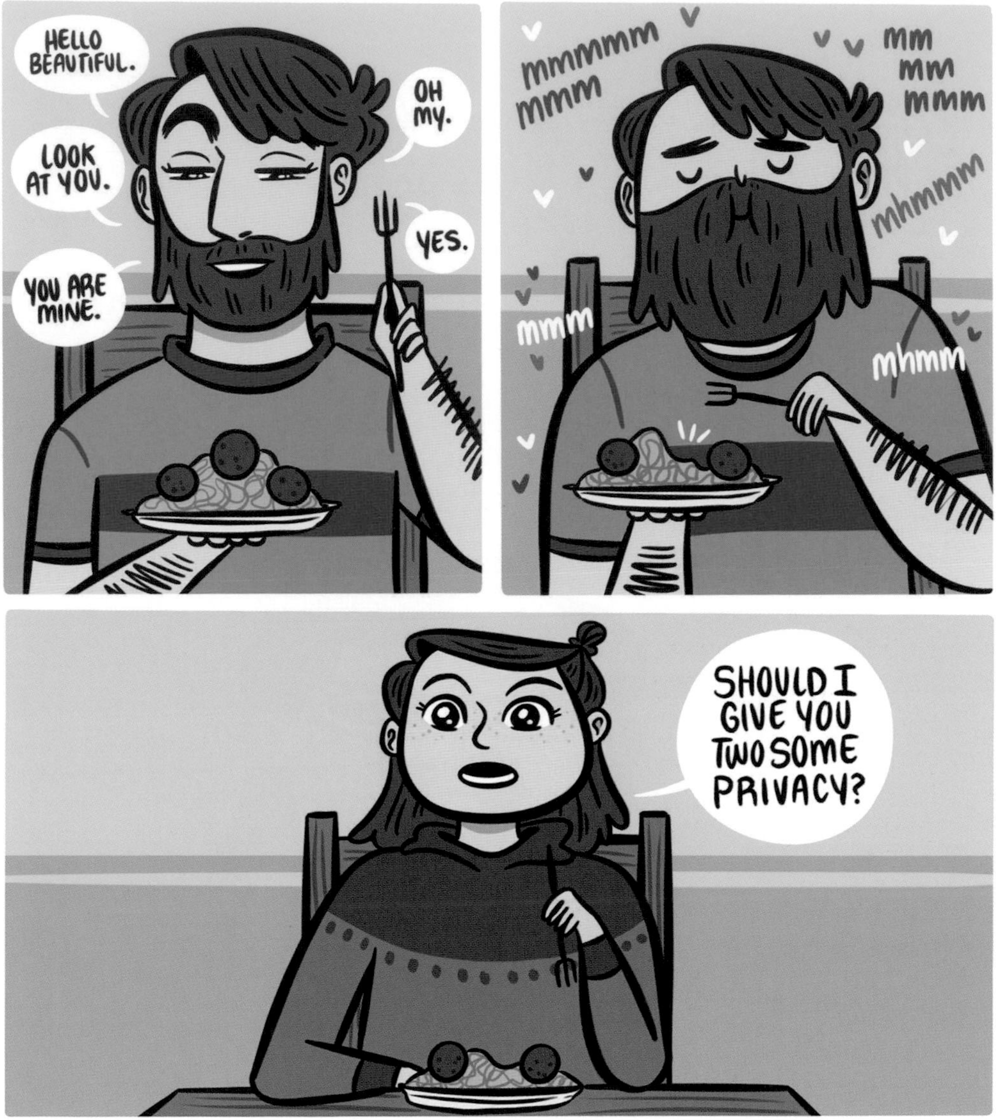
HELLO BEAUTIFUL.
LOOK AT YOU.
YOU ARE MINE.
OH MY.
YES.
mmmmm mmm
mm mm mmm
mhmmm
mmm
mhmm
SHOULD I GIVE YOU TWO SOME PRIVACY?

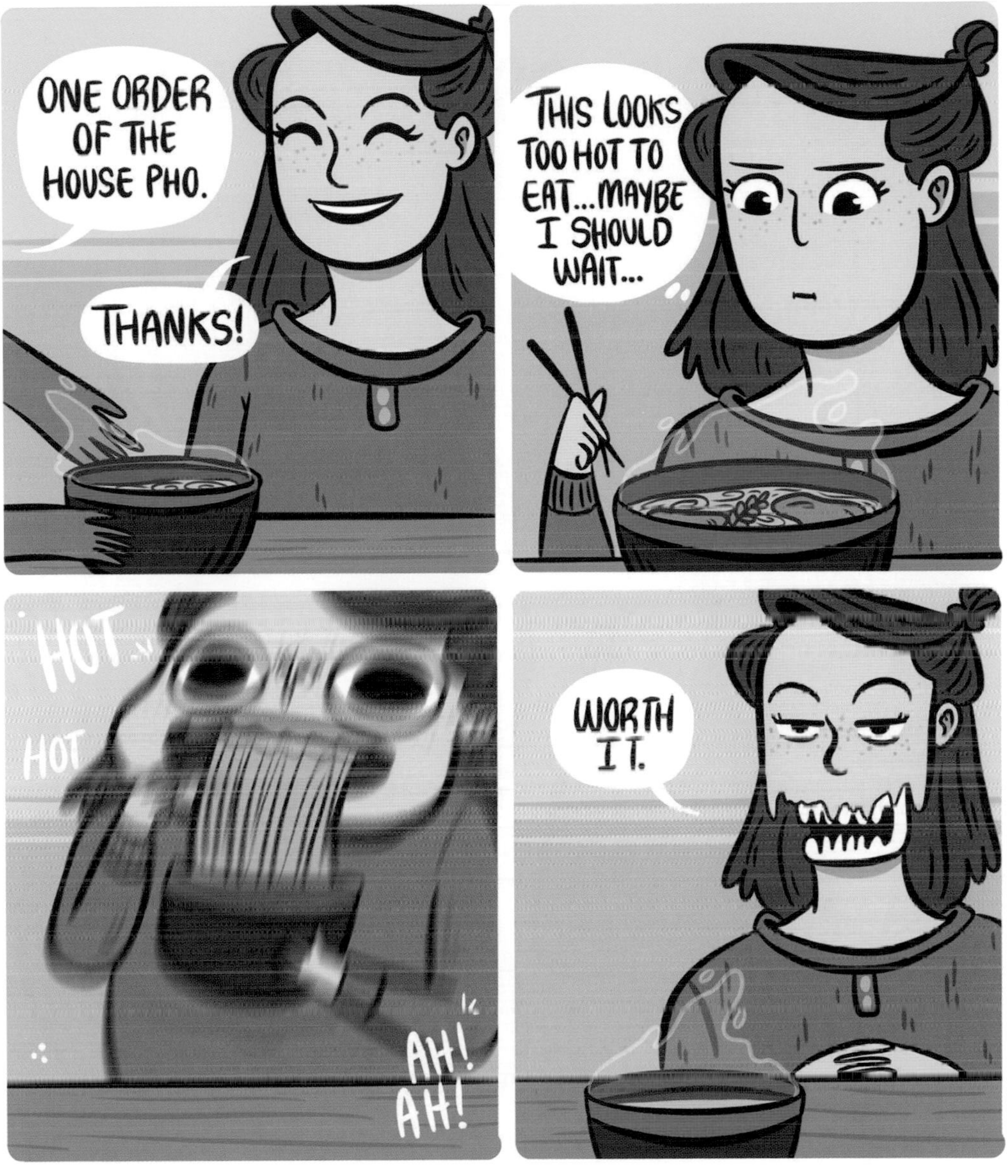
ONE ORDER OF THE HOUSE PHO.
THANKS!
THIS LOOKS TOO HOT TO EAT...MAYBE I SHOULD WAIT...
HOT
HOT
AH! AH!
WORTH IT.

TWO KINDS OF PEOPLE

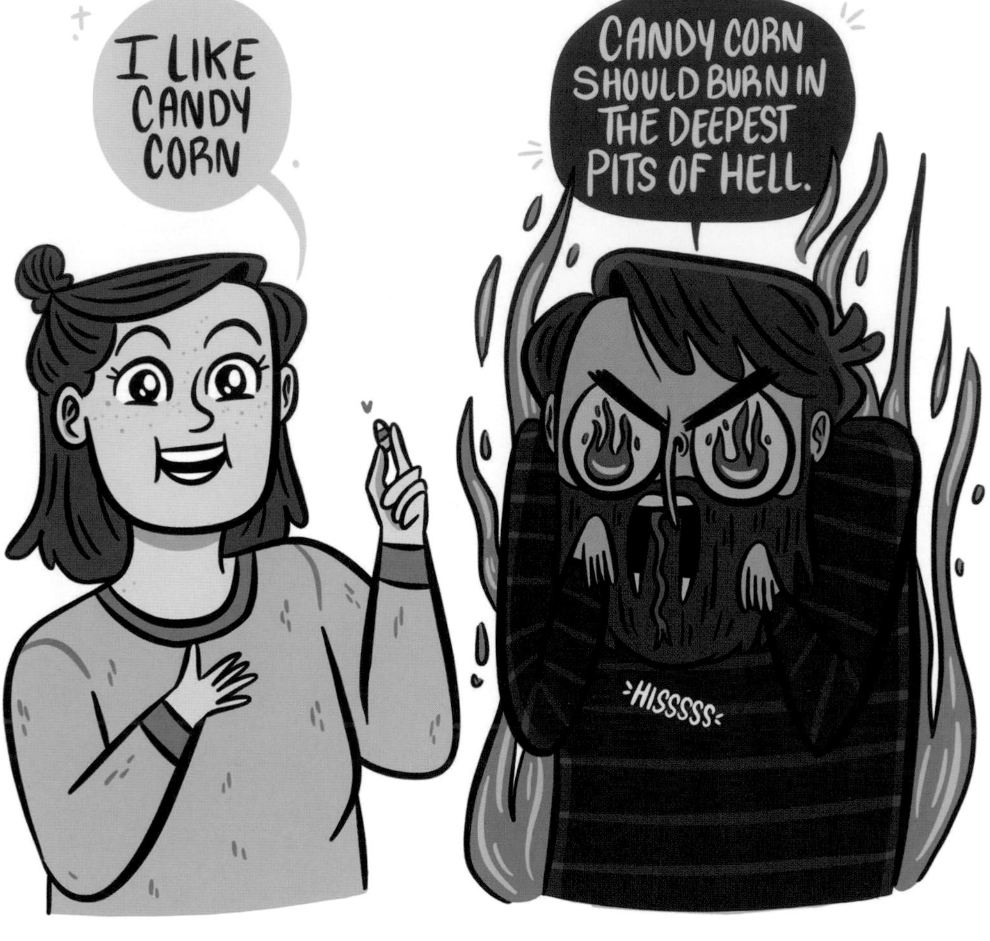
I LIKE CANDY CORN
CANDY CORN SHOULD BURN IN THE DEEPEST PITS OF HELL.
HISSSSS

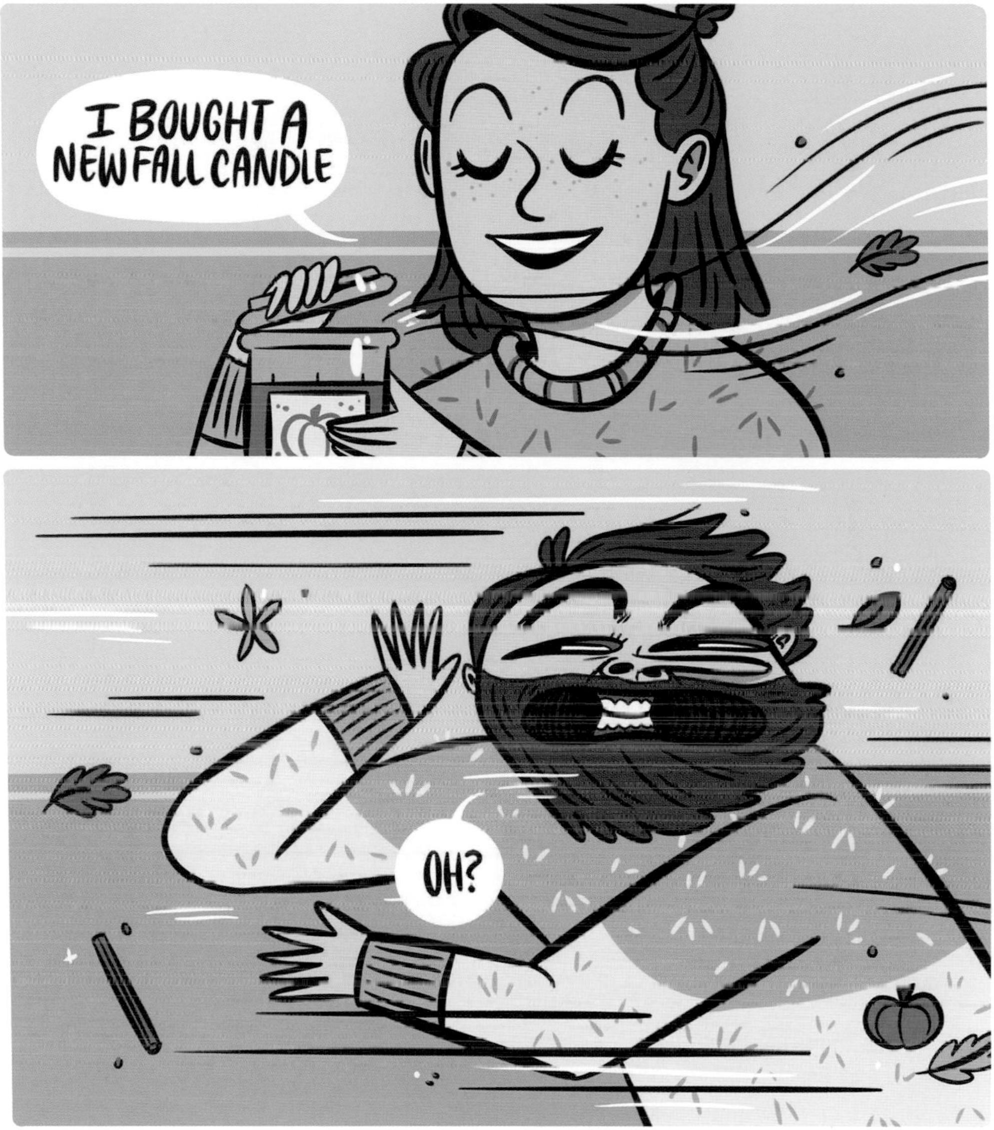
I BOUGHT A NEW FALL CANDLE
OH?

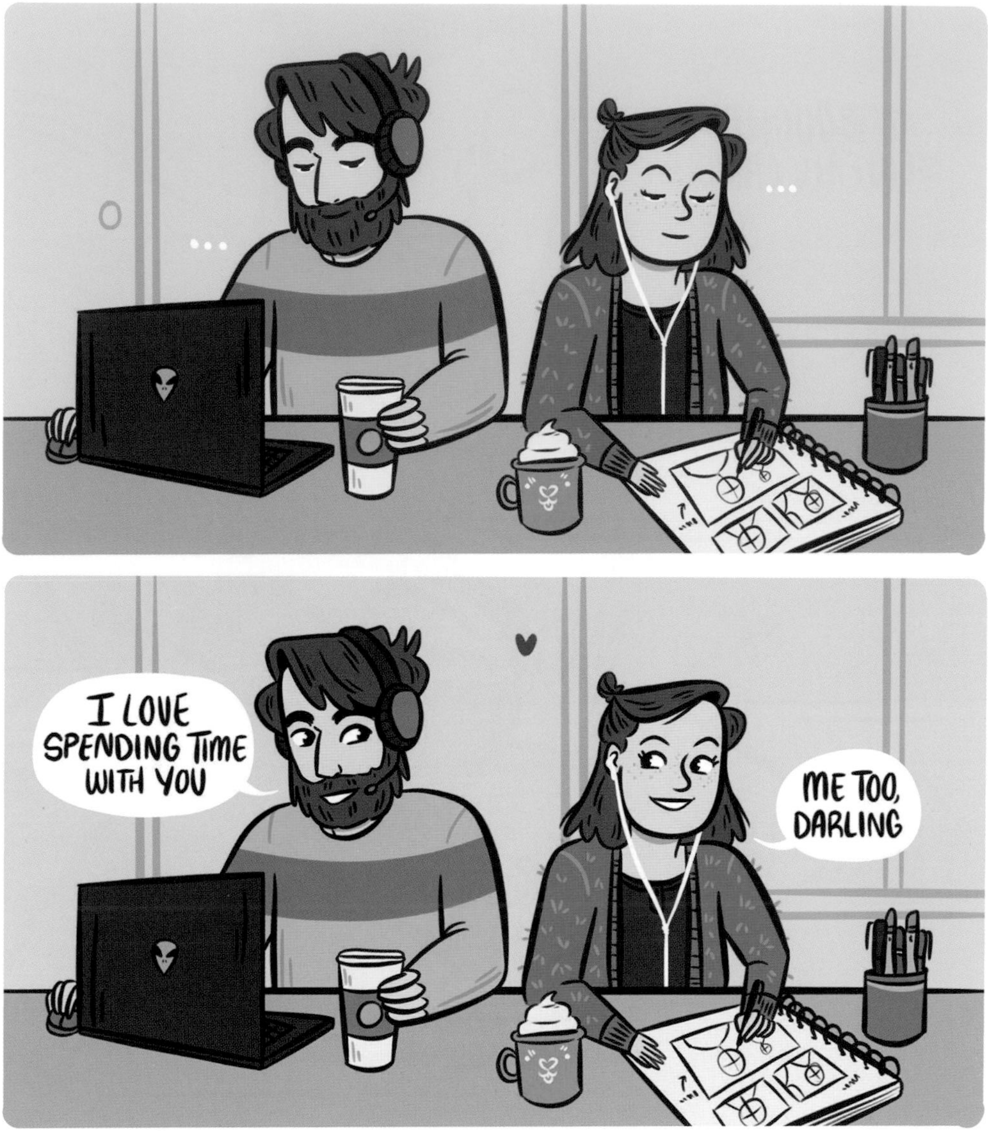
...
...
I LOVE SPENDING TIME WITH YOU
ME TOO, DARLING

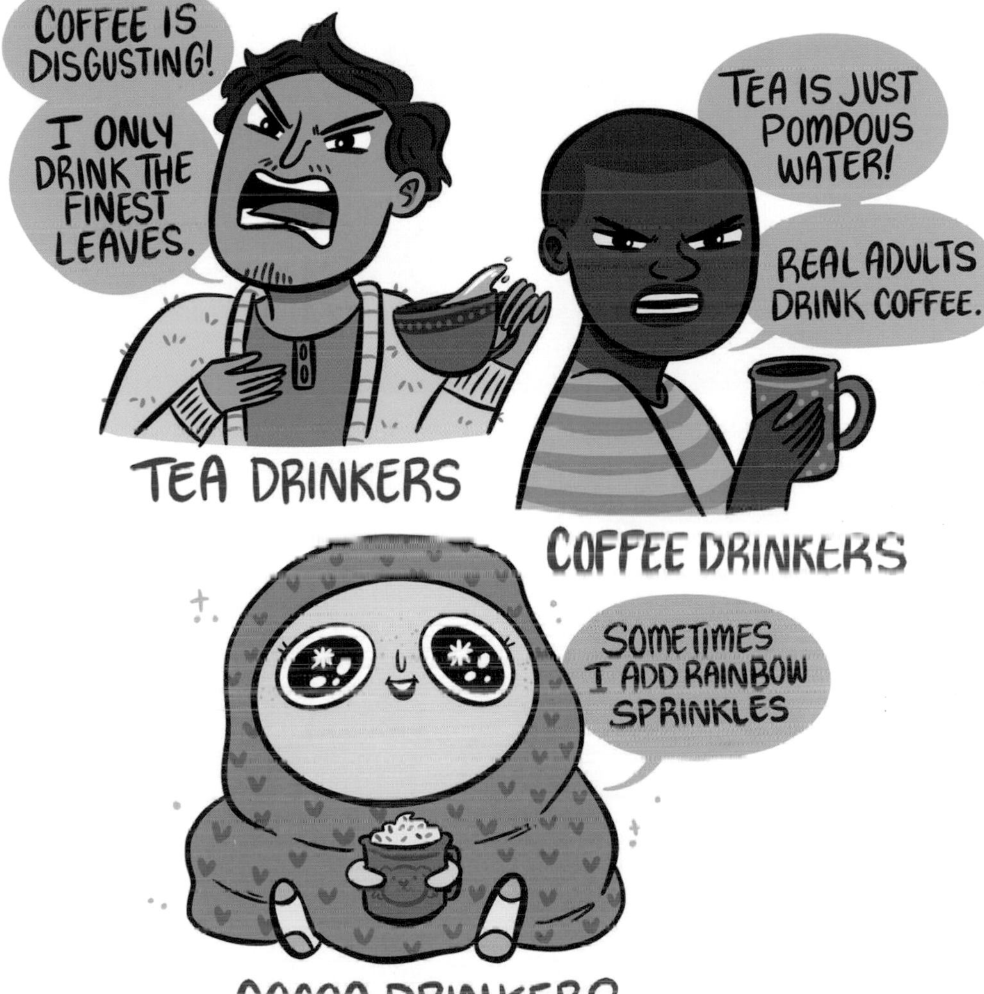
COFFEE IS DISGUSTING!
I ONLY DRINK THE FINEST LEAVES.
TEA DRINKERS
TEA IS JUST POMPOUS WATER!
REAL ADULTS DRINK COFFEE.
COFFEE DRINKERS
SOMETIMES I ADD RAINBOW SPRINKLES
COCOA DRINKERS

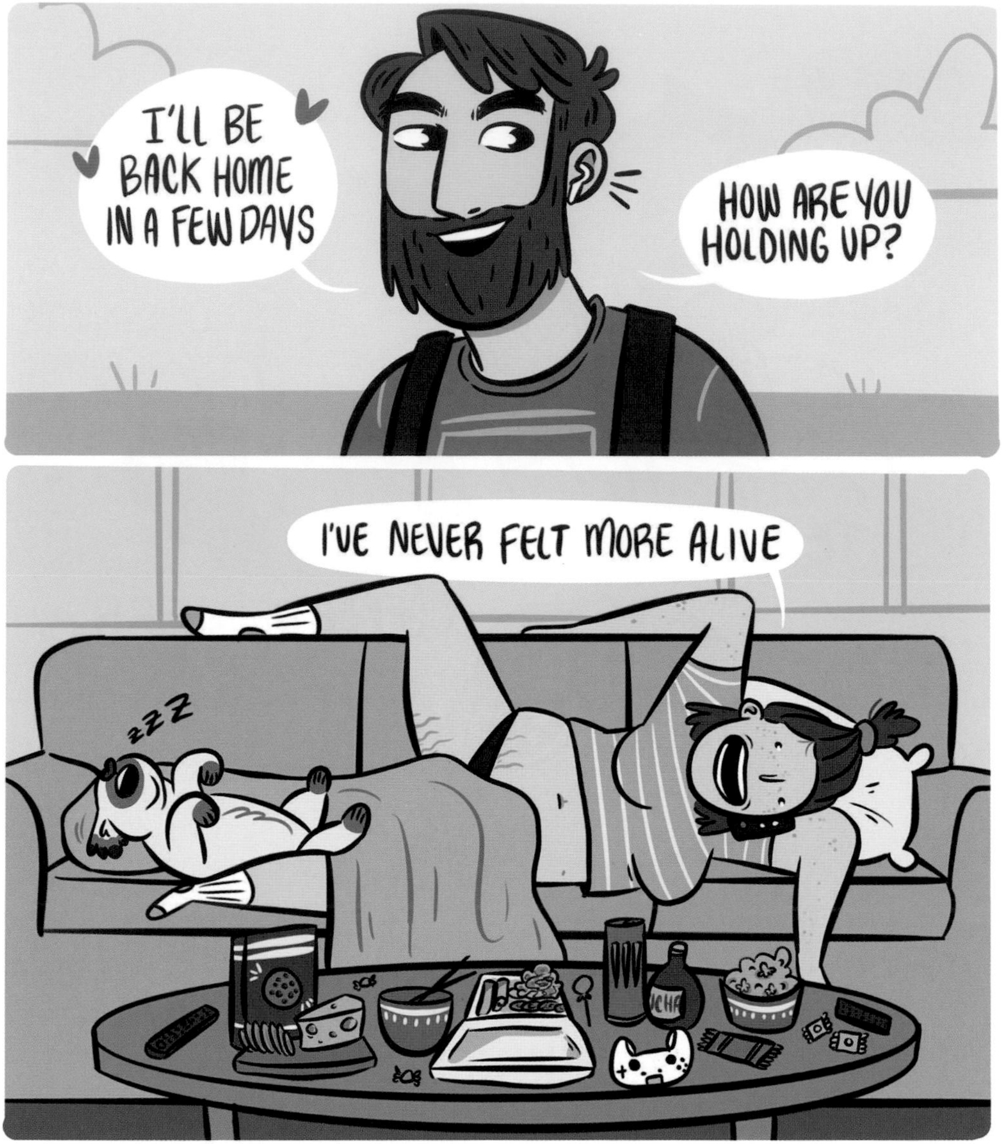
I'LL BE BACK HOME IN A FEW DAYS
HOW ARE YOU HOLDING UP?
I'VE NEVER FELT MORE ALIVE

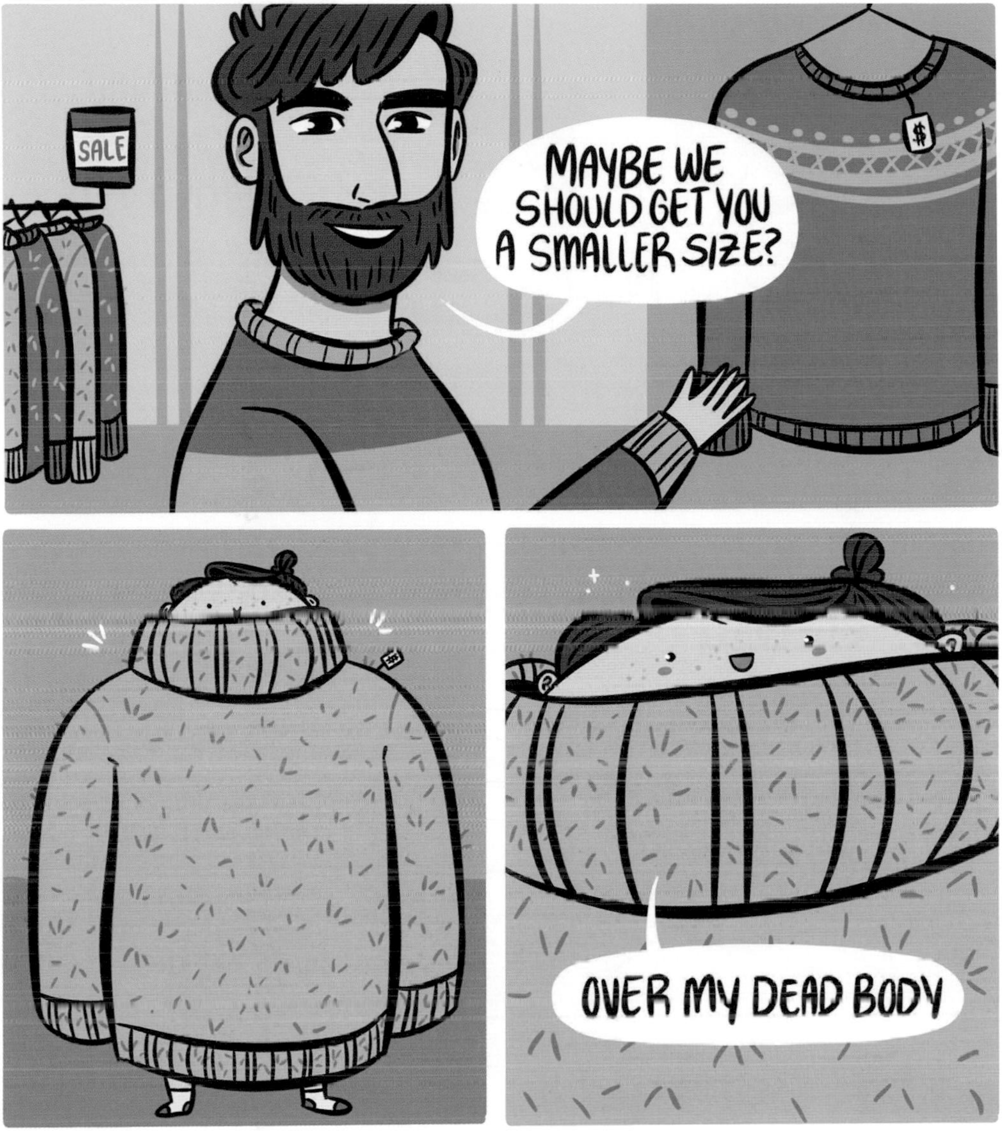
SALE
MAYBE WE SHOULD GET YOU A SMALLER SIZE?
OVER MY DEAD BODY

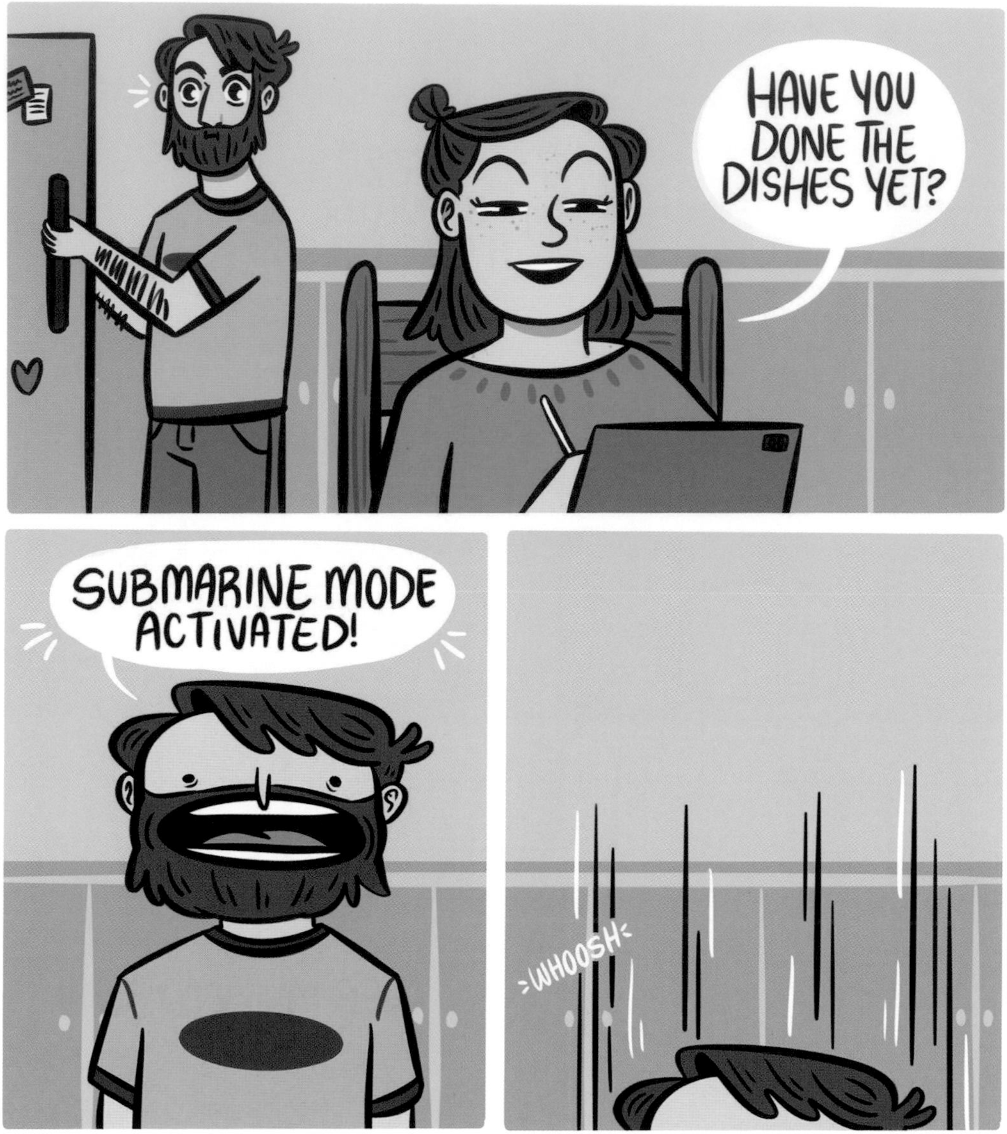
HAVE YOU DONE THE DISHES YET?
SUBMARINE MODE ACTIVATED!
WHOOSH

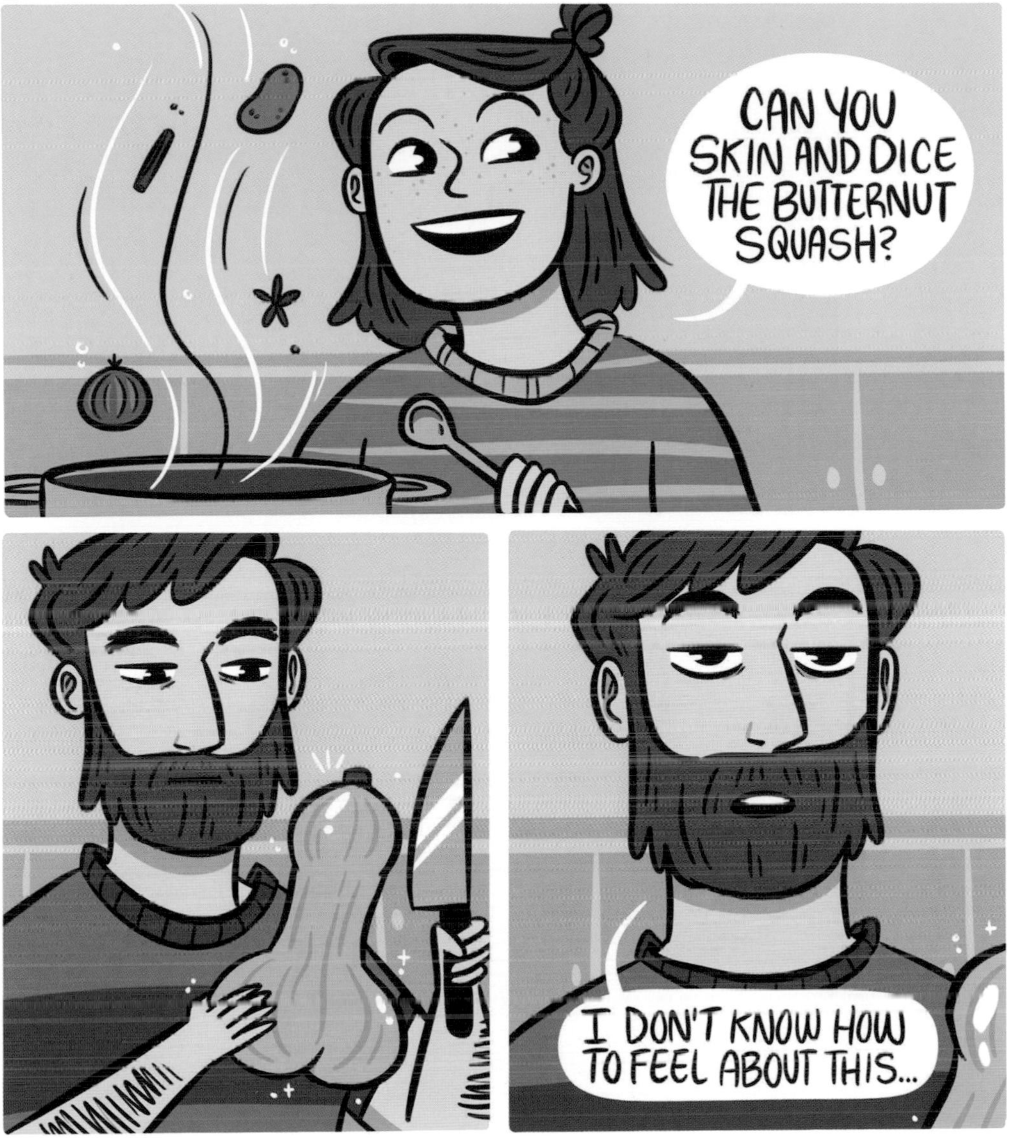
CAN YOU SKIN AND DICE THE BUTTERNUT SQUASH?
I DON'T KNOW HOW TO FEEL ABOUT THIS...

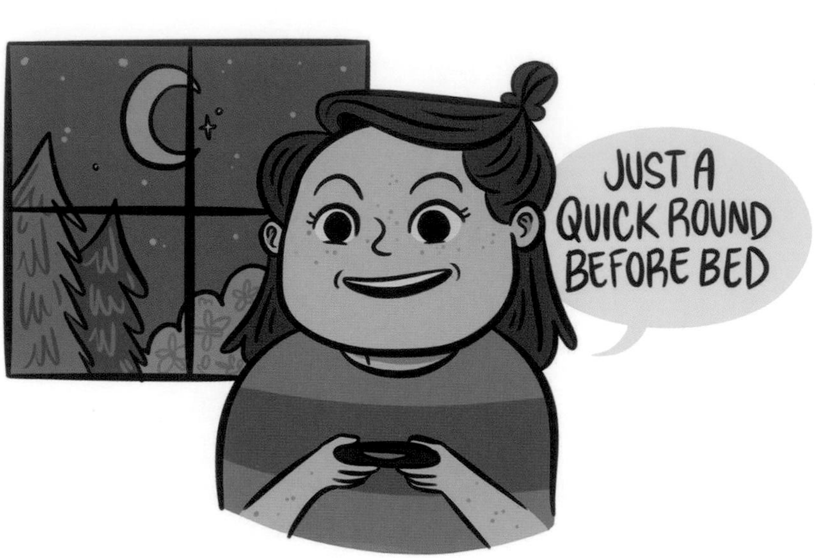
JUST A QUICK ROUND BEFORE BED

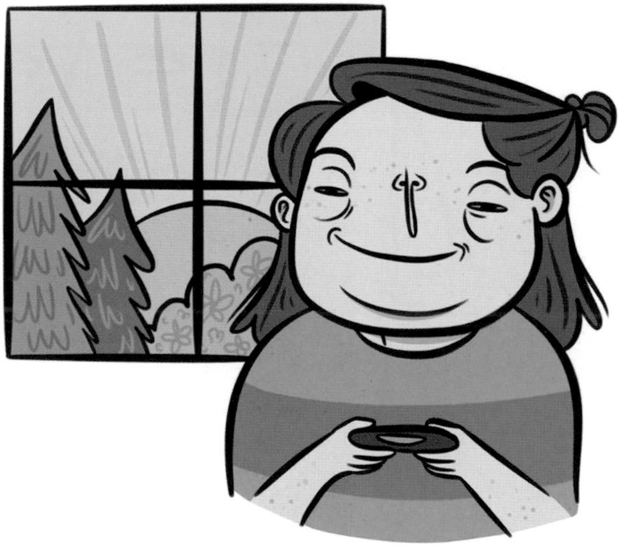

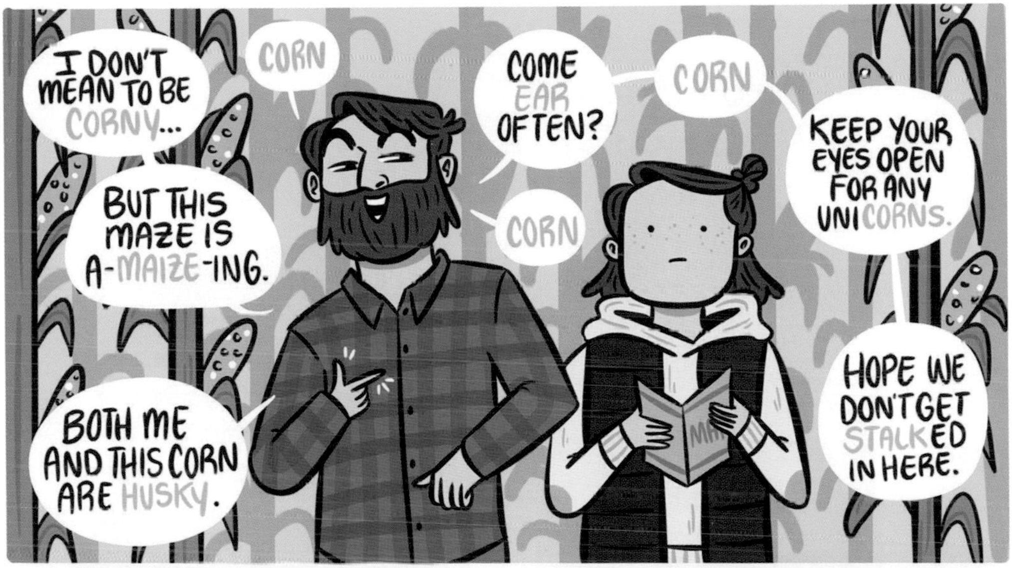
I DON'T MEAN TO BE CORNY...
BUT THIS MAZE IS A-MAIZE-ING.
BOTH ME AND THIS CORN ARE HUSKY.
CORN
COME EAR OFTEN?
CORN
CORN
KEEP YOUR EYES OPEN FOR ANY UNICORNS.
HOPE WE DON'T GET STALKED IN HERE.

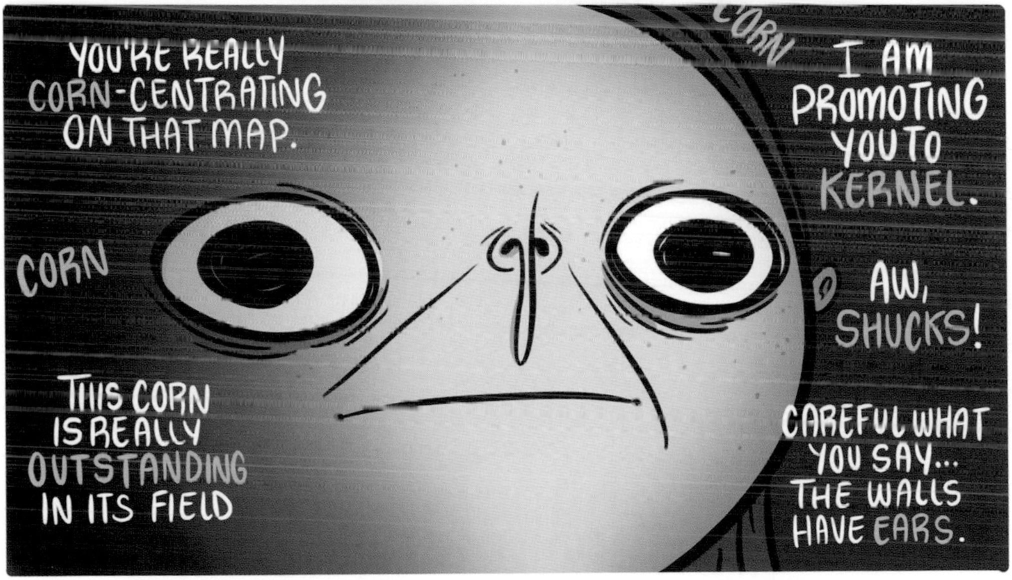
YOU'RE REALLY CORN-CENTRATING ON THAT MAP.
CORN
THIS CORN IS REALLY OUTSTANDING IN ITS FIELD
CORN
I AM PROMOTING YOU TO KERNEL.
AW, SHUCKS!
CAREFUL WHAT YOU SAY... THE WALLS HAVE EARS.

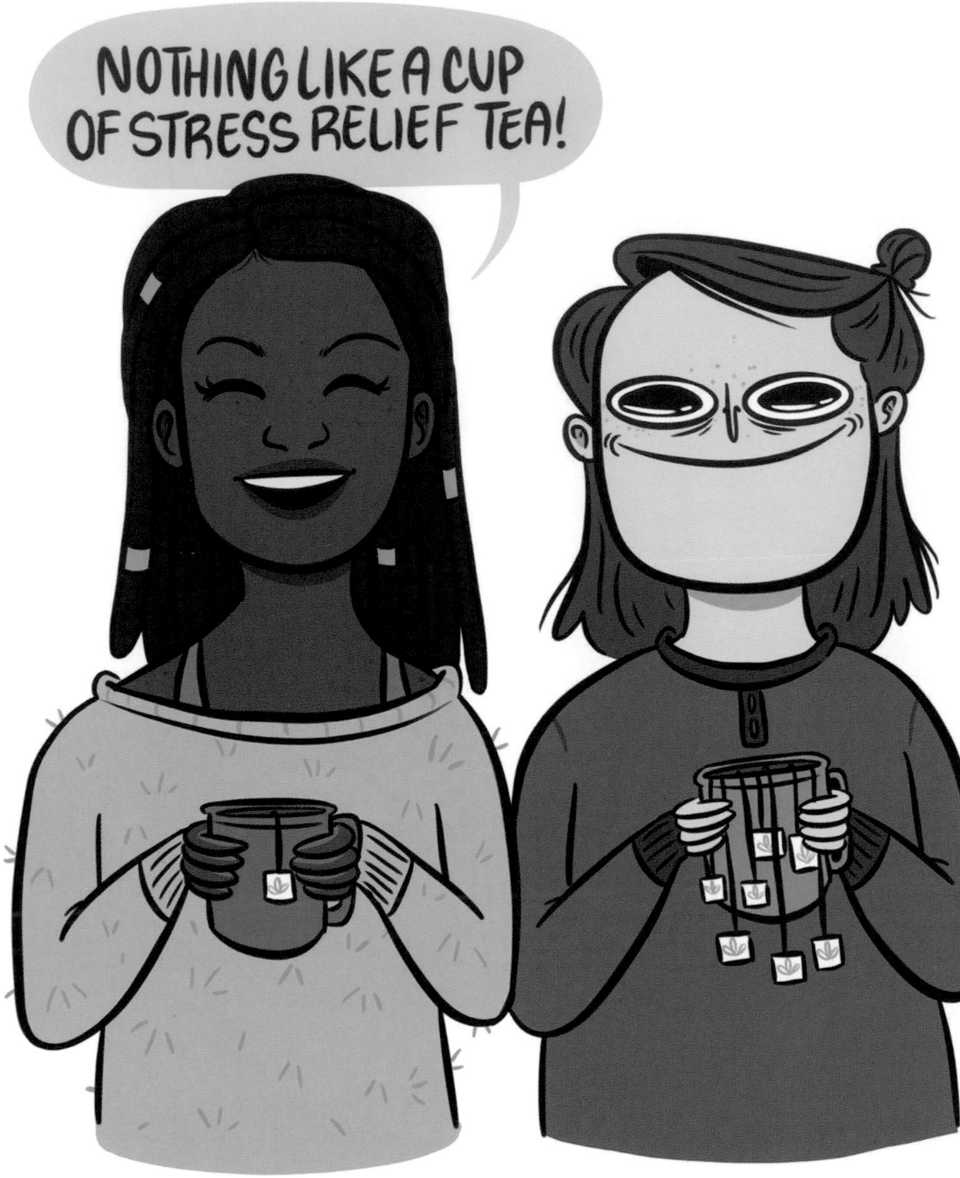
NOTHING LIKE A CUP OF STRESS RELIEF TEA!

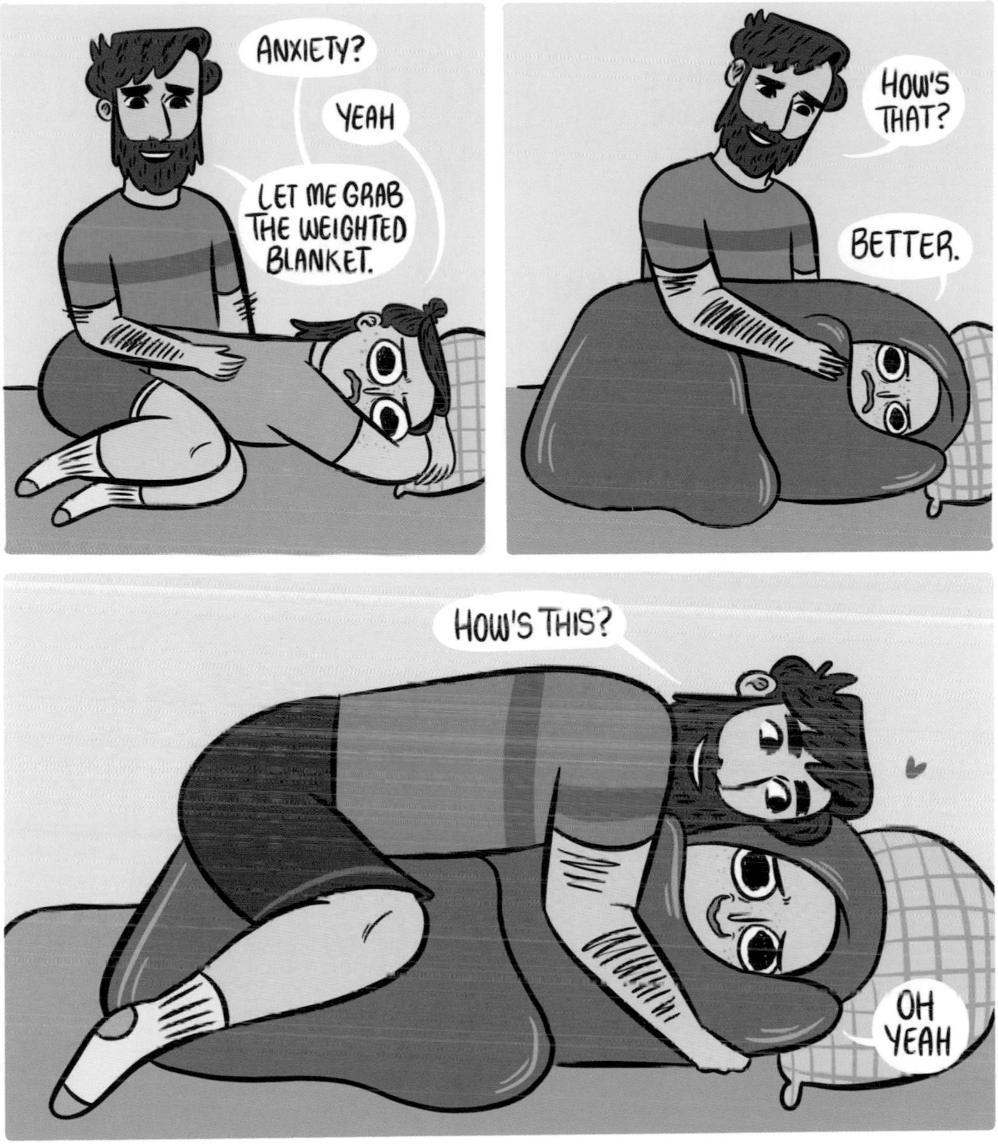
ANXIETY?
YEAH
LET ME GRAB THE WEIGHTED BLANKET.
HOW'S THAT?
BETTER.
HOW'S THIS?
OH YEAH

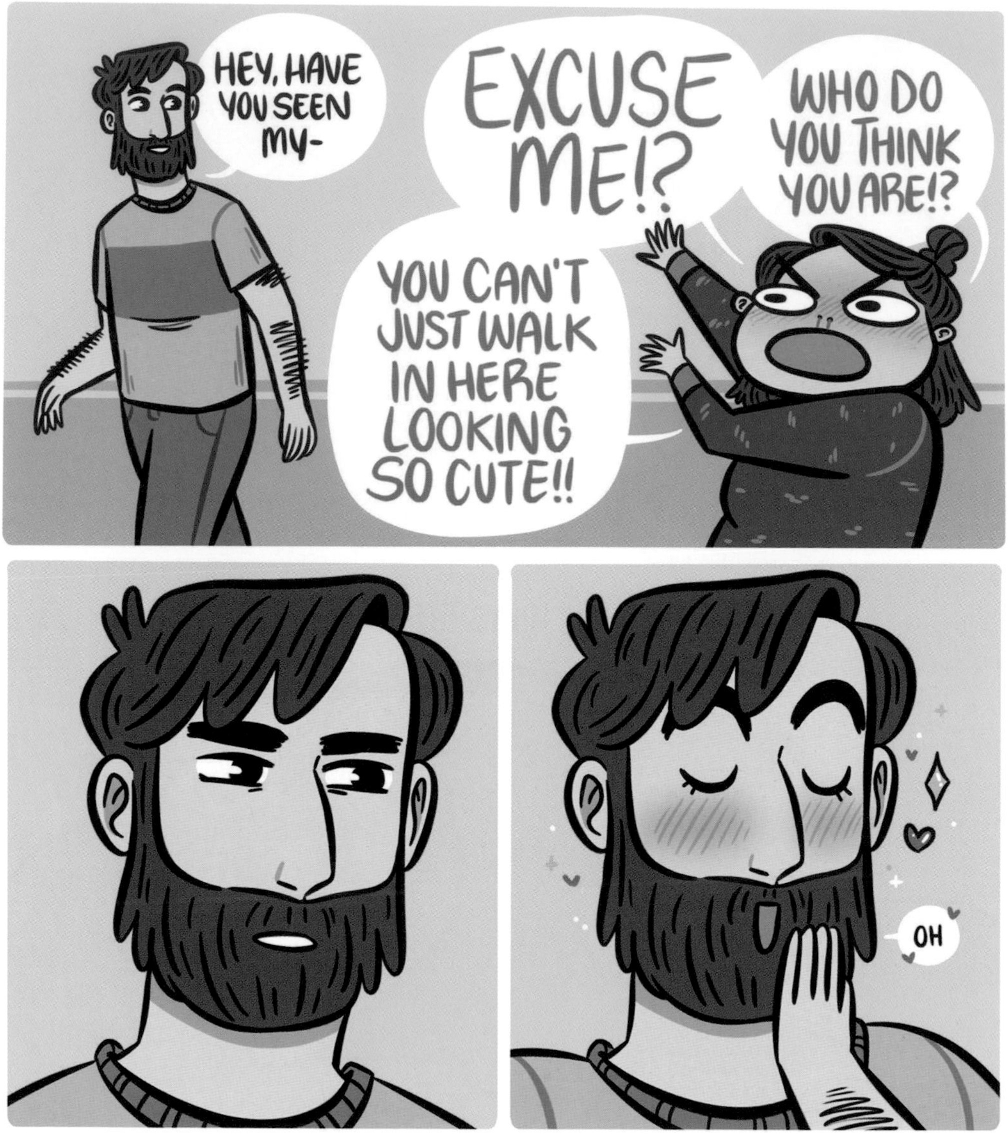
HEY, HAVE YOU SEEN MY-
EXCUSE ME!?
WHO DO YOU THINK YOU ARE!?
YOU CAN'T JUST WALK IN HERE LOOKING SO CUTE!!
OH

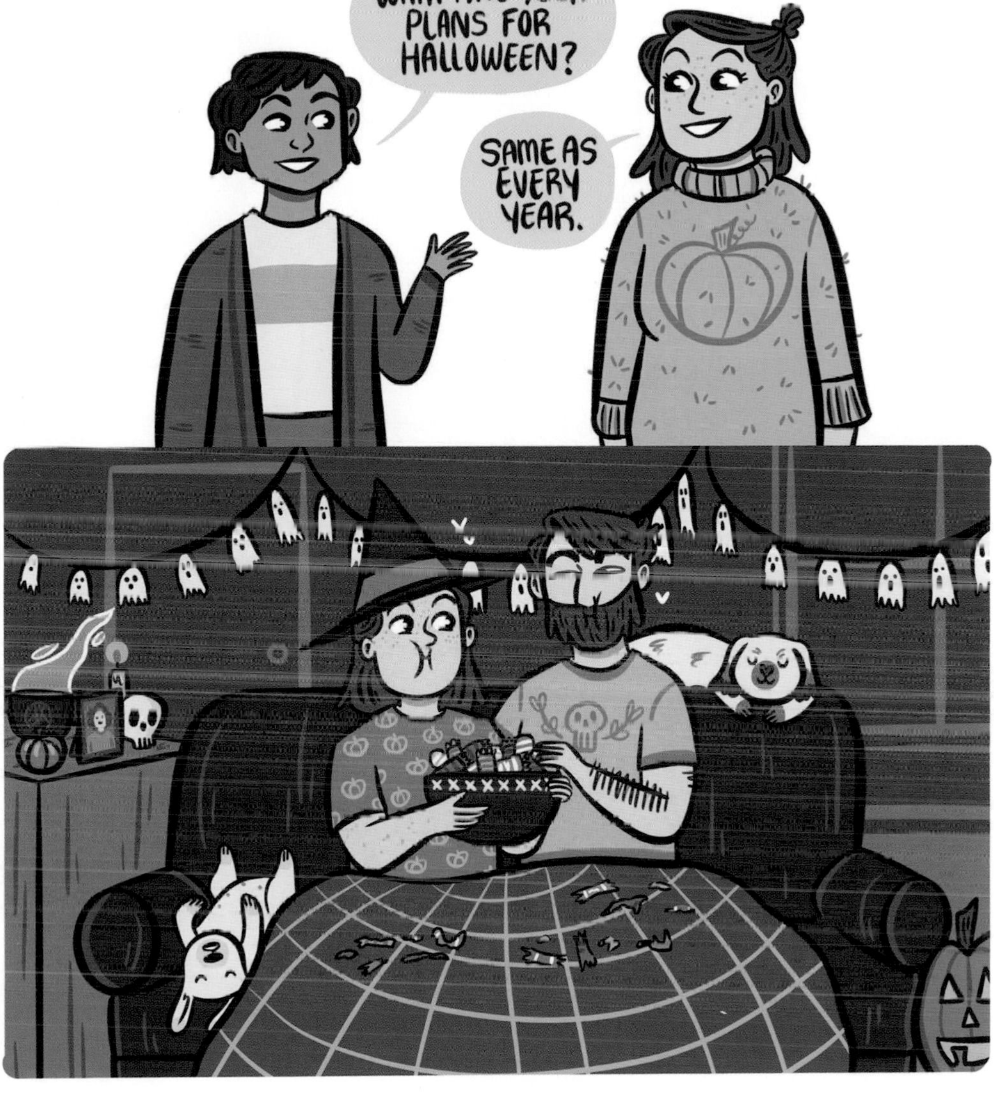
WHAT ARE YOUR PLANS FOR HALLOWEEN?
SAME AS EVERY YEAR.

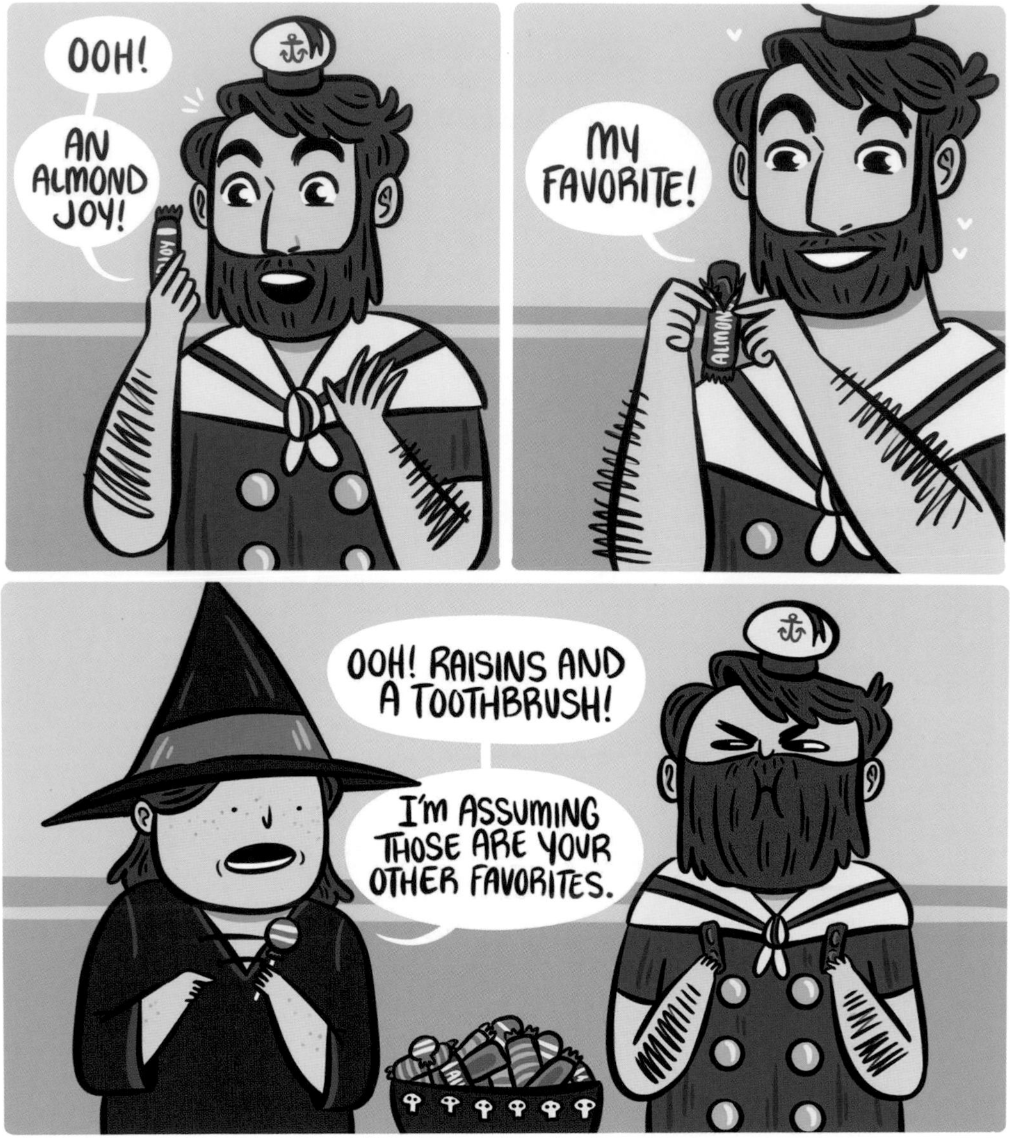
OOH!
AN ALMOND JOY!
JOY
MY FAVORITE!
ALMON
OOH! RAISINS AND A TOOTHBRUSH!
I'M ASSUMING THOSE ARE YOUR OTHER FAVORITES.

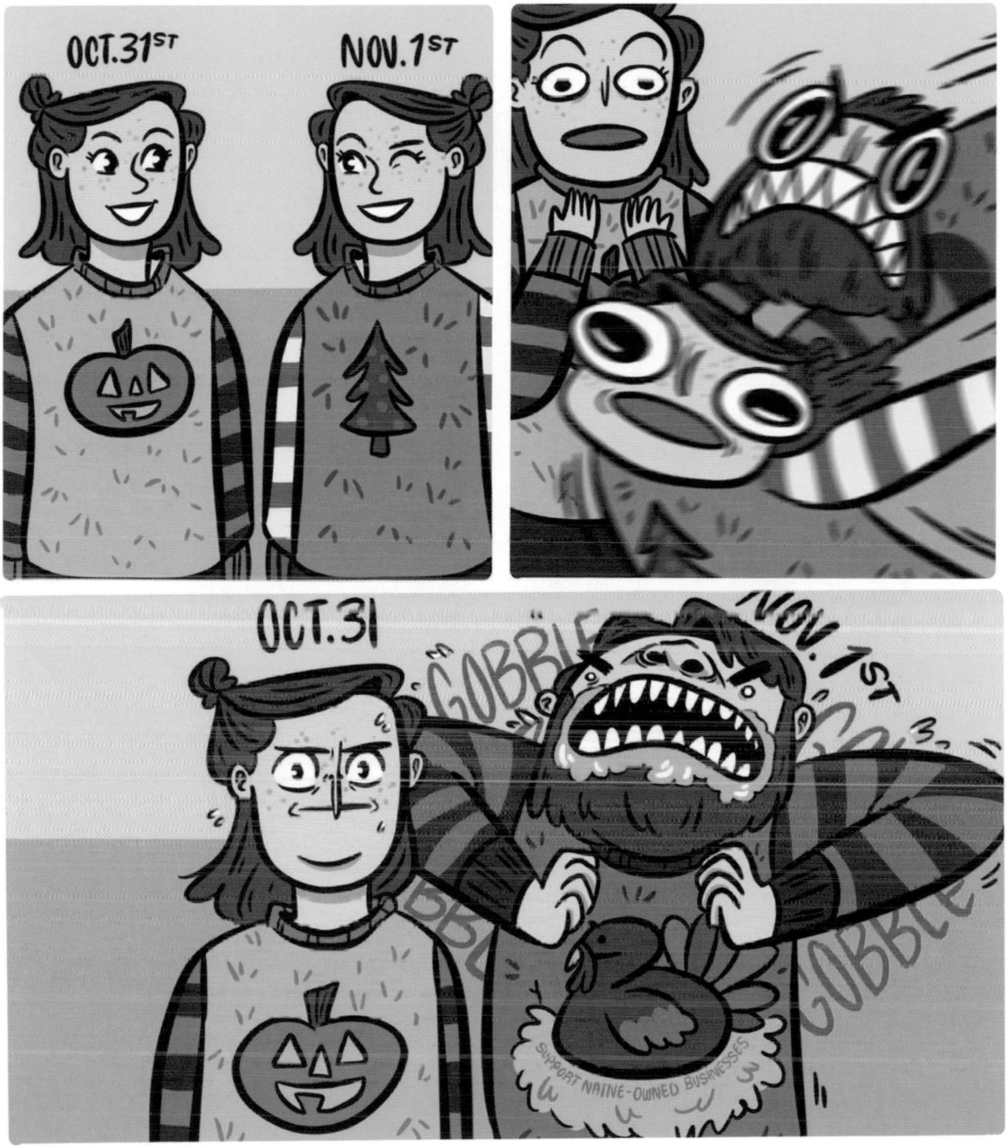
OCT.31ST
NOV.1ST
OCT.31
NOV.1ST
GOBBLE
GOBBLE
SUPPORT NATIVE-OWNED BUSINESSES

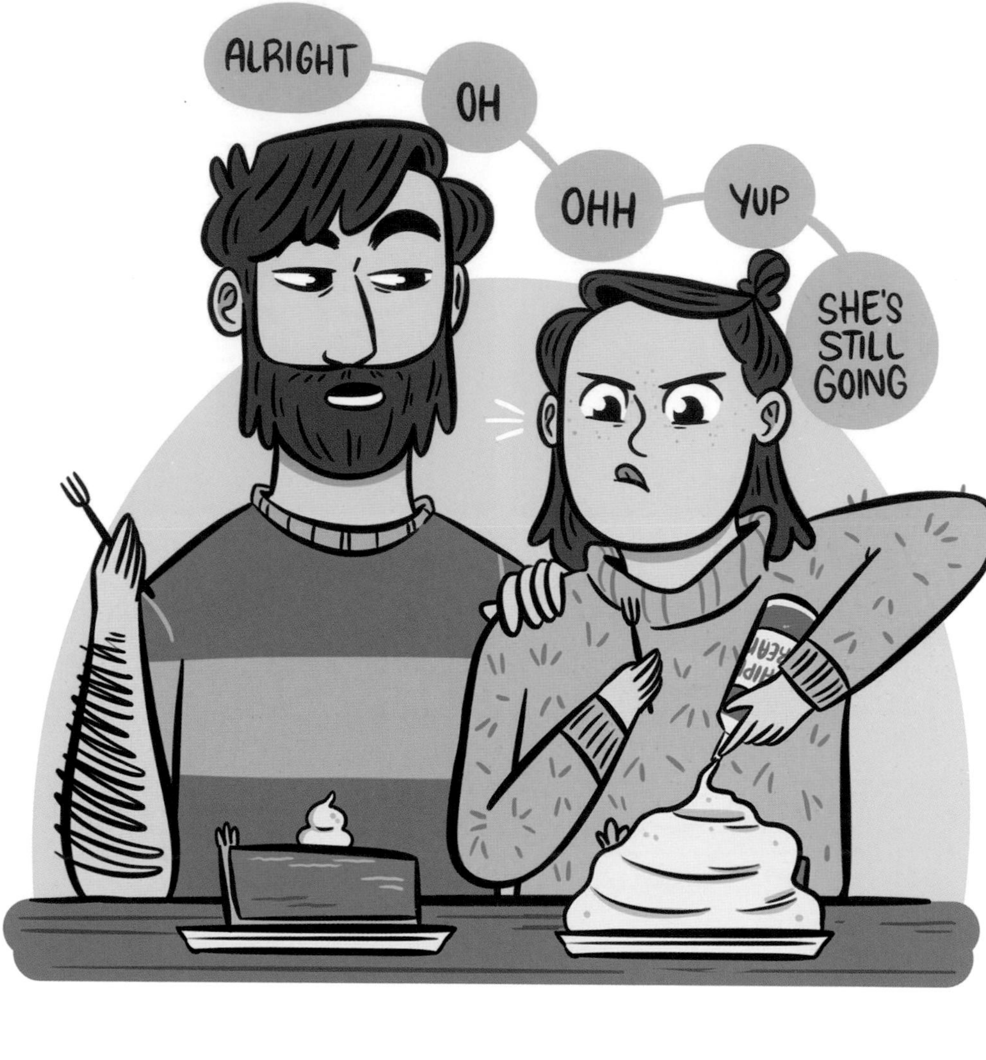
ALRIGHT
OH
OHH
YUP
SHE'S STILL GOING

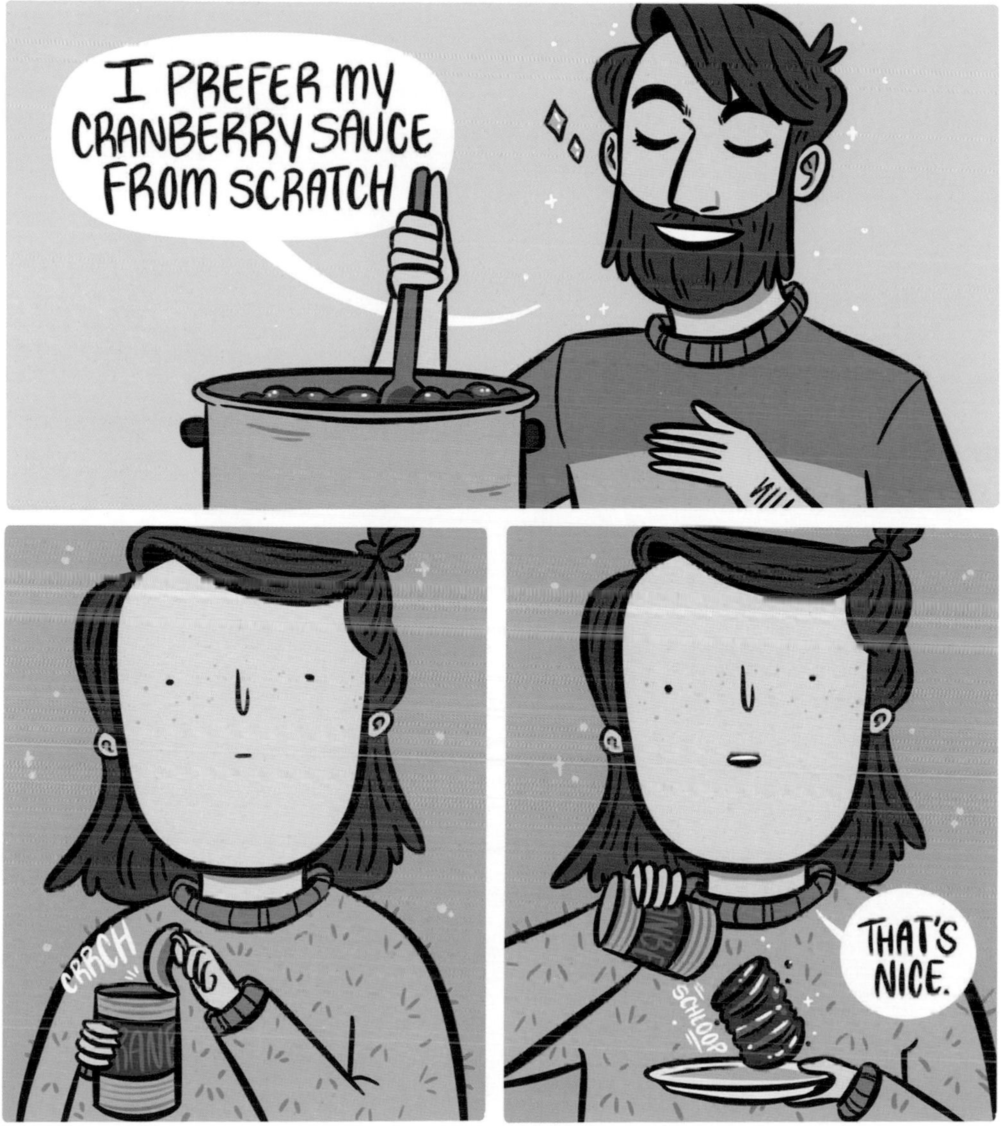
I PREFER MY CRANBERRY SAUCE FROM SCRATCH
CRRCH
SCHLOOP
THAT'S NICE.

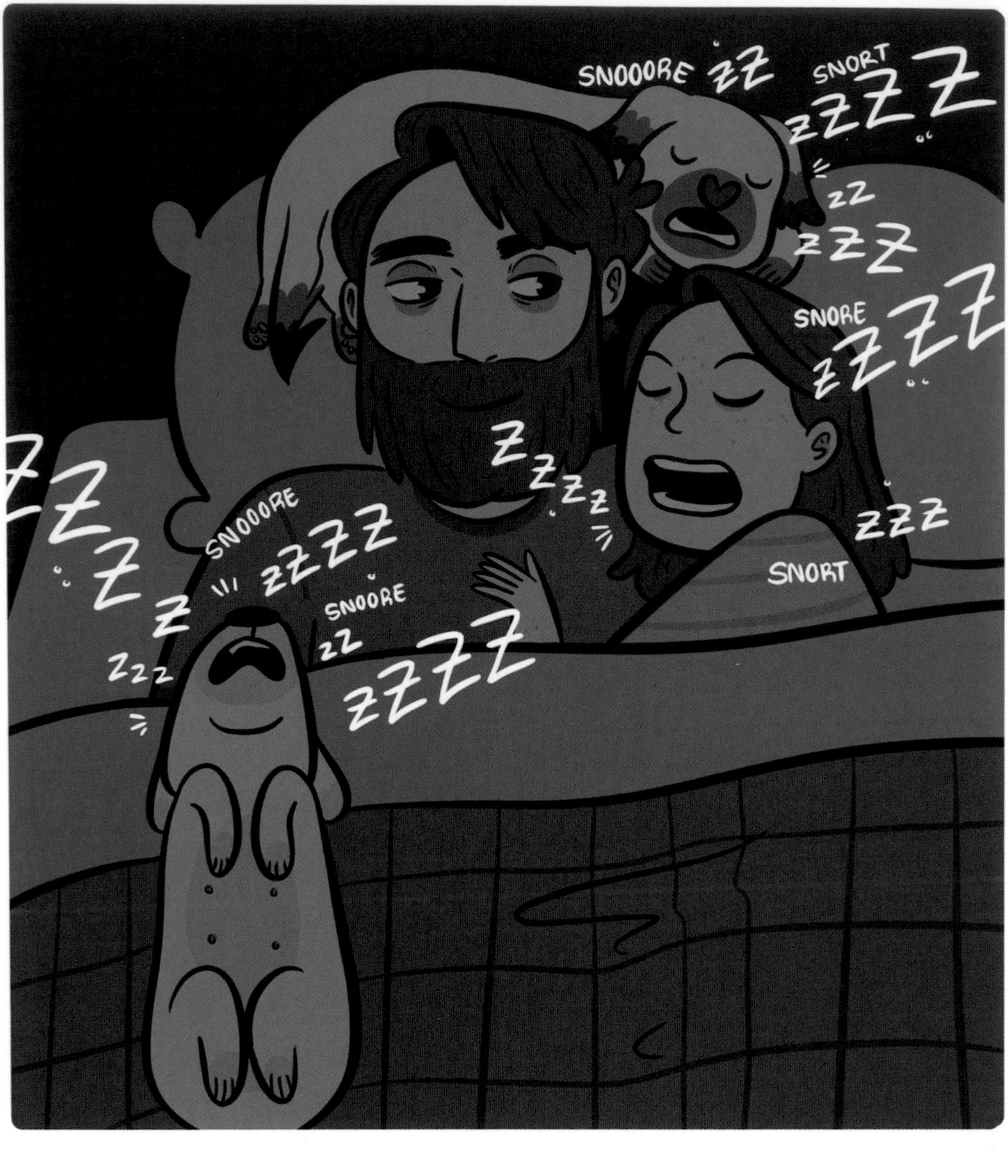
SNOOORE ZZ
SNORT ZZZZ
ZZ
ZZZ
SNORE ZZZZ
ZZZ
SNORT
ZZZZZ
Zzzz
SNOOORE ZZZZ
SNOORE ZZ
ZZZZZ
Zzz

WAKING FROM A NAP

EXPECTATION:

REALITY:

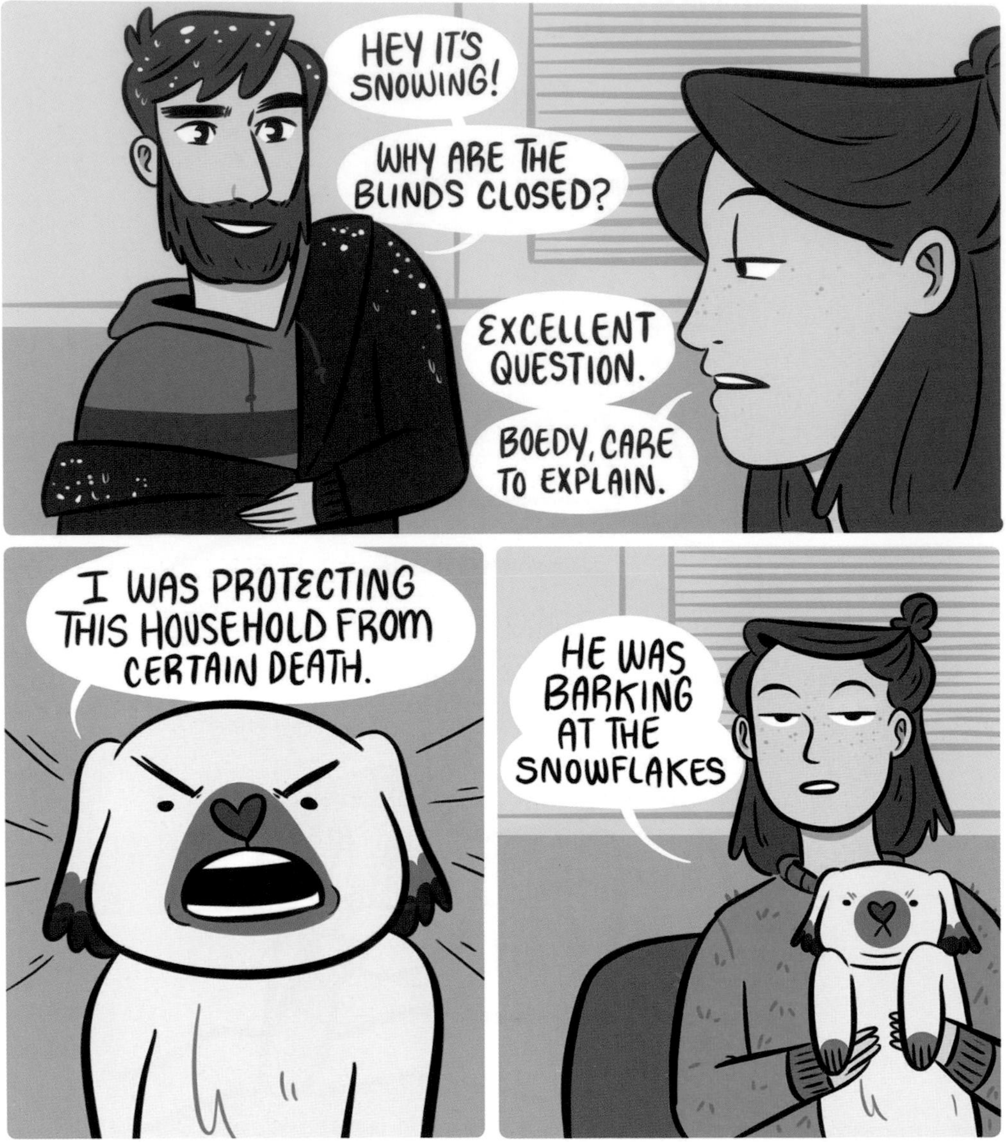
HEY IT'S SNOWING!
WHY ARE THE BLINDS CLOSED?
EXCELLENT QUESTION.
BOEDY, CARE TO EXPLAIN.
I WAS PROTECTING THIS HOUSEHOLD FROM CERTAIN DEATH.
HE WAS BARKING AT THE SNOWFLAKES

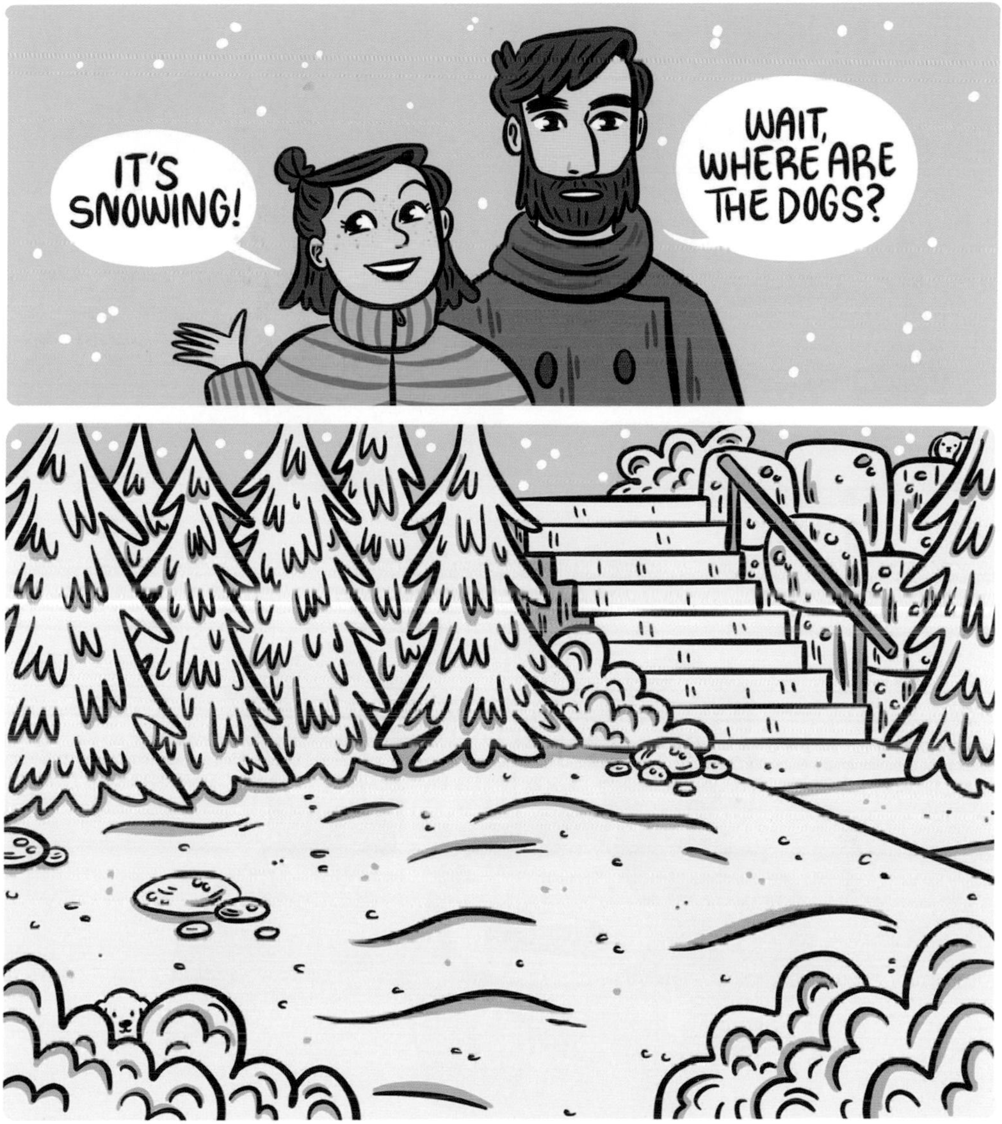
IT'S SNOWING!
WAIT, WHERE ARE THE DOGS?

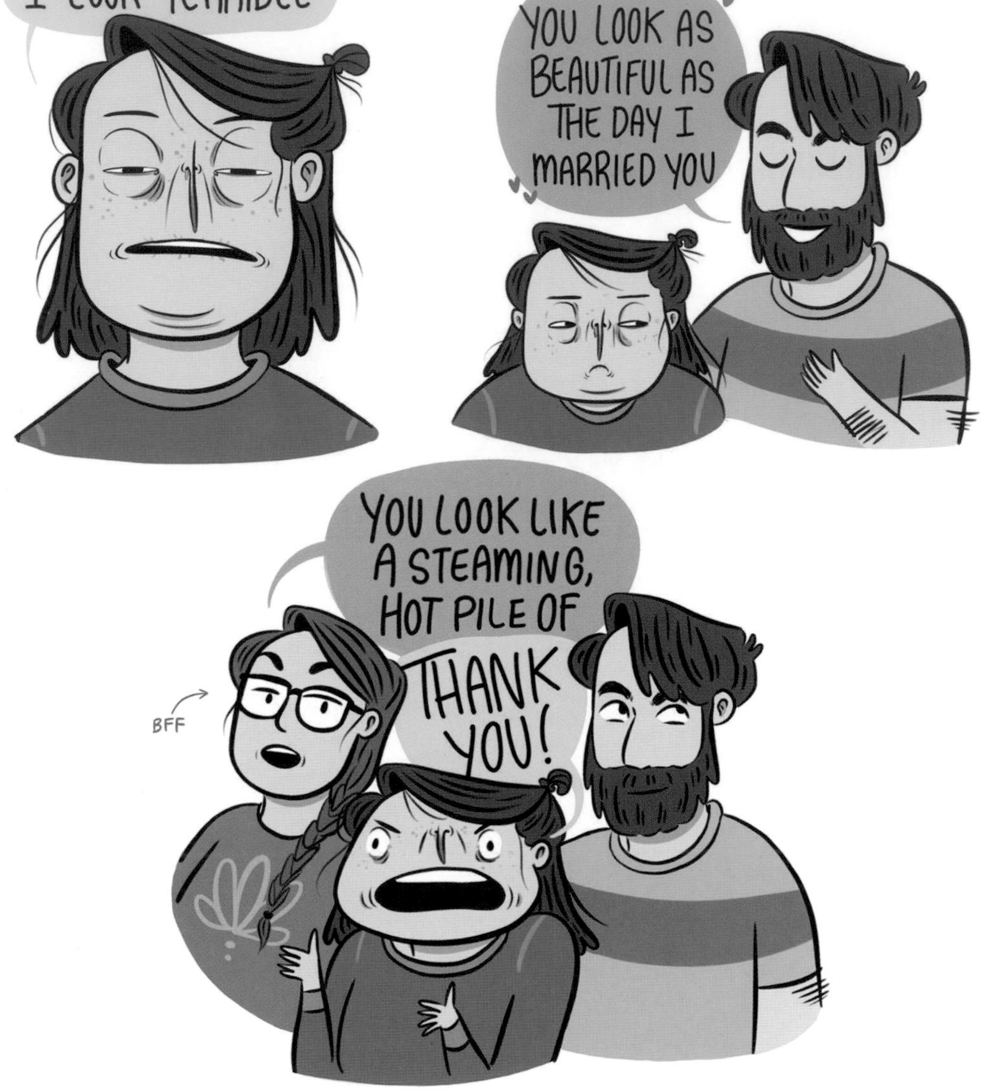
I LOOK TERRIBLE
YOU LOOK AS BEAUTIFUL AS THE DAY I MARRIED YOU
BFF
YOU LOOK LIKE A STEAMING, HOT PILE OF
THANK YOU!

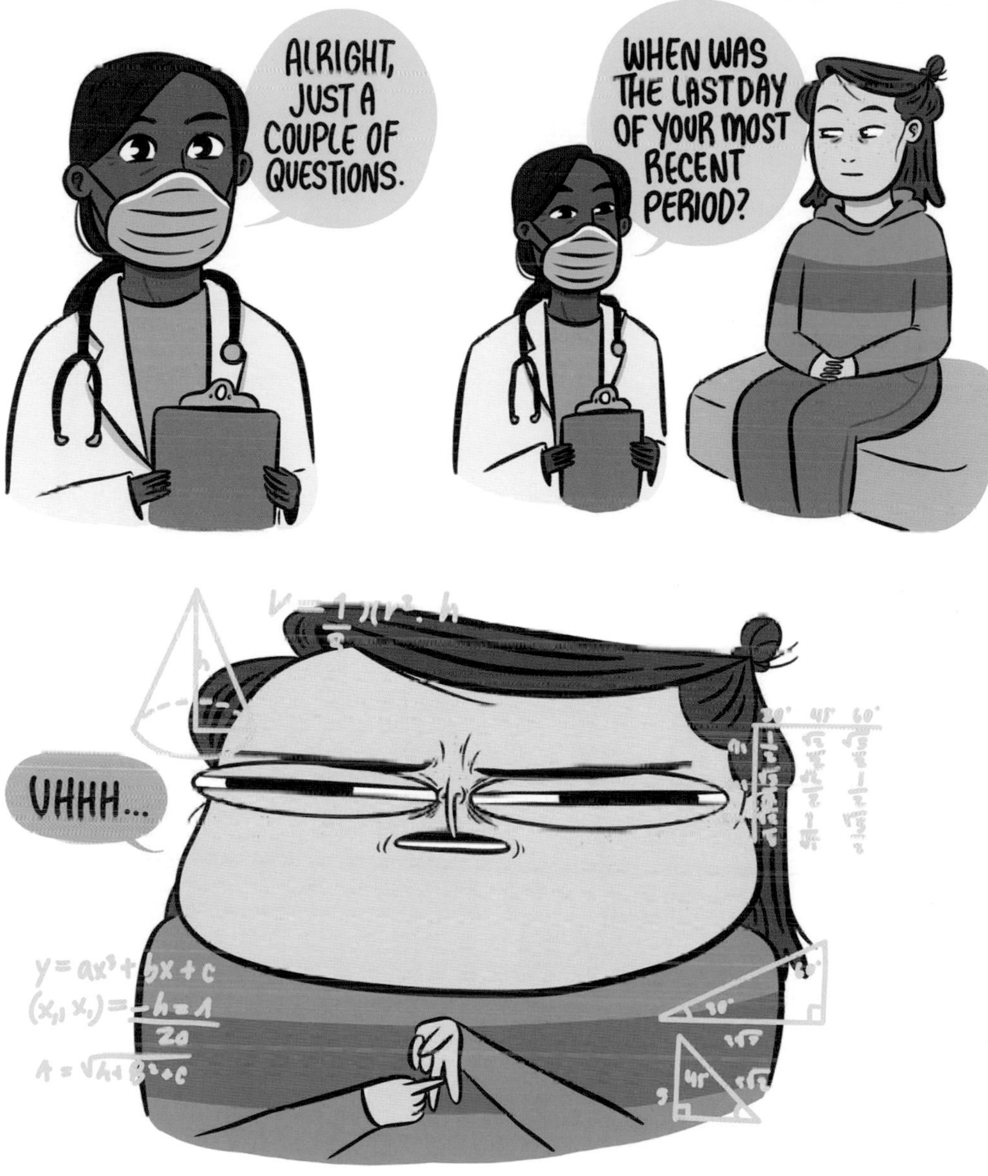
ALRIGHT, JUST A COUPLE OF QUESTIONS.
WHEN WAS THE LAST DAY OF YOUR MOST RECENT PERIOD?
UHHH...

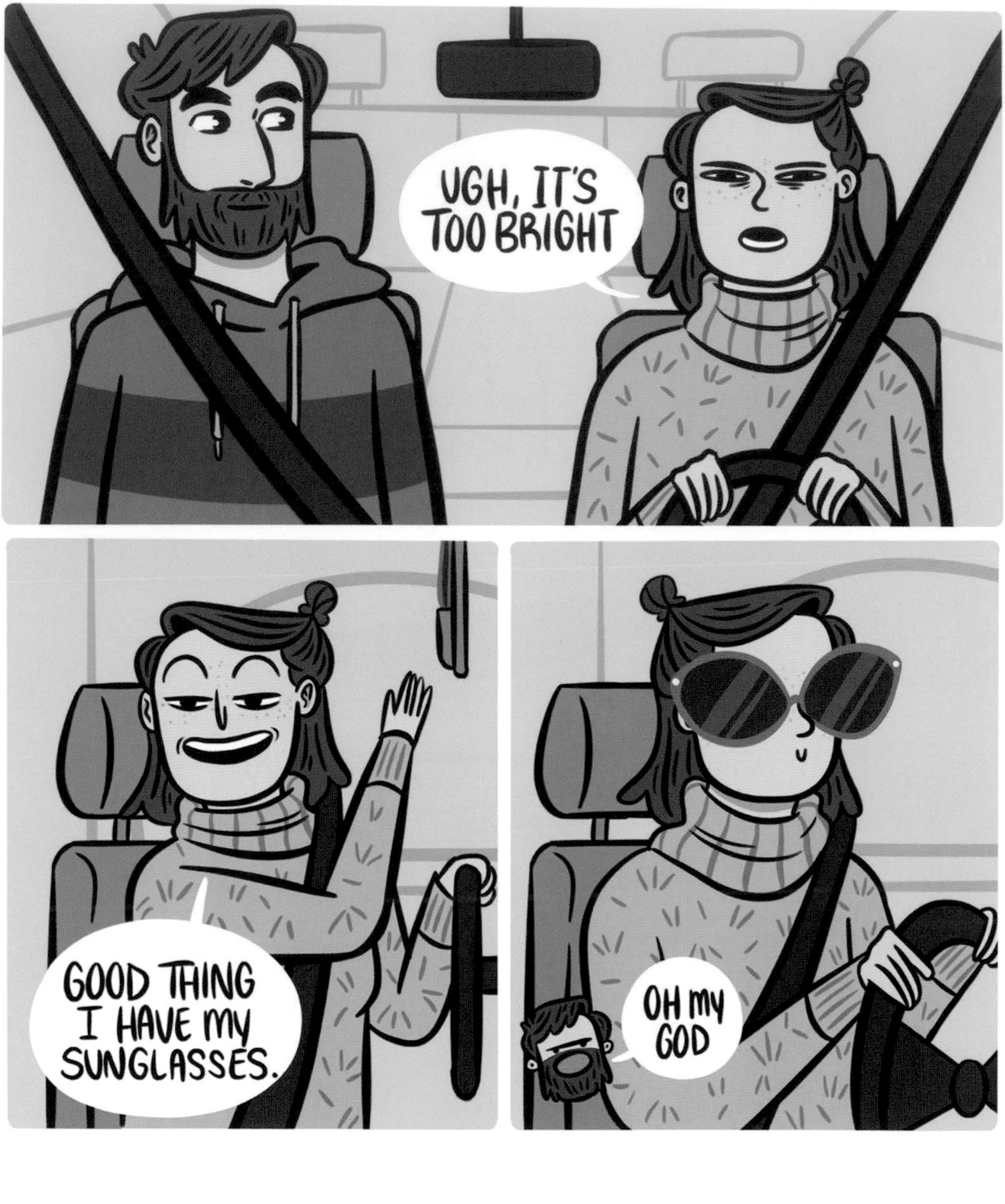
UGH, IT'S TOO BRIGHT
GOOD THING I HAVE MY SUNGLASSES.
OH MY GOD

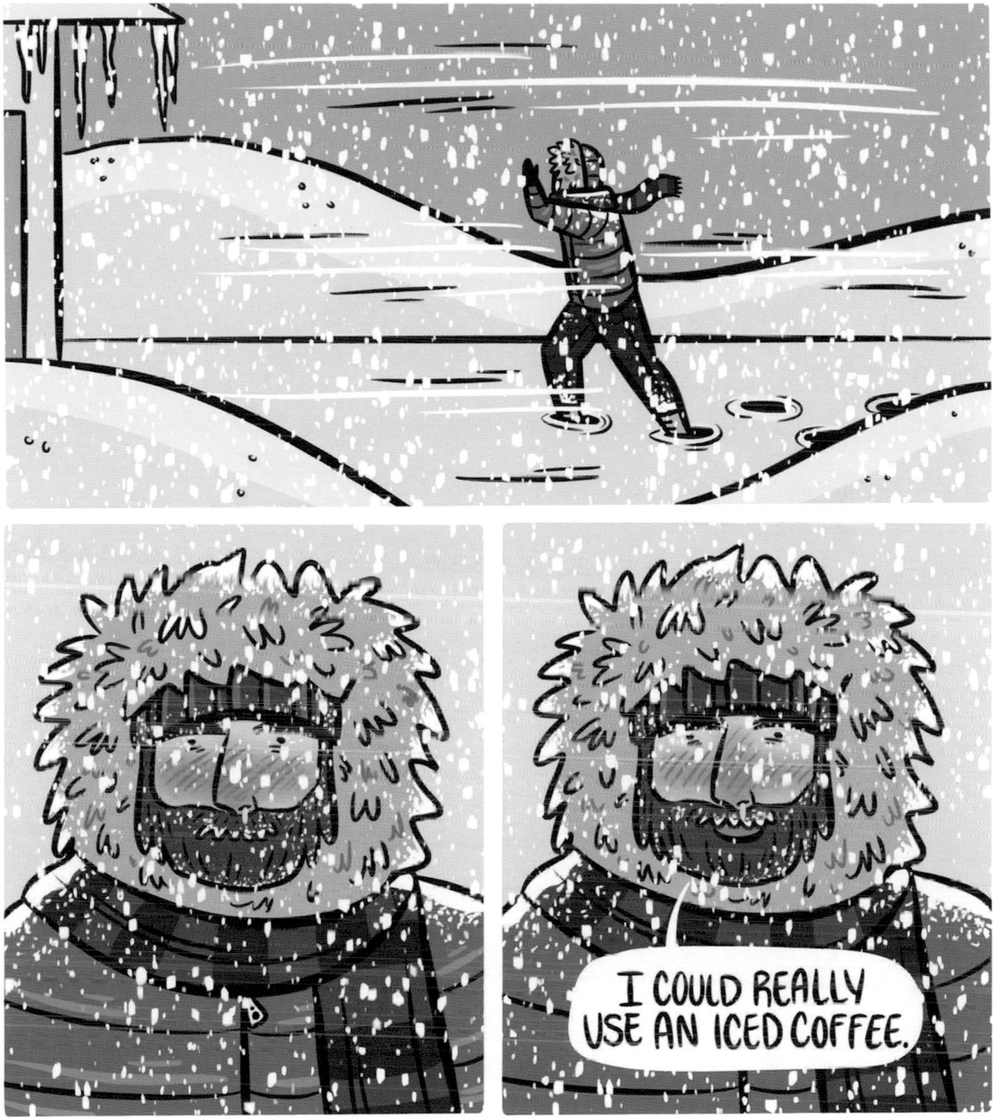
I COULD REALLY USE AN ICED COFFEE.

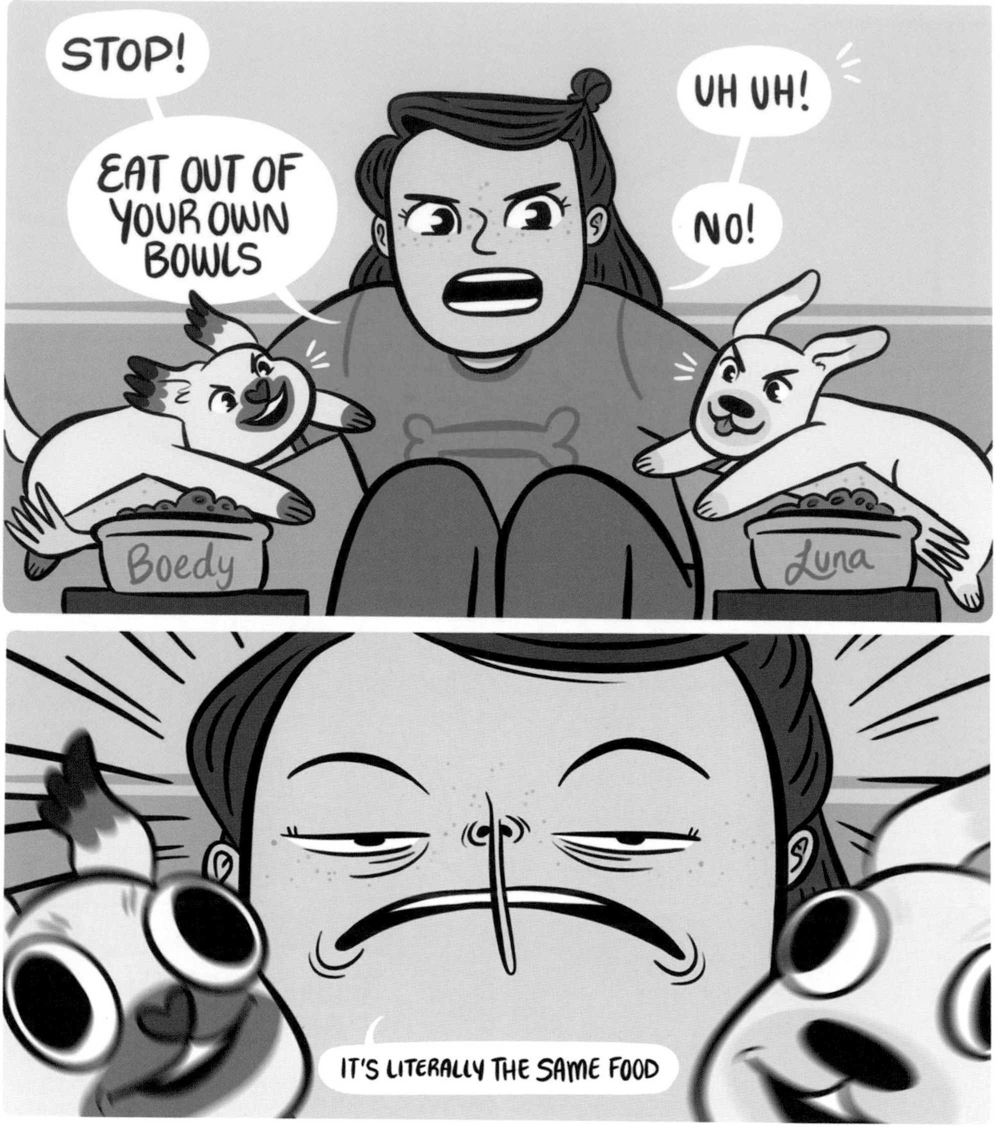
STOP!
EAT OUT OF YOUR OWN BOWLS
UH UH!
NO!
Boedy
Luna
IT'S LITERALLY THE SAME FOOD

START OF DECEMBER:

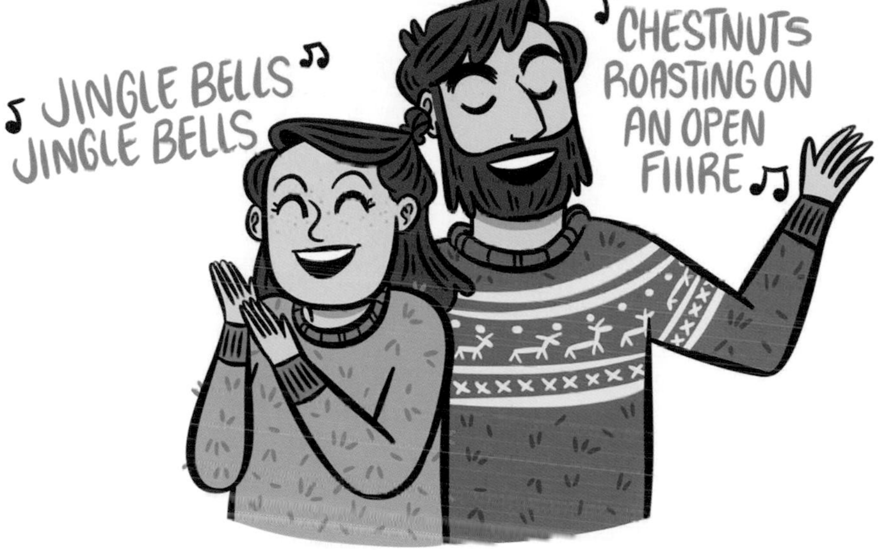
JINGLE BELLS
JINGLE BELLS
CHESTNUTS
ROASTING ON
AN OPEN
FIIIRE

END OF DECEMBER:

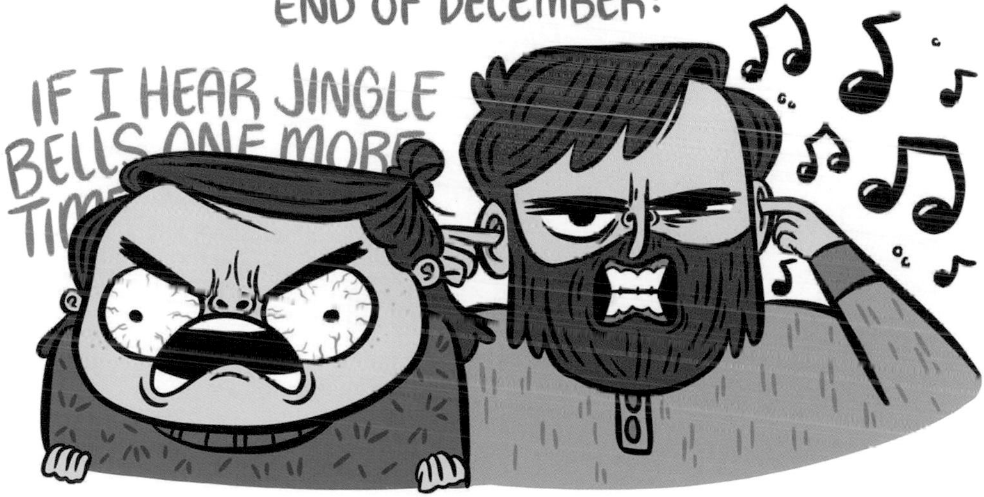
IF I HEAR JINGLE
BELLS ONE MOR

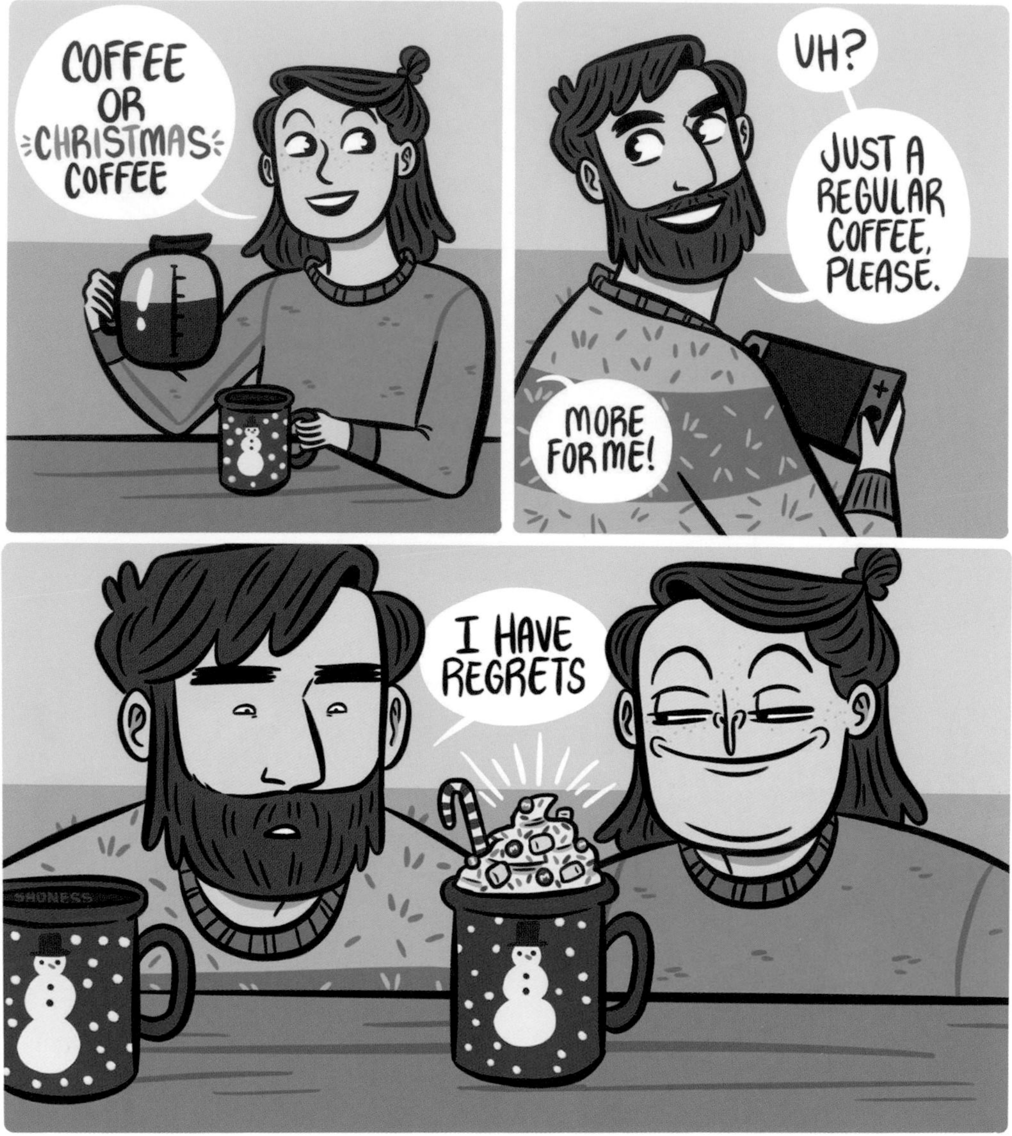
COFFEE OR CHRISTMAS COFFEE
UH?
JUST A REGULAR COFFEE, PLEASE.
MORE FOR ME!
I HAVE REGRETS

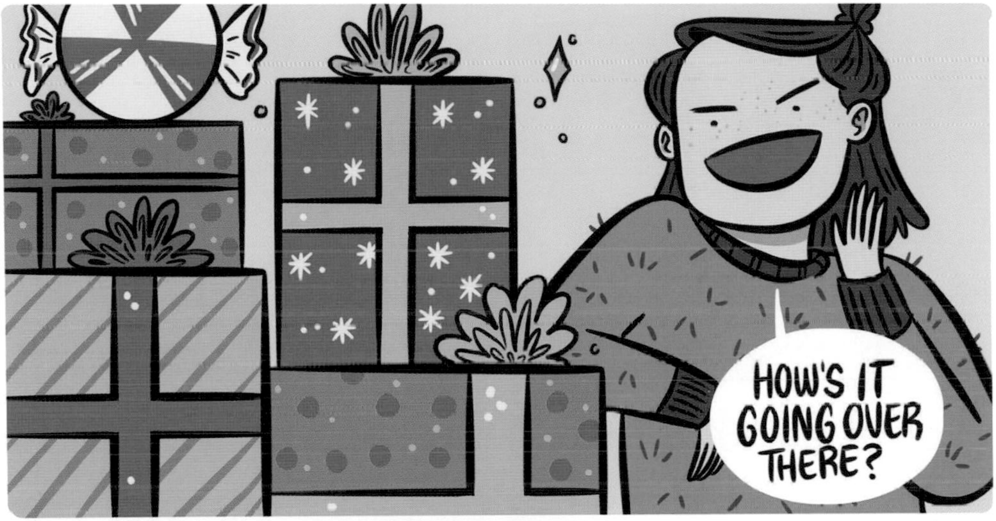
HOW'S IT GOING OVER THERE?

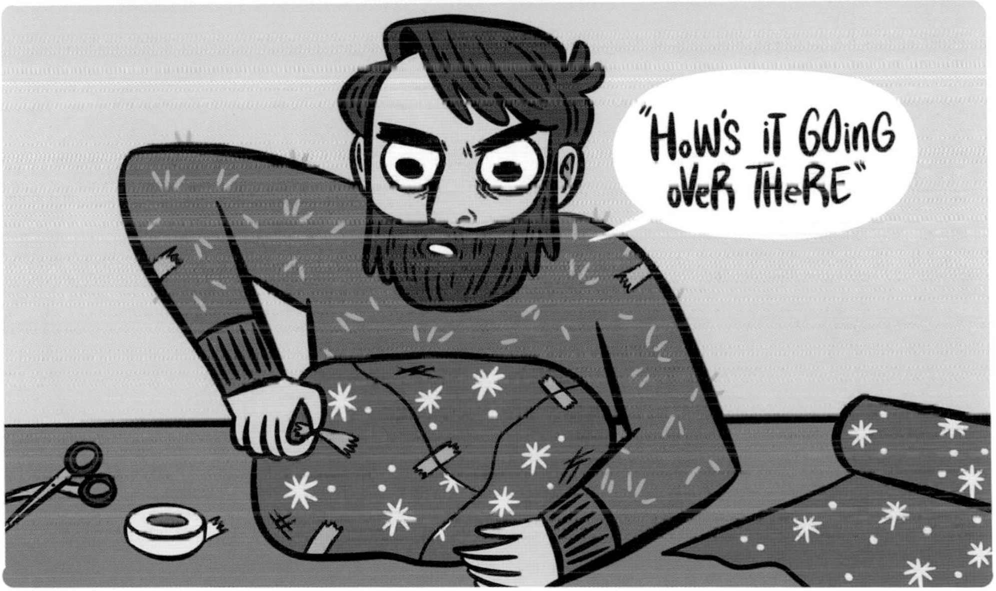
"HoW'S iT GOinG oVeR THeRE"

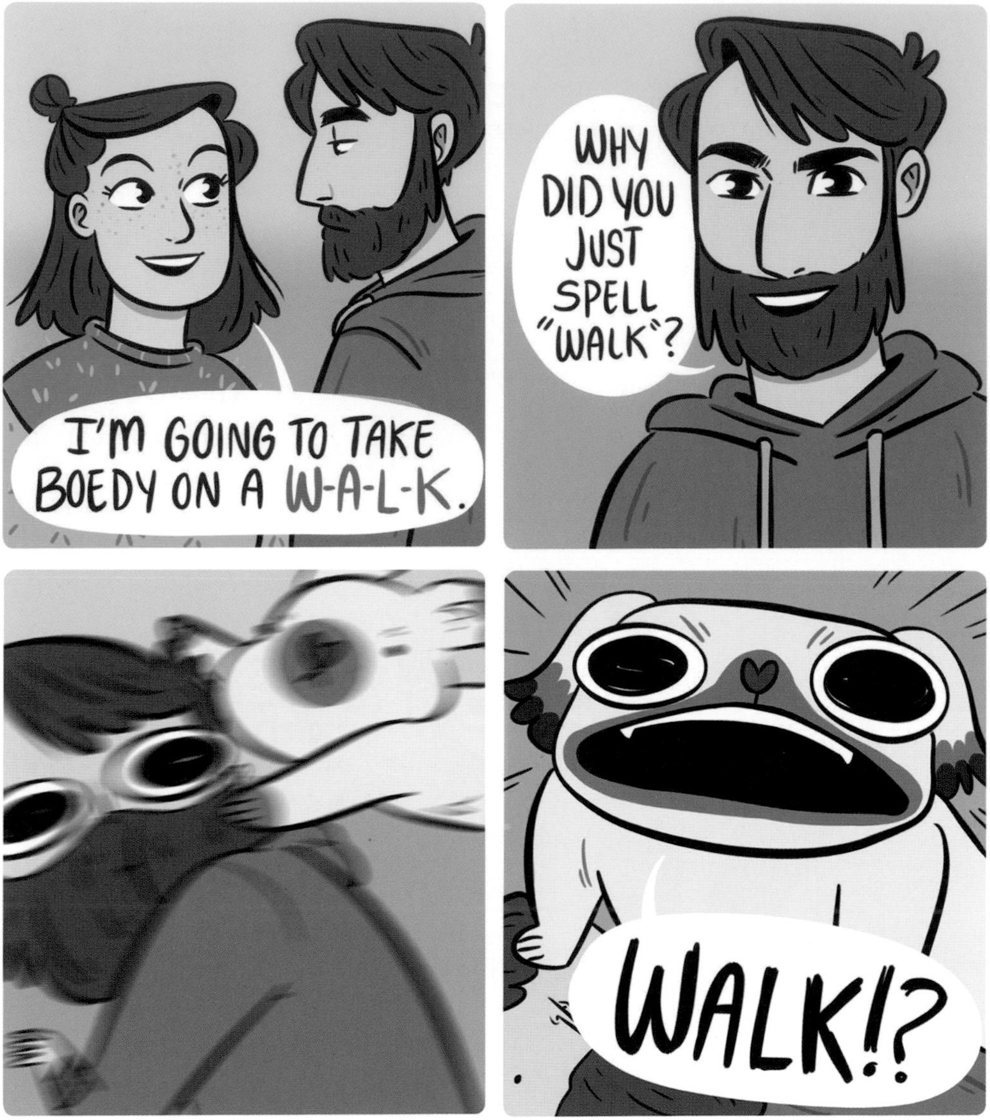
I'M GOING TO TAKE BOEDY ON A W-A-L-K.
WHY DID YOU JUST SPELL "WALK"?
WALK!?

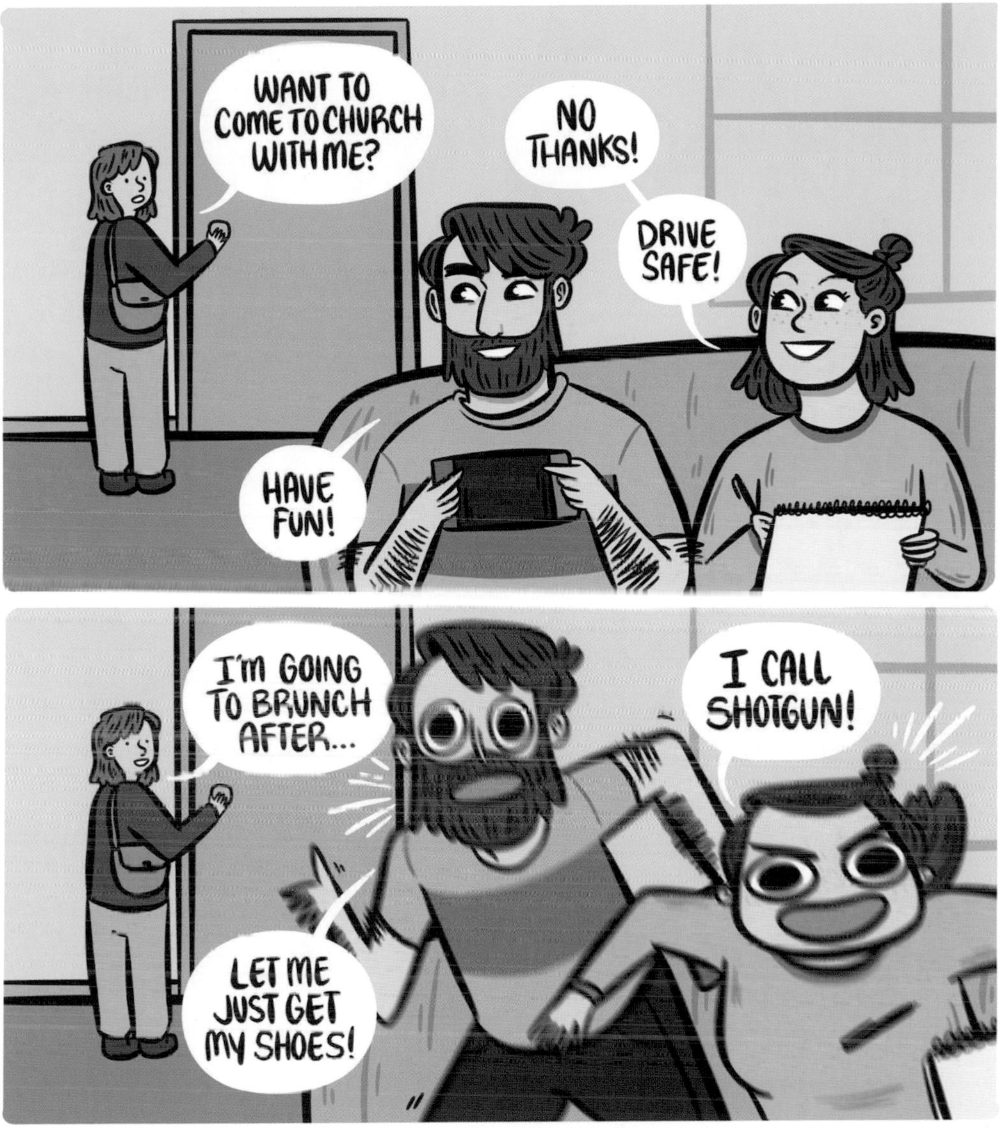
WANT TO COME TO CHURCH WITH ME?
NO THANKS!
DRIVE SAFE!
HAVE FUN!
I'M GOING TO BRUNCH AFTER...
I CALL SHOTGUN!
LET ME JUST GET MY SHOES!

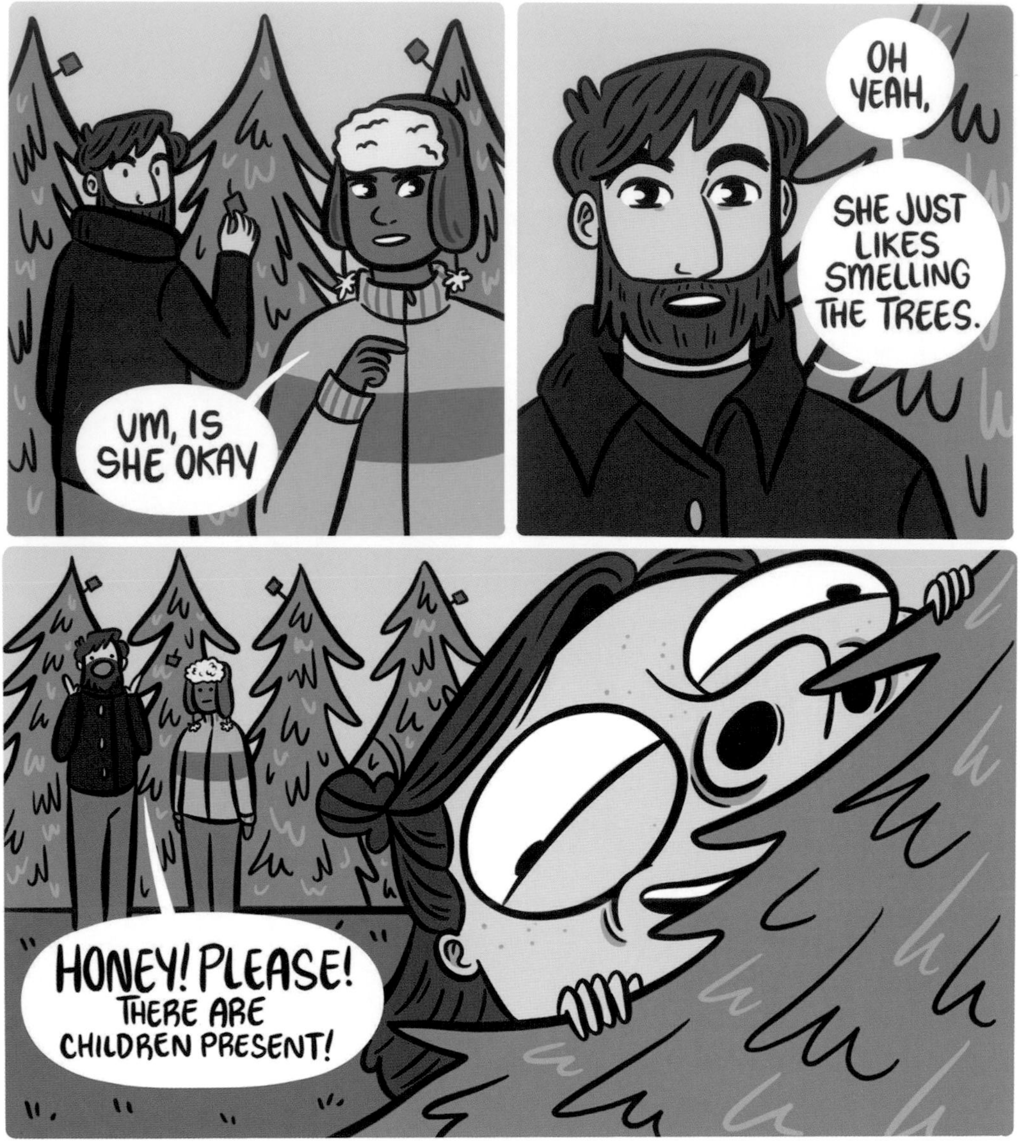
UM, IS SHE OKAY
OH YEAH,
SHE JUST LIKES SMELLING THE TREES.
HONEY! PLEASE! THERE ARE CHILDREN PRESENT!

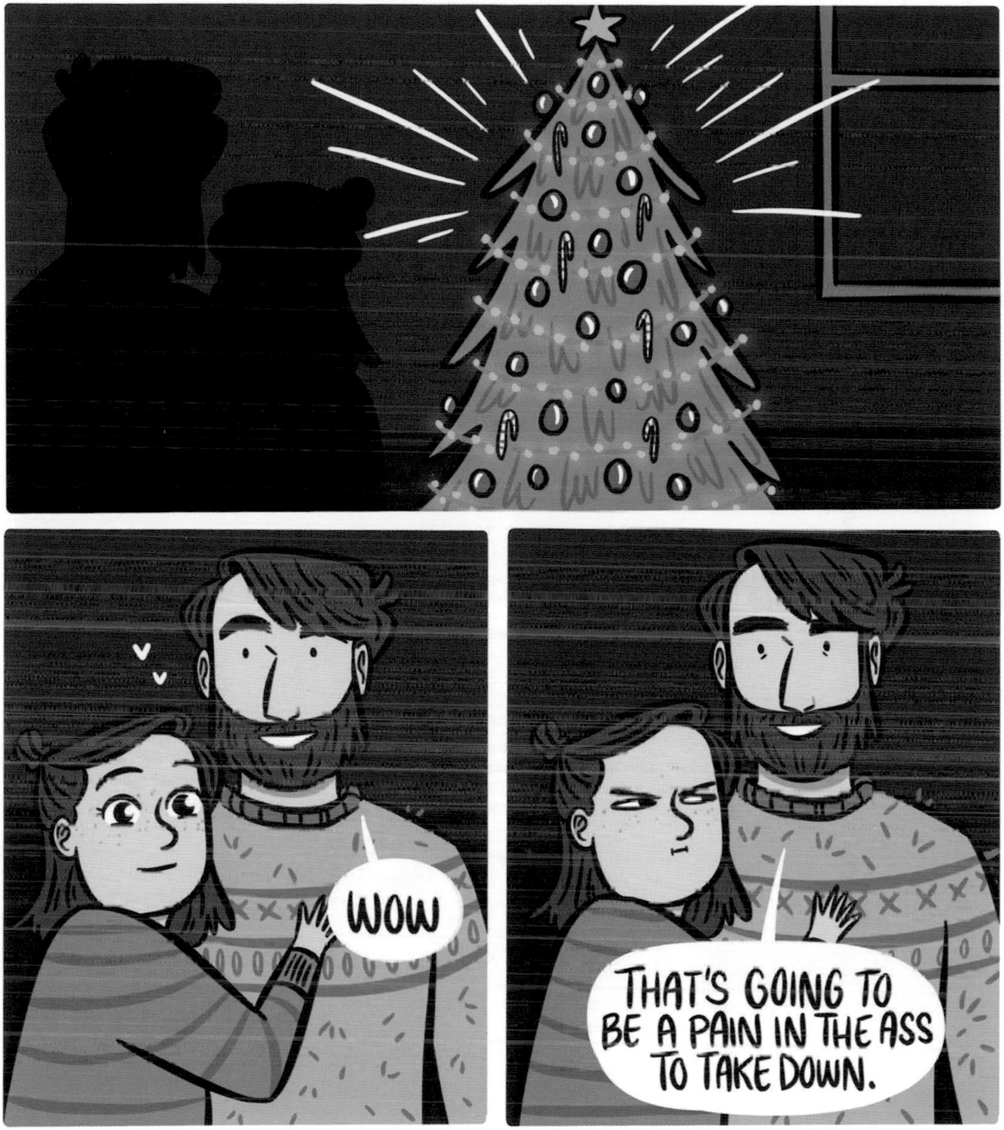
WOW
THAT'S GOING TO BE A PAIN IN THE ASS TO TAKE DOWN.

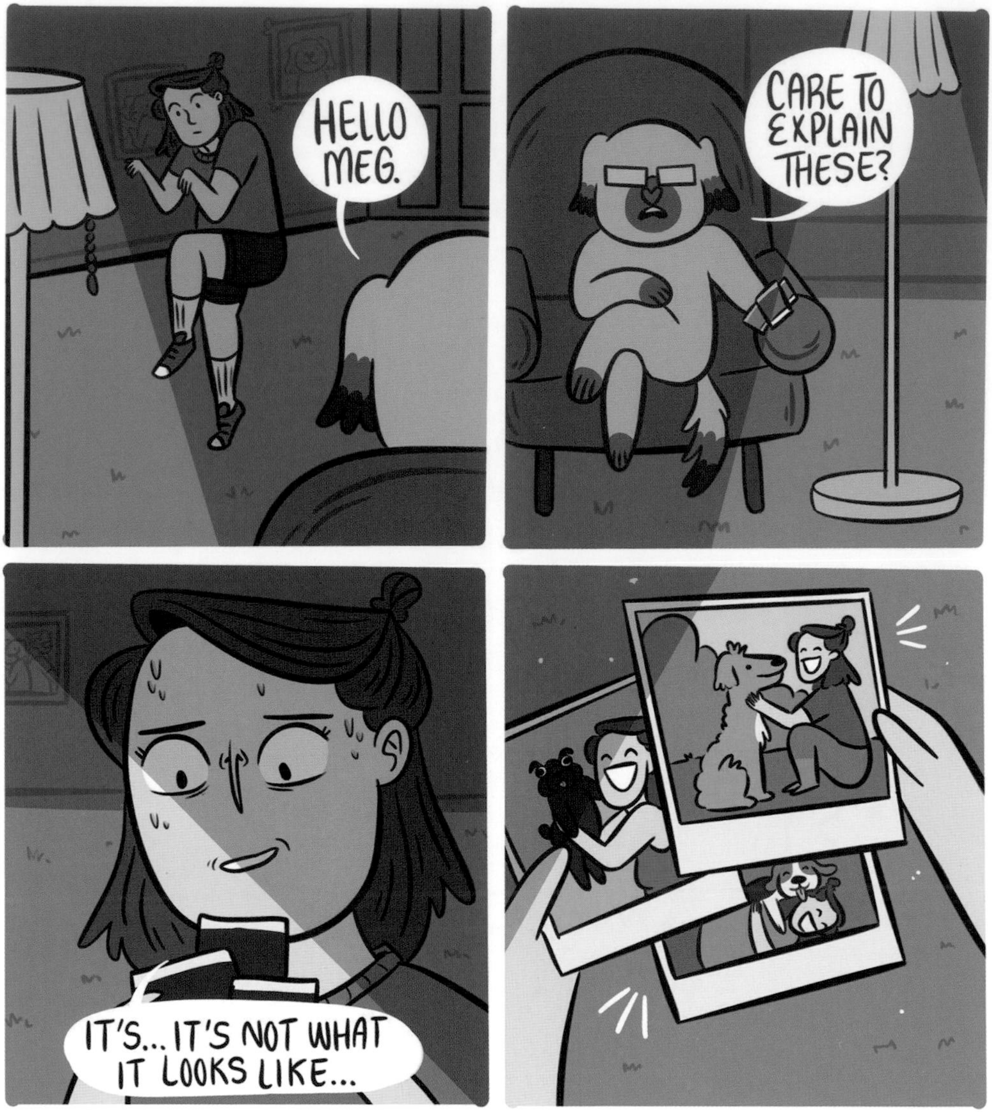
HELLO MEG.
CARE TO EXPLAIN THESE?
IT'S... IT'S NOT WHAT IT LOOKS LIKE...

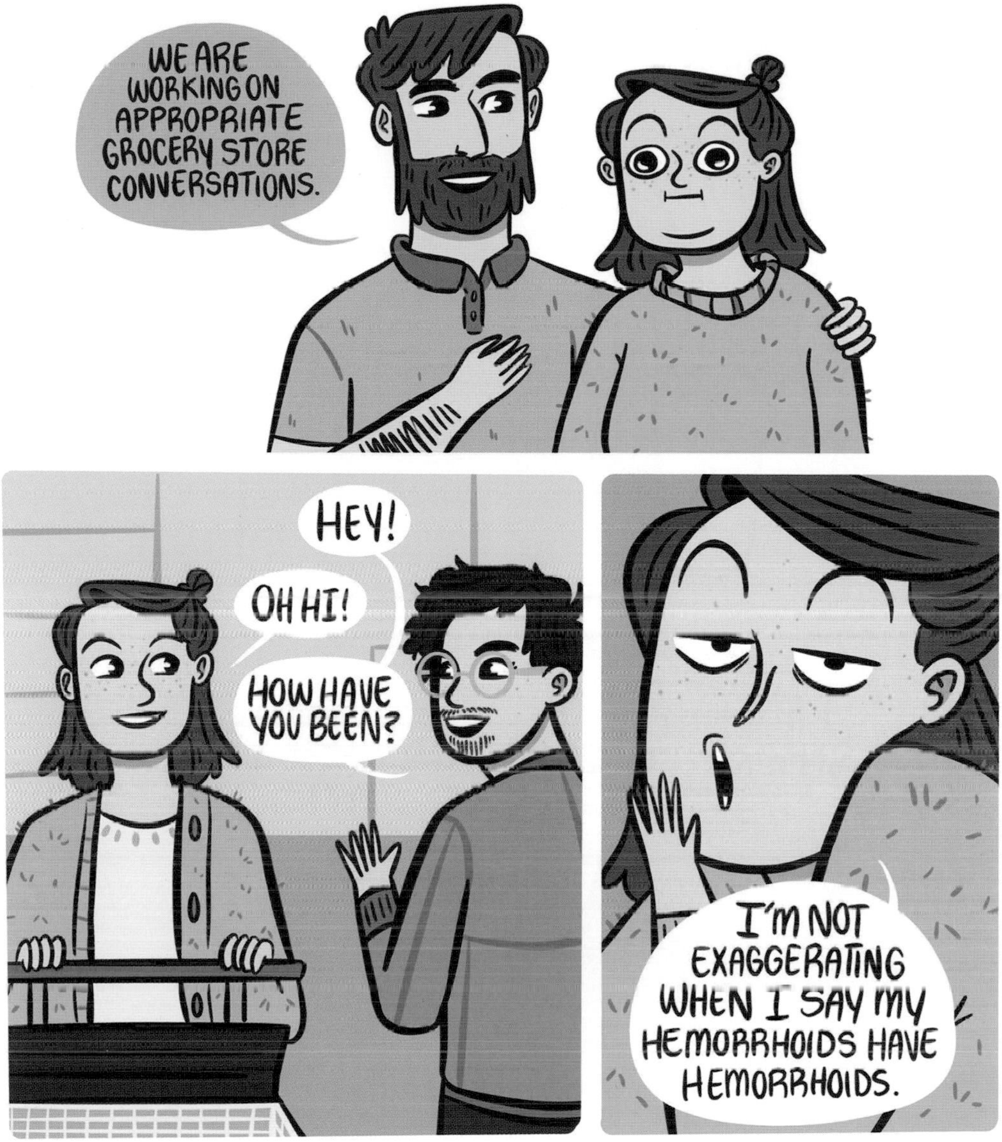
WE ARE WORKING ON APPROPRIATE GROCERY STORE CONVERSATIONS.
HEY!
OH HI!
HOW HAVE YOU BEEN?
I'M NOT EXAGGERATING WHEN I SAY MY HEMORRHOIDS HAVE HEMORRHOIDS.

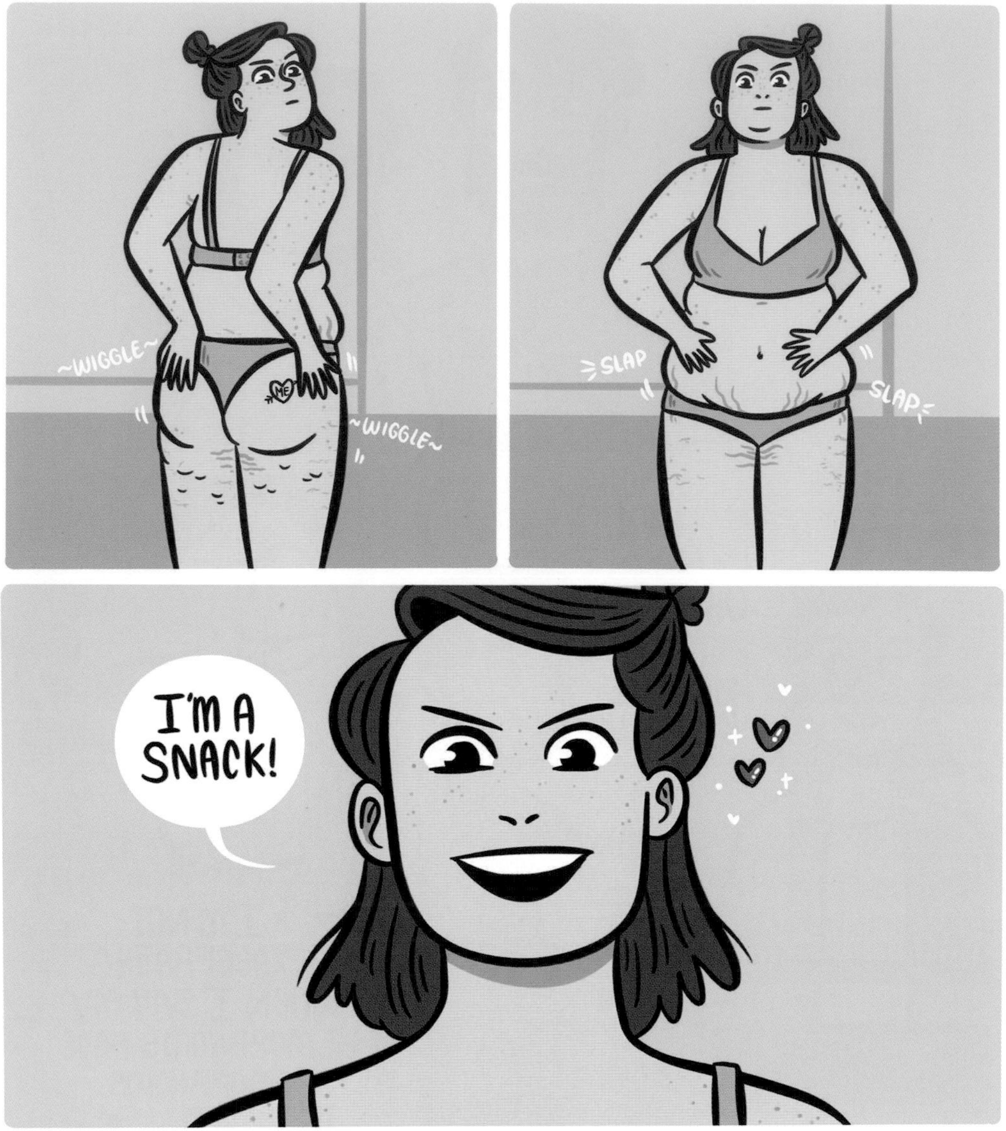
~WIGGLE~
ME
~WIGGLE~
SLAP
SLAP
I'M A SNACK!

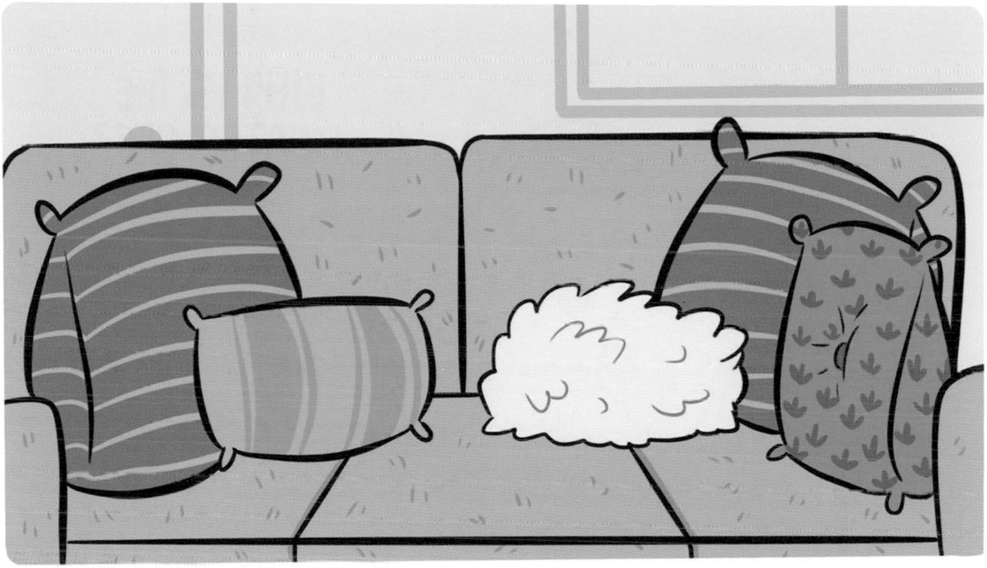

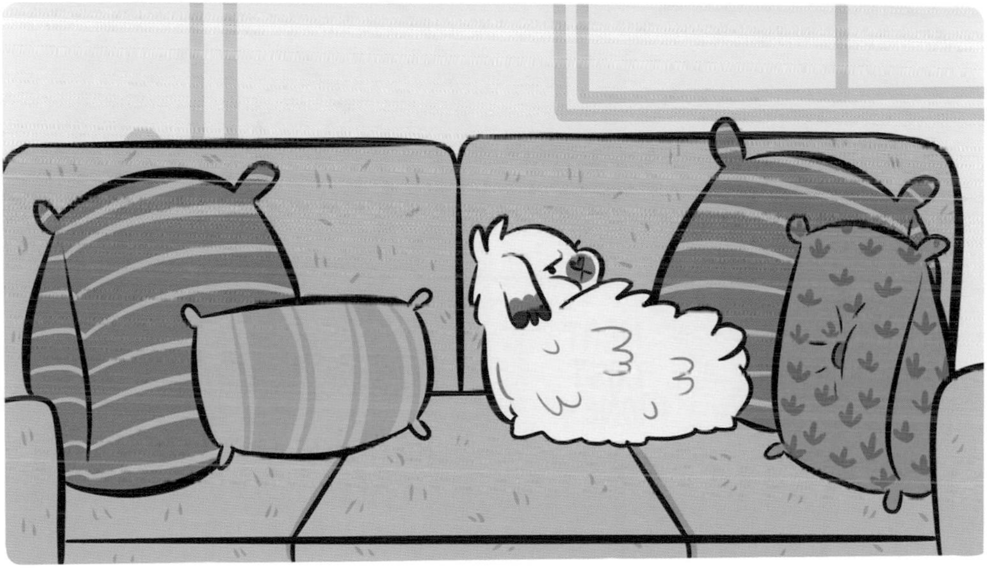

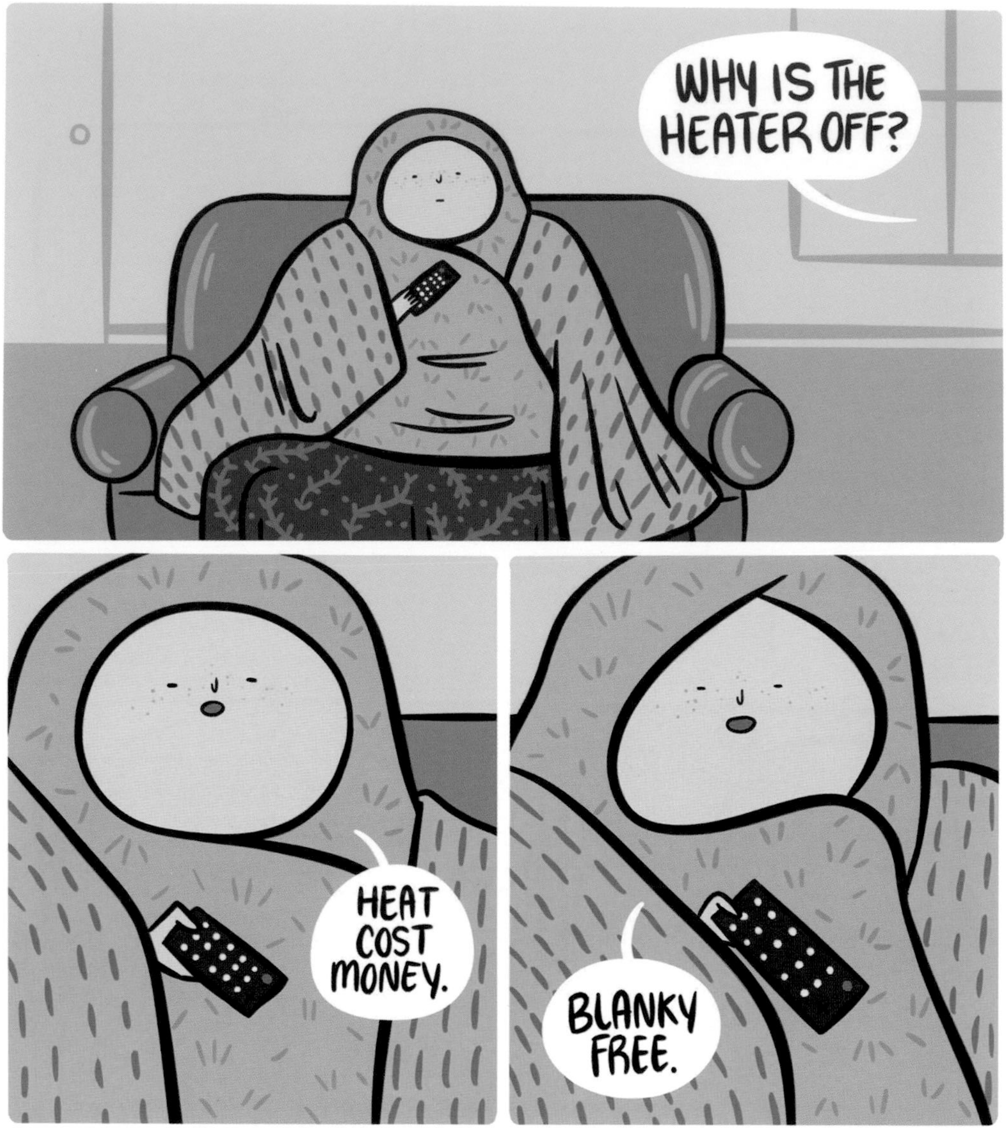
WHY IS THE HEATER OFF?
HEAT COST MONEY.
BLANKY FREE.

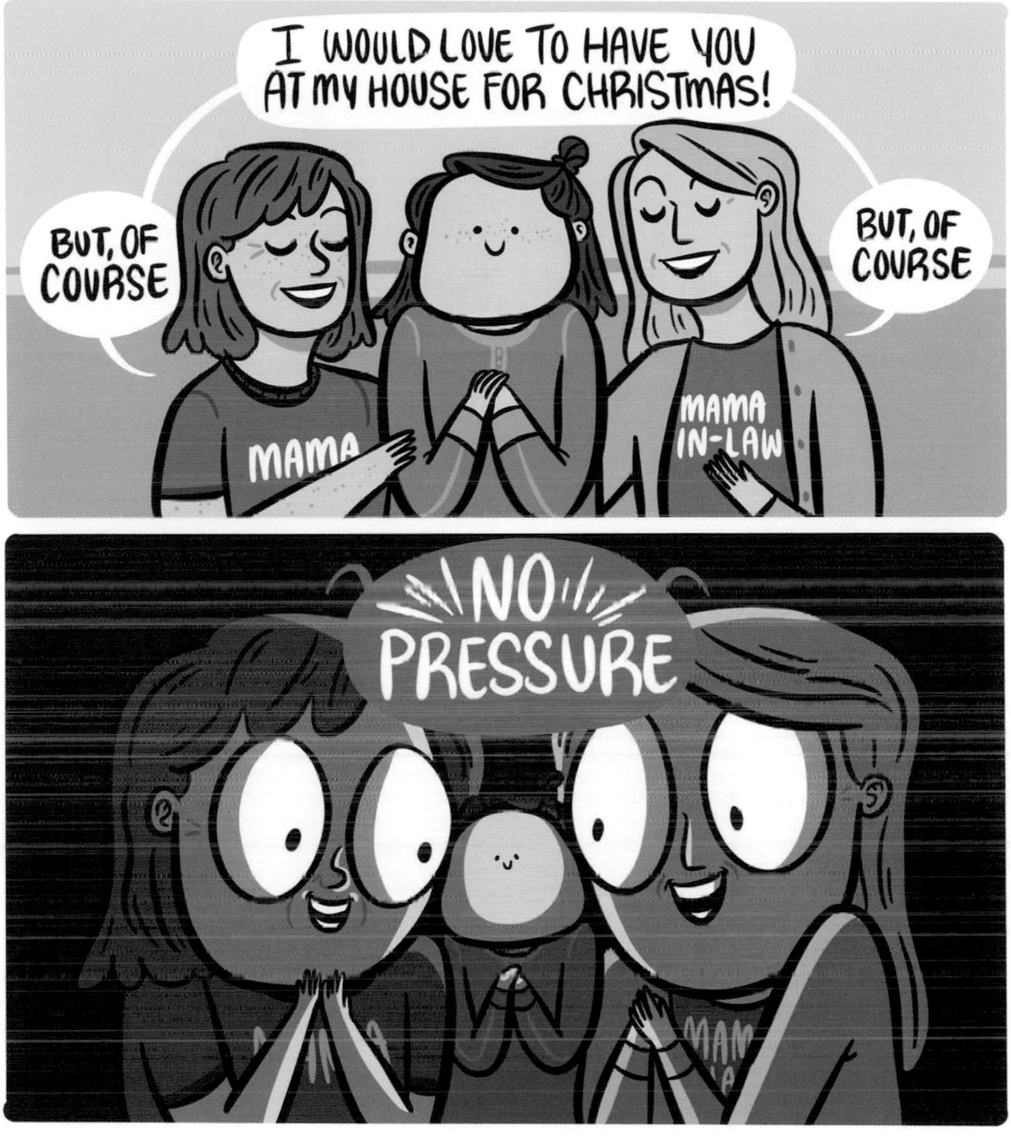
I WOULD LOVE TO HAVE YOU AT MY HOUSE FOR CHRISTMAS!
BUT, OF COURSE
BUT, OF COURSE
MAMA
MAMA IN-LAW
NO PRESSURE

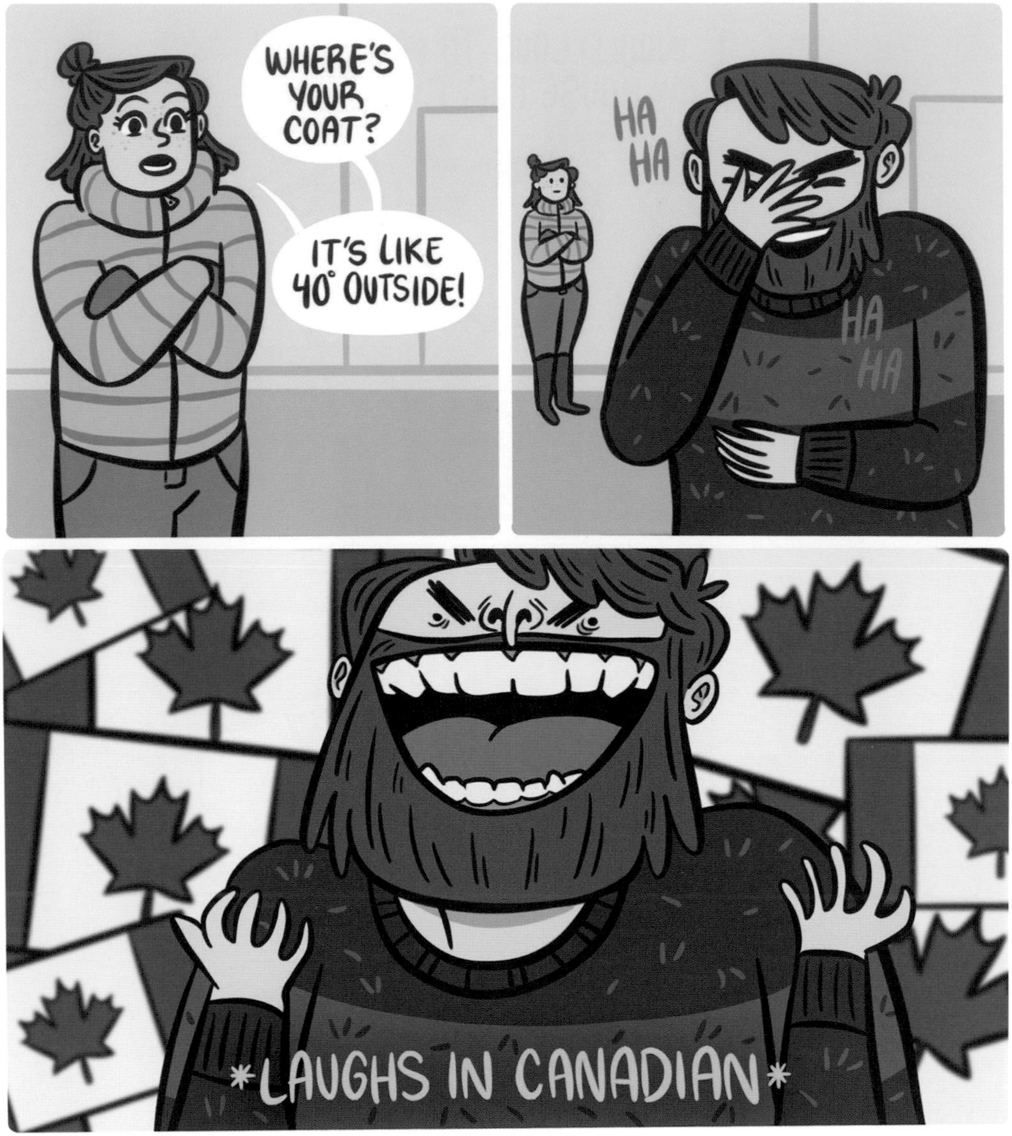
WHERE'S YOUR COAT?
IT'S LIKE 40° OUTSIDE!
HA HA
HA HA
LAUGHS IN CANADIAN

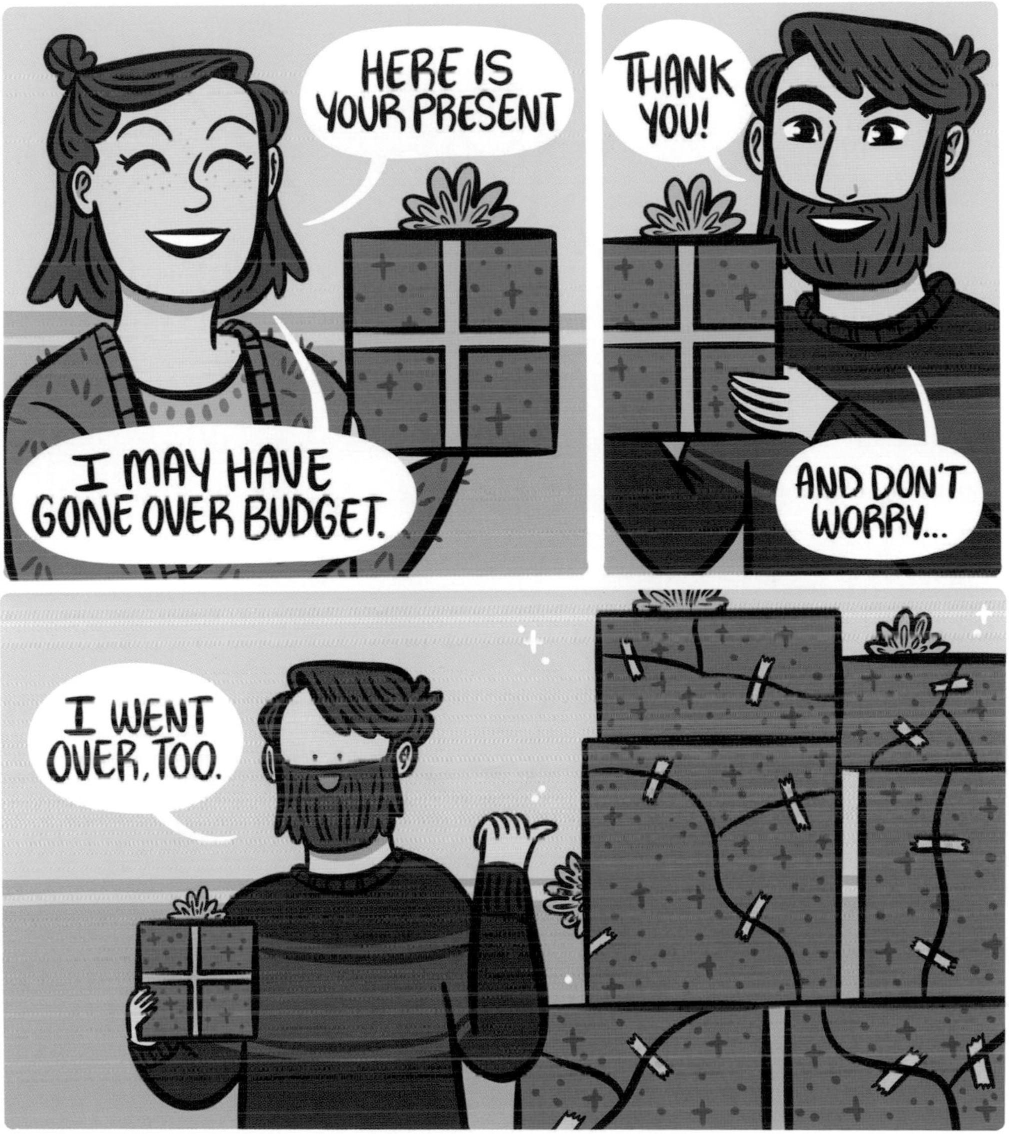
HERE IS YOUR PRESENT
I MAY HAVE GONE OVER BUDGET.
THANK YOU!
AND DON'T WORRY...
I WENT OVER, TOO.

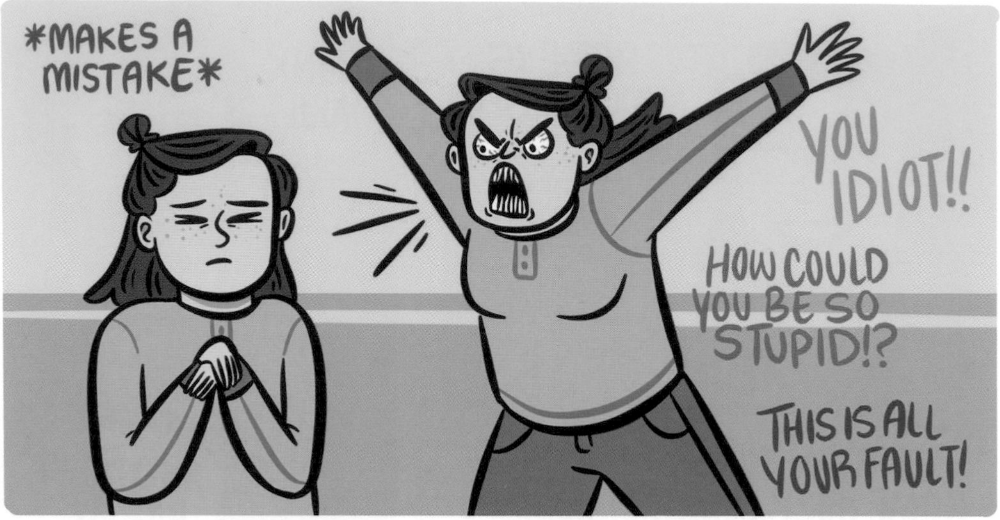
MAKES A MISTAKE
YOU IDIOT!!
HOW COULD YOU BE SO STUPID!?
THIS IS ALL YOUR FAULT!

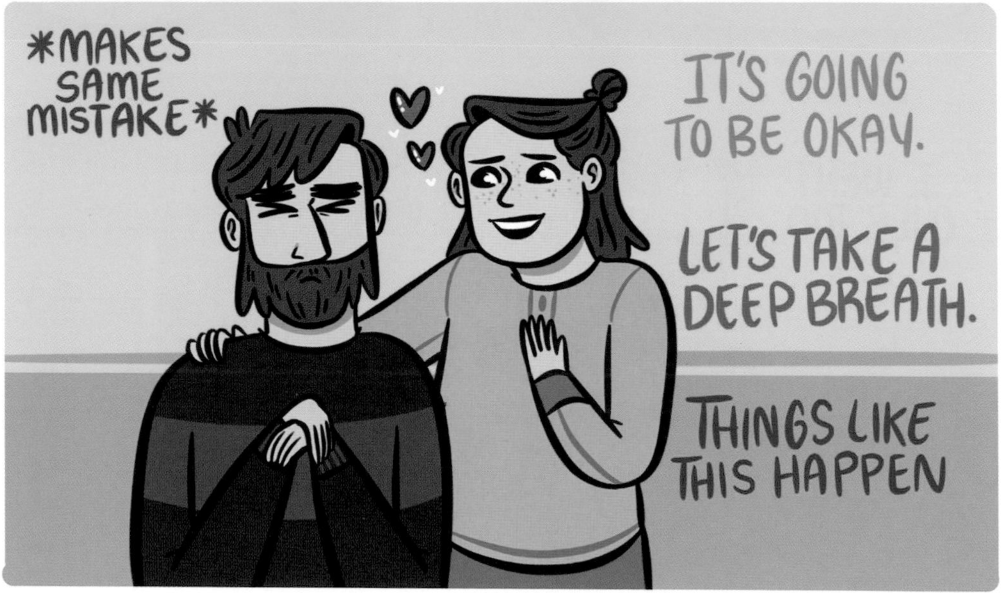
MAKES SAME MISTAKE
IT'S GOING TO BE OKAY.
LET'S TAKE A DEEP BREATH.
THINGS LIKE THIS HAPPEN

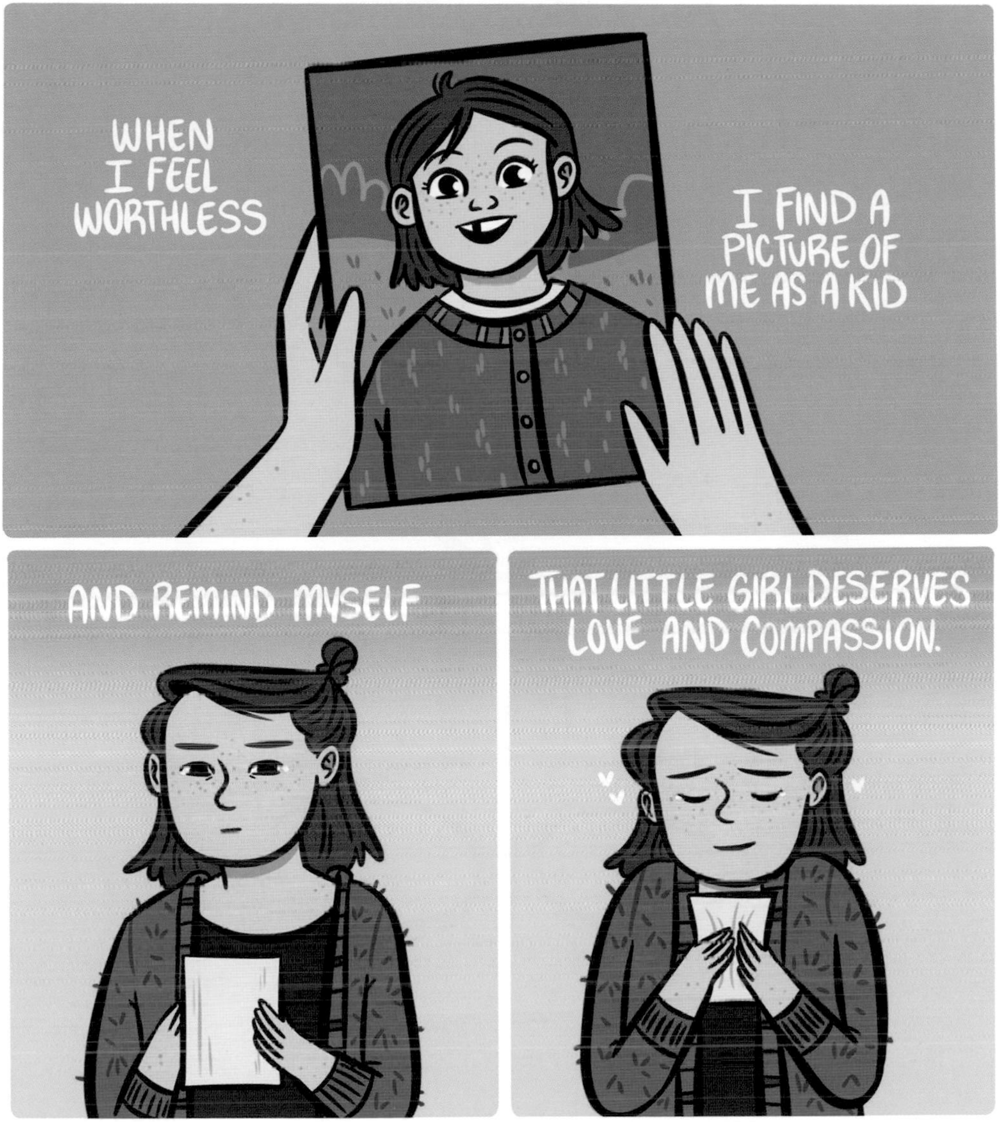
WHEN I FEEL WORTHLESS
I FIND A PICTURE OF ME AS A KID
AND REMIND MYSELF
THAT LITTLE GIRL DESERVES LOVE AND COMPASSION.

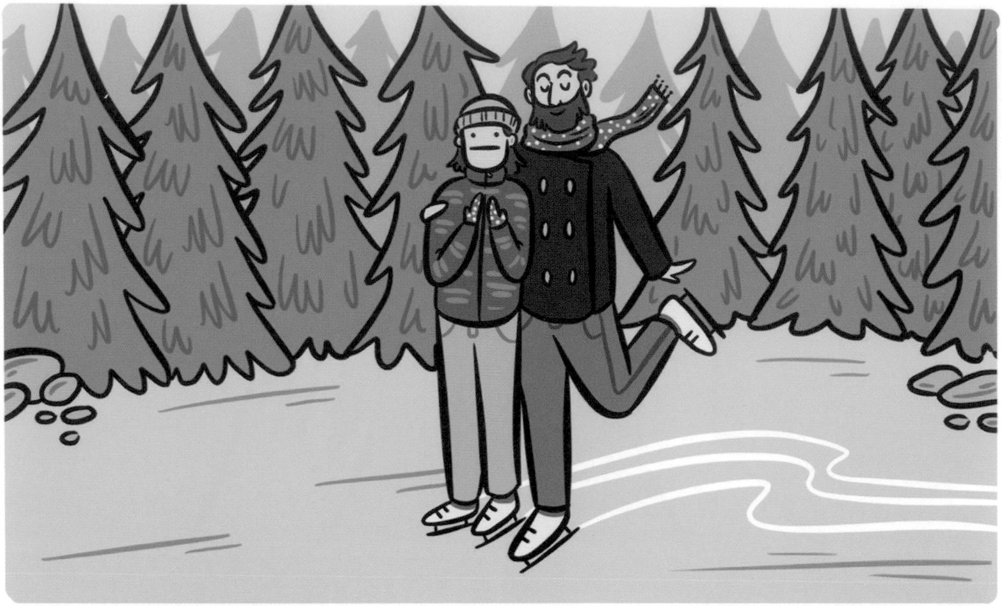

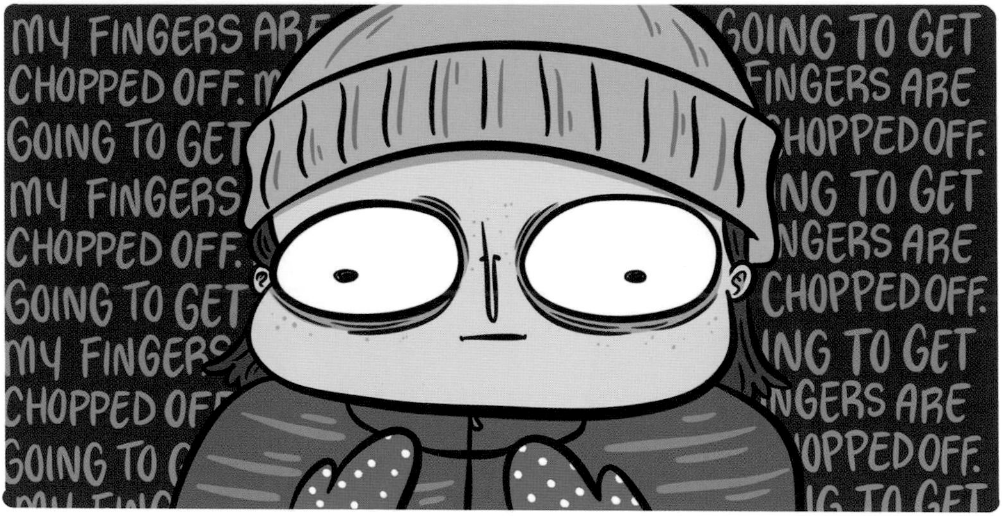
MY FINGERS ARE ... GOING TO GET
CHOPPED OFF. ... FINGERS ARE
GOING TO GET ... CHOPPED OFF.
MY FINGERS ... NG TO GET
CHOPPED OFF. ... NGERS ARE
GOING TO GET ... CHOPPED OFF.
MY FINGERS ... NG TO GET
CHOPPED OF ... NGERS ARE
GOING TO ... OPPED OFF.

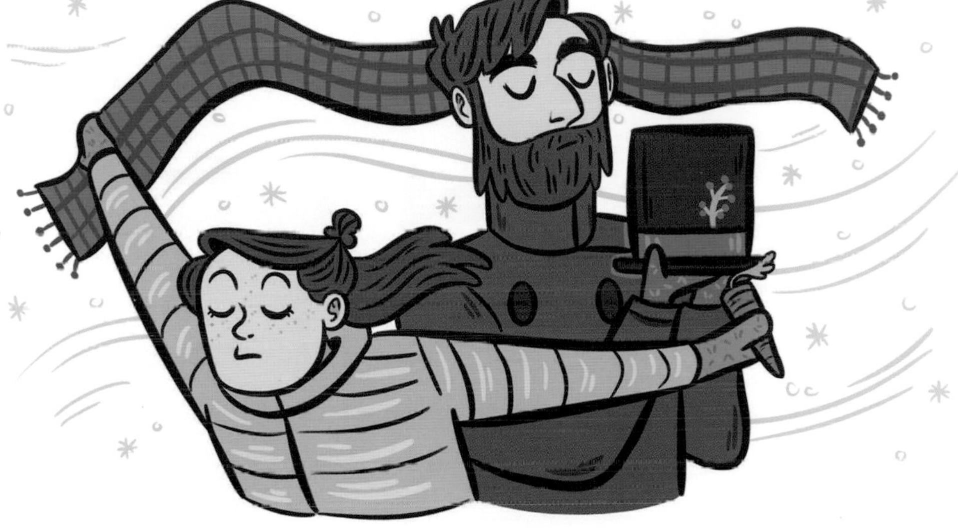

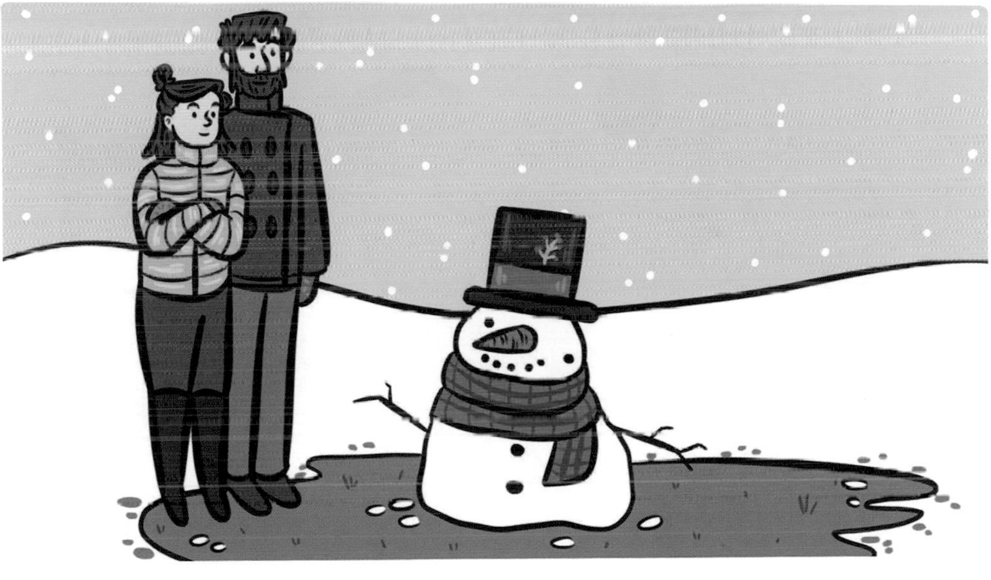

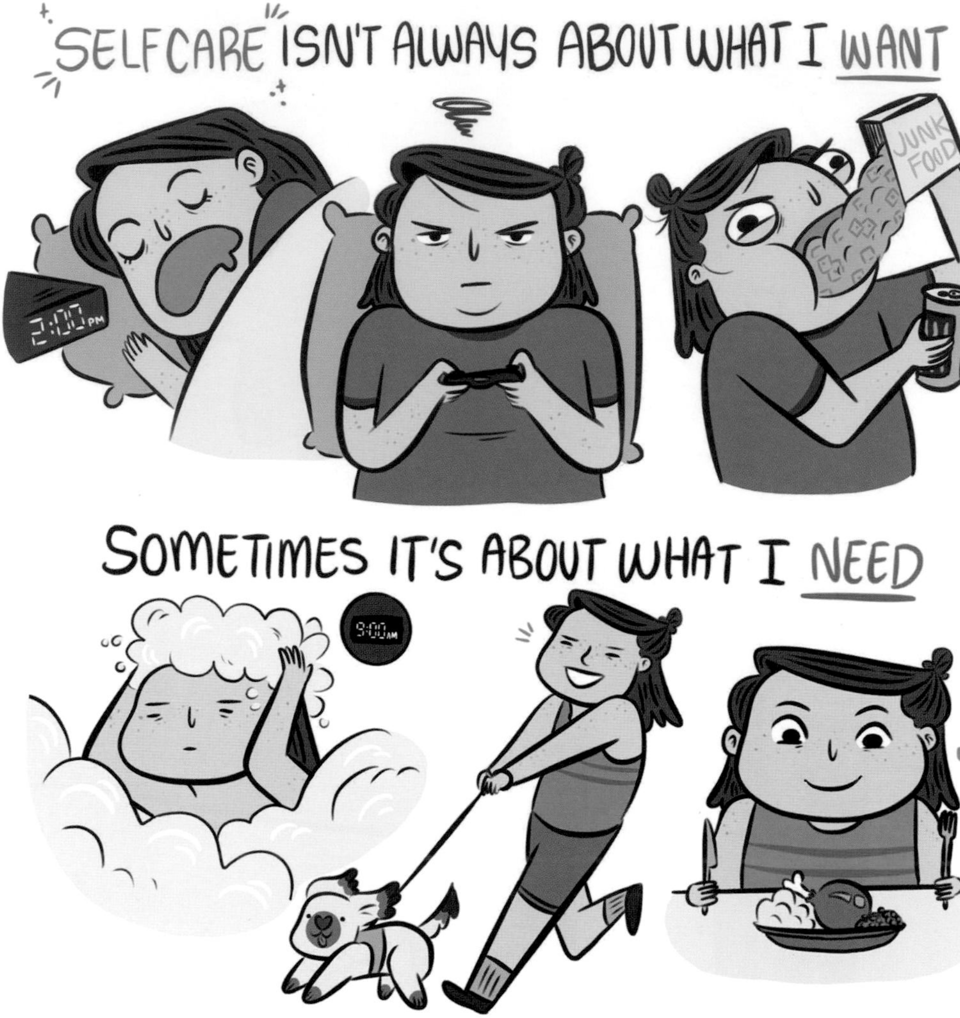
SELFCARE ISN'T ALWAYS ABOUT WHAT I WANT
2:00 PM
JUNK FOOD
SOMETIMES IT'S ABOUT WHAT I NEED
9:00 AM

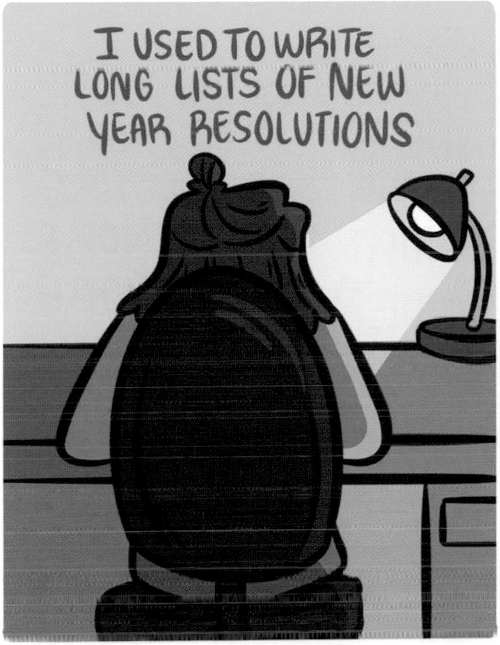
I USED TO WRITE LONG LISTS OF NEW YEAR RESOLUTIONS

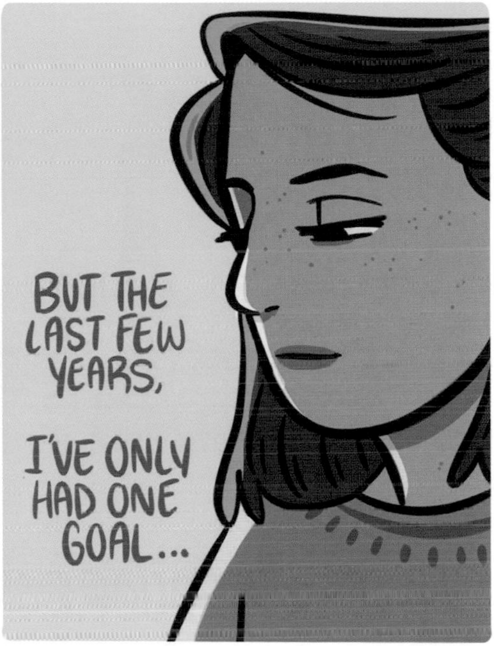
BUT THE LAST FEW YEARS,
I'VE ONLY HAD ONE GOAL...

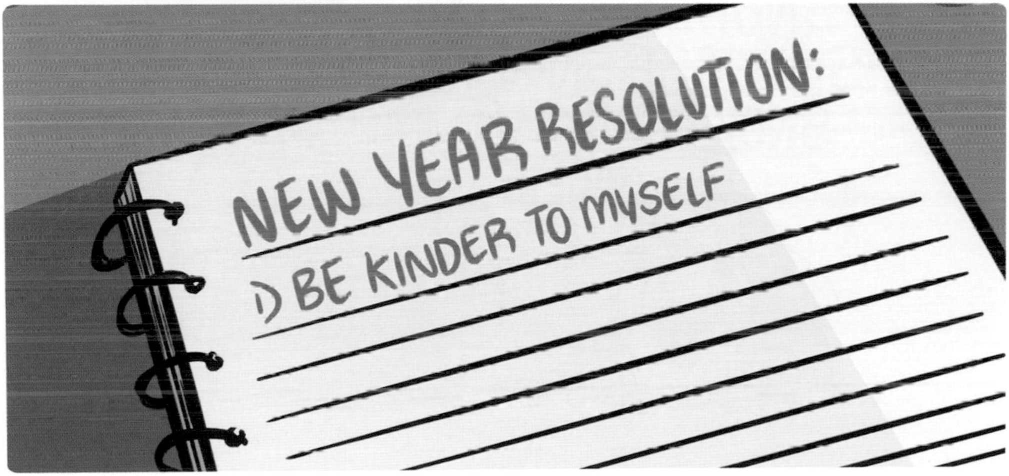
NEW YEAR RESOLUTION:
1) BE KINDER TO MYSELF

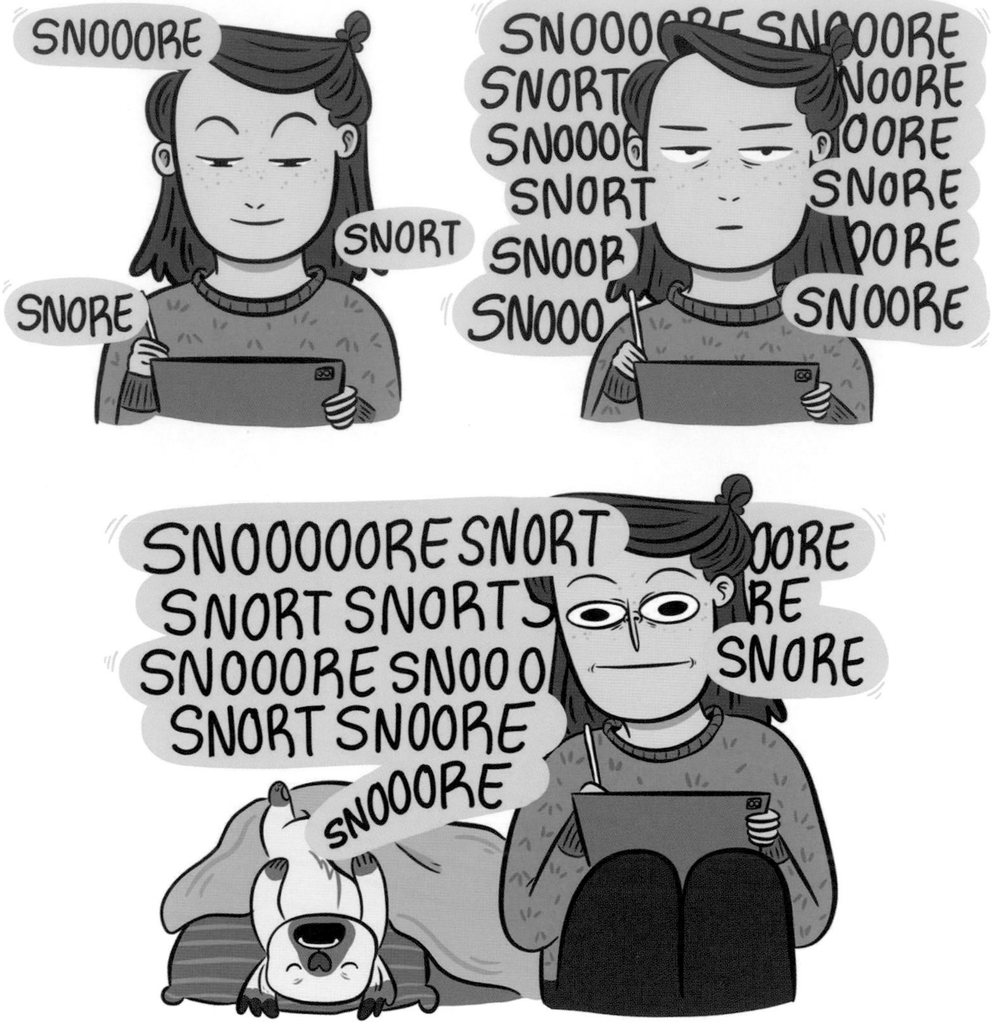
SNOOORE
SNORT
SNORE
SNORT
SNORT
SNORE
SNOORE
SNOOOOORE SNORT
SNORT SNORT
SNOOORE
SNORT SNOORE
SNORE
SNOOORE

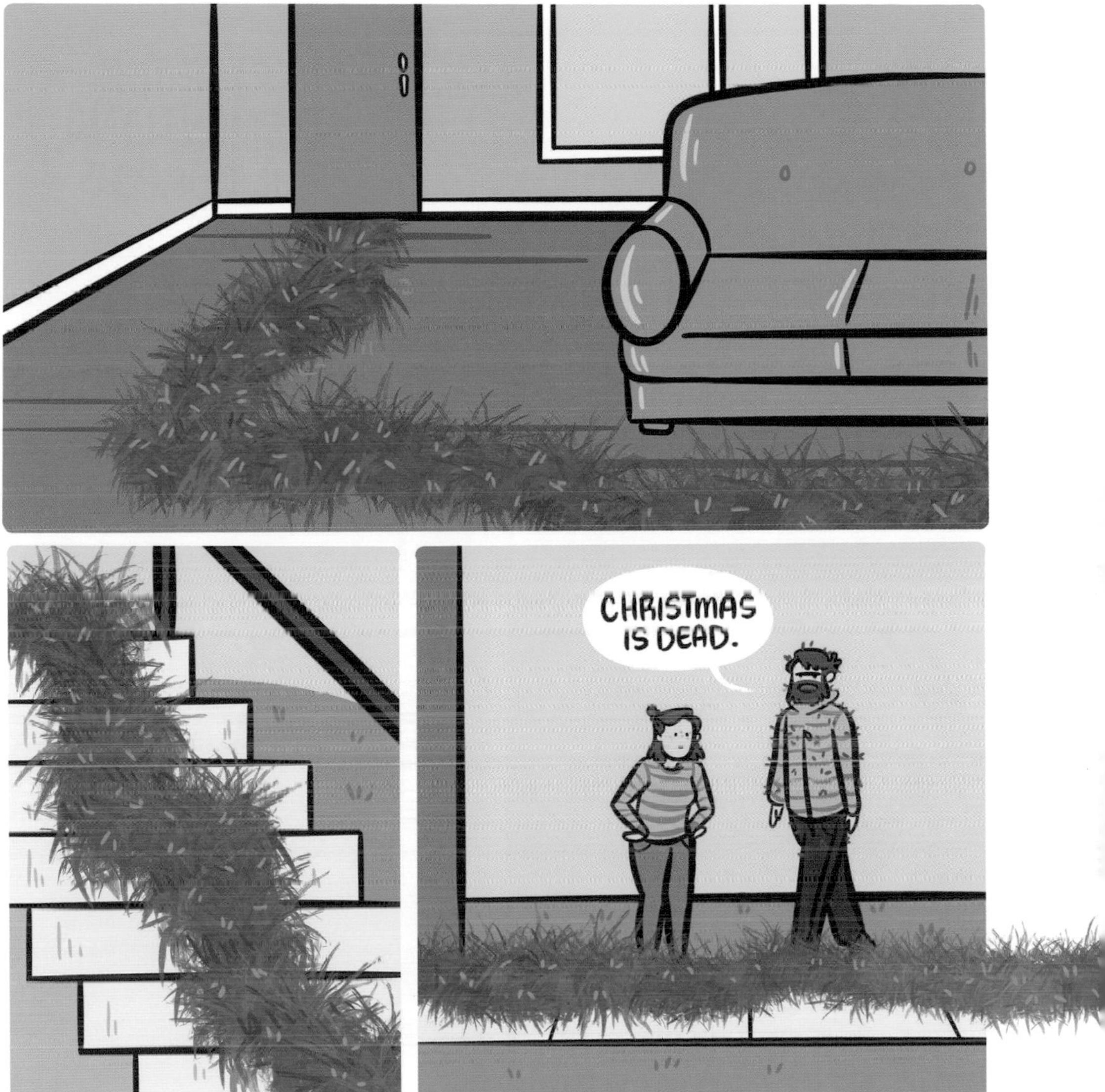
CHRISTMAS IS DEAD.

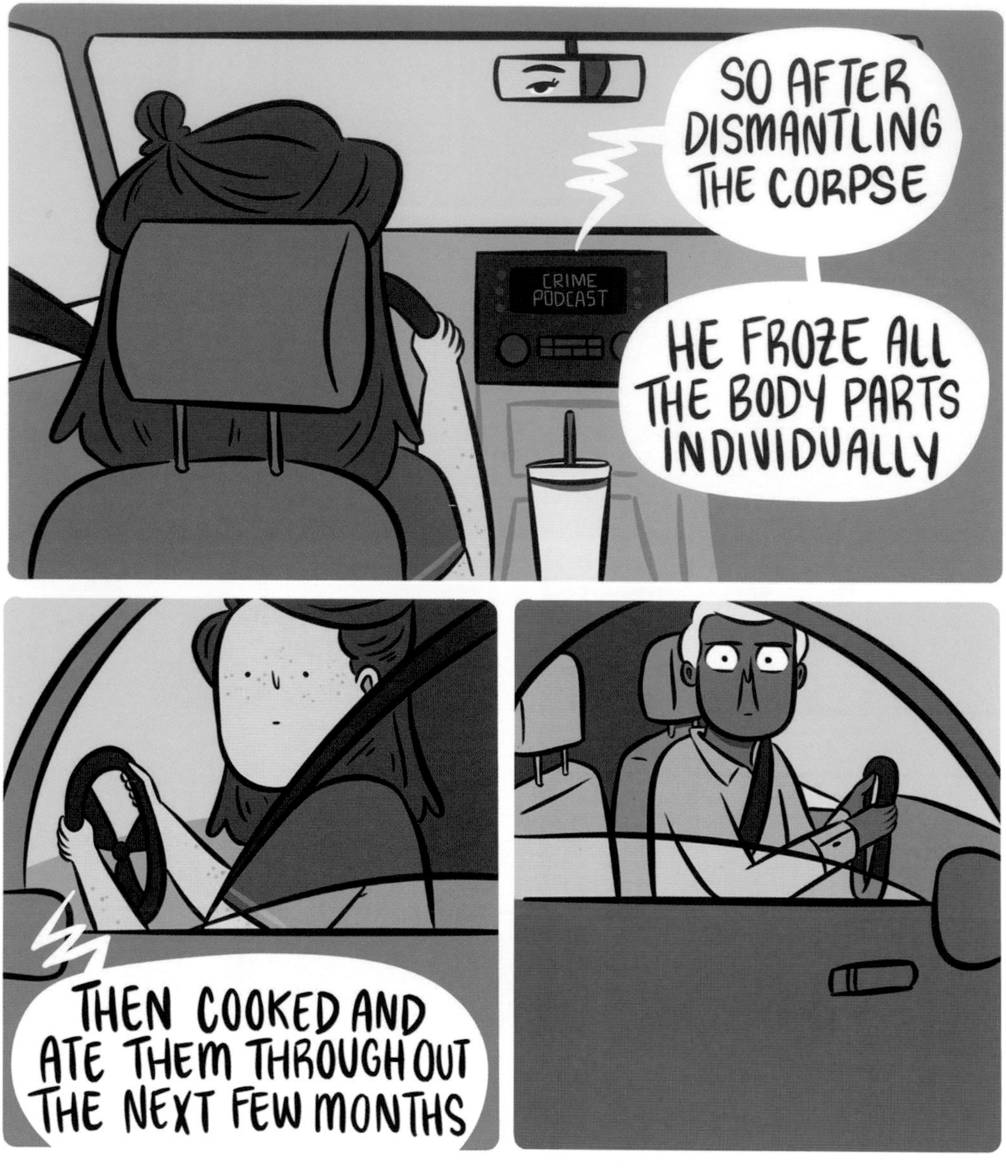
SO AFTER DISMANTLING THE CORPSE
CRIME PODCAST
HE FROZE ALL THE BODY PARTS INDIVIDUALLY
THEN COOKED AND ATE THEM THROUGHOUT THE NEXT FEW MONTHS

YEAH, YEAH VALENTINE'S DAY IS GREAT

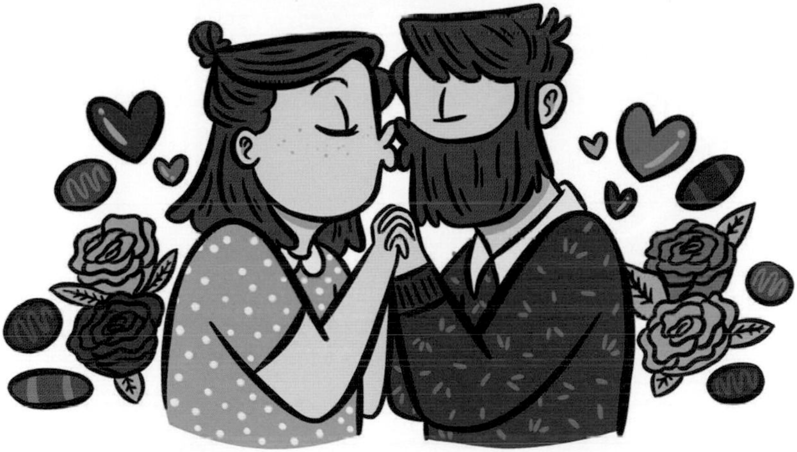

BUT, THE REAL HOLIDAY IS
FEBRUARY 15th

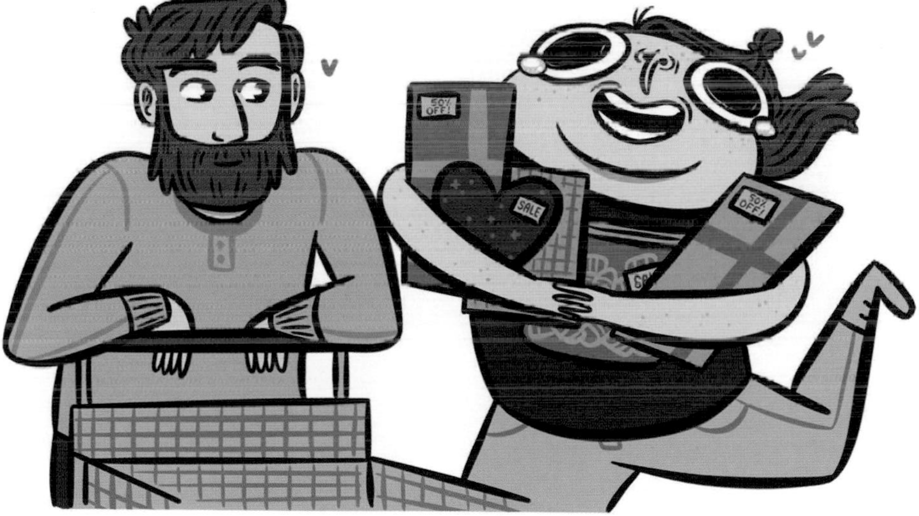

50% OFF!
SALE
50% OFF!

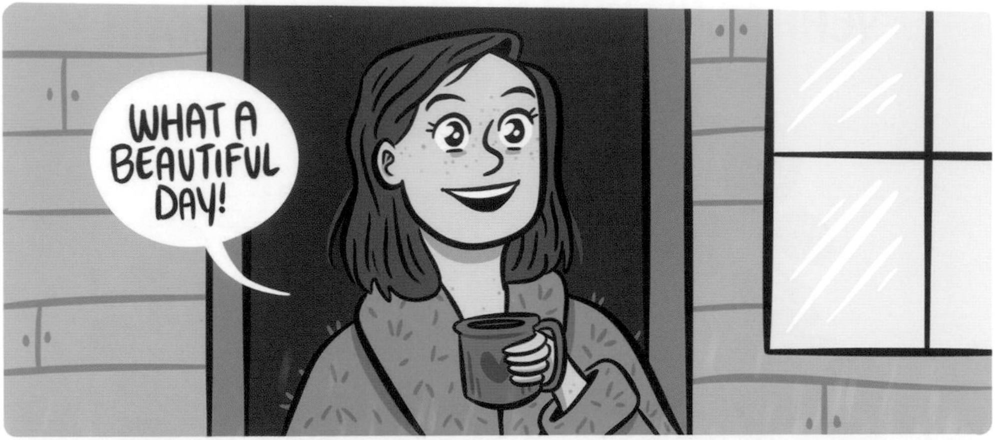
WHAT A BEAUTIFUL DAY!

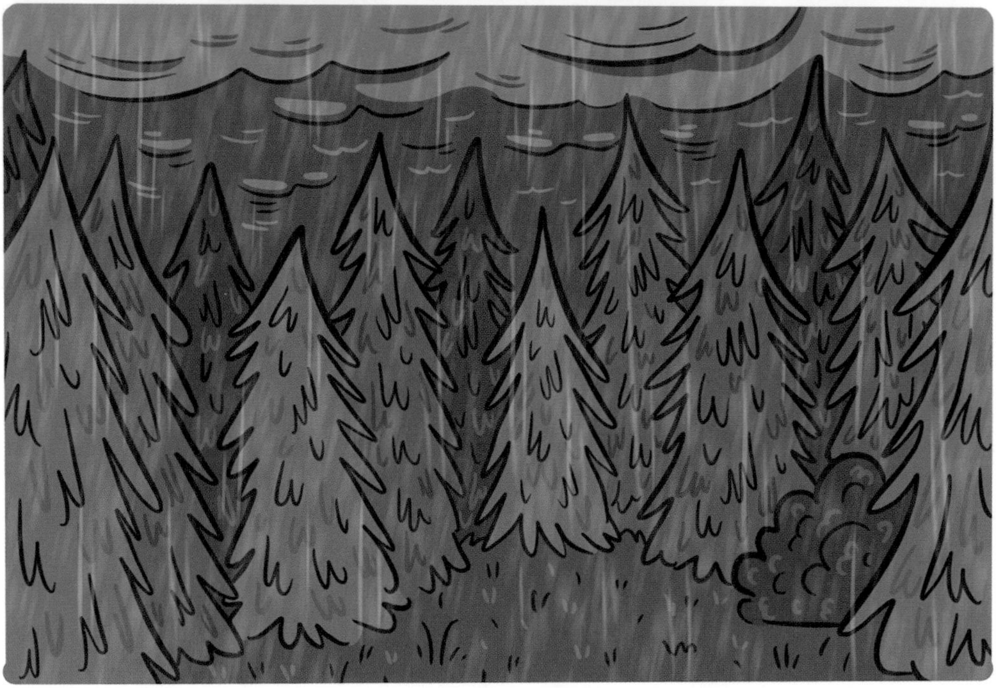

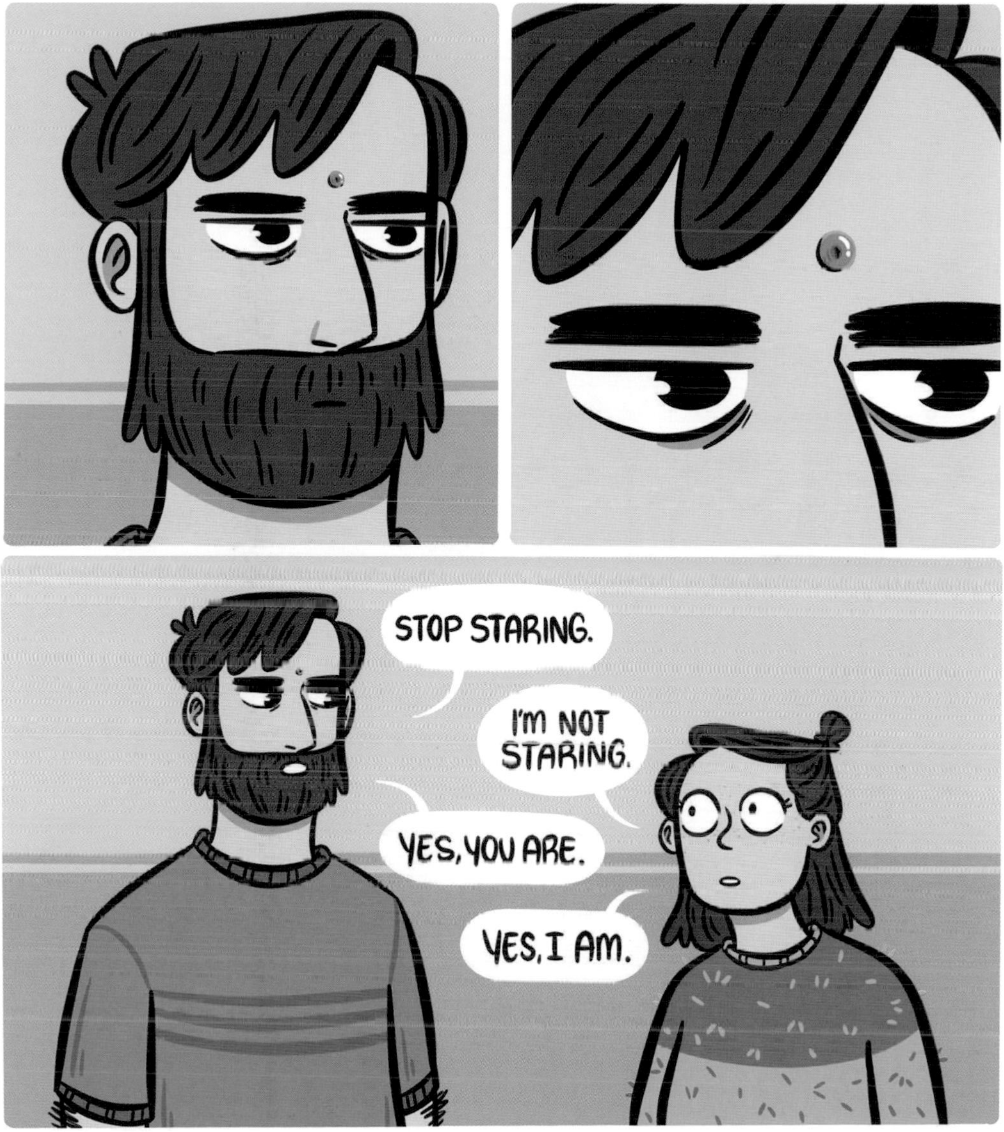
STOP STARING.
I'M NOT STARING.
YES, YOU ARE.
YES, I AM.

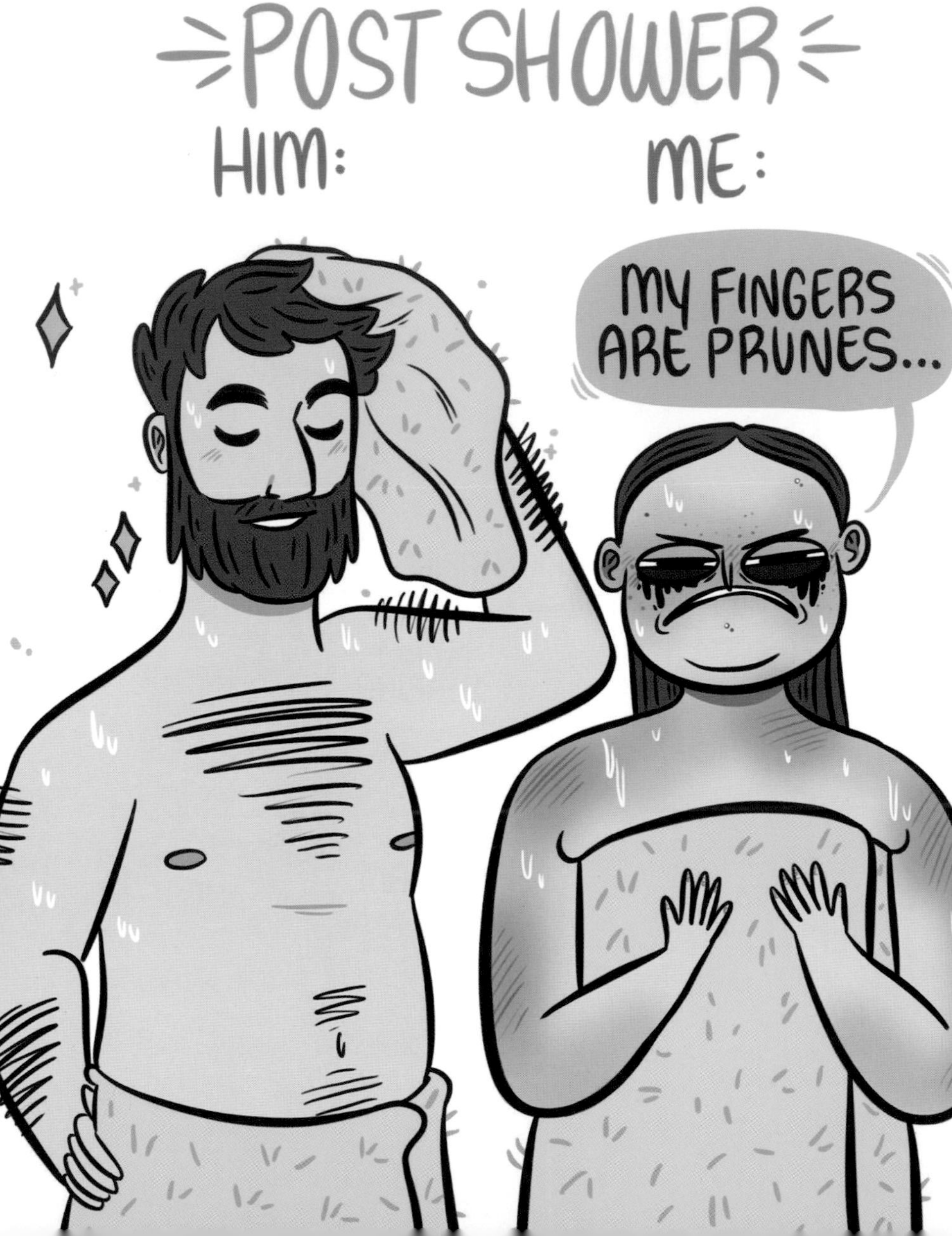
POST SHOWER
HIM:
ME:
MY FINGERS ARE PRUNES...

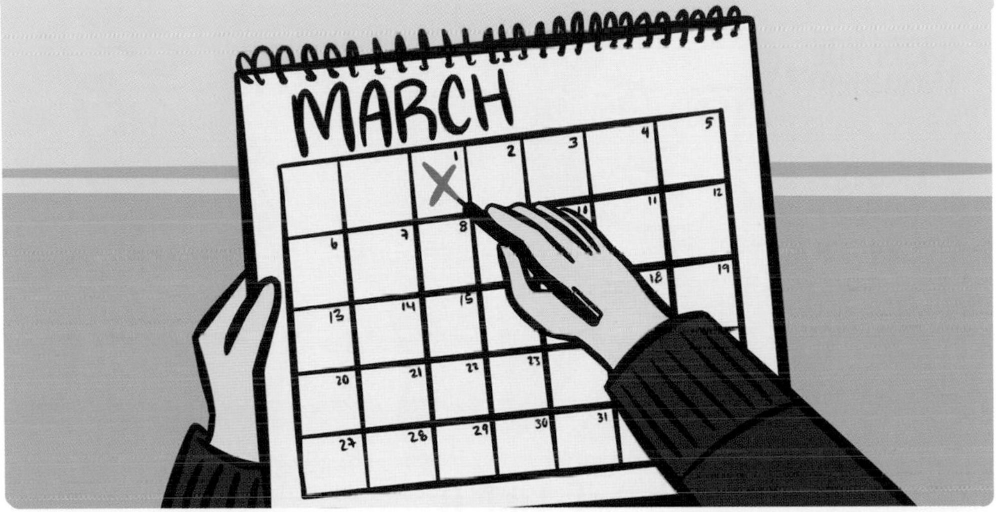
MARCH

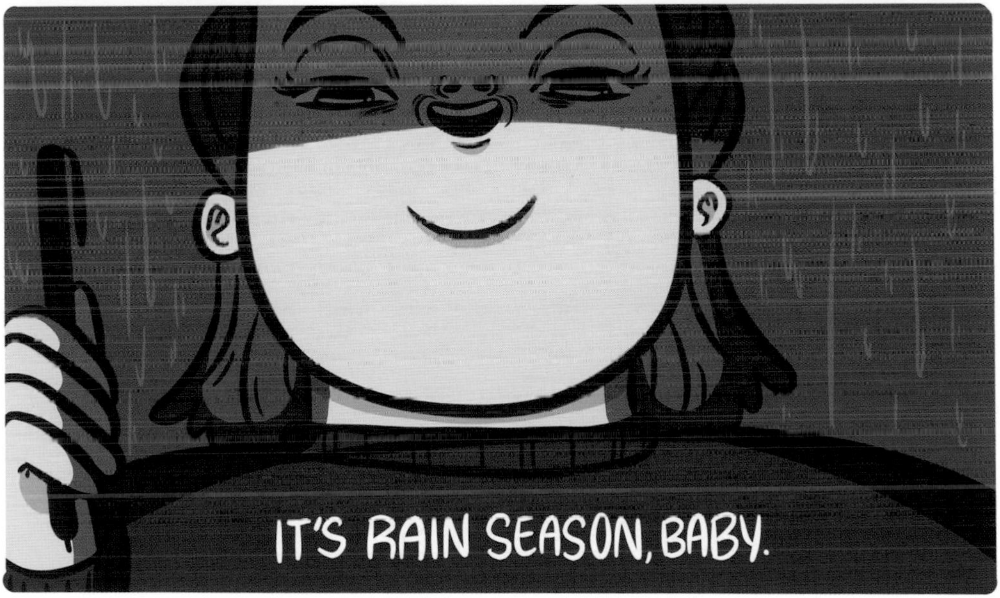
IT'S RAIN SEASON, BABY.

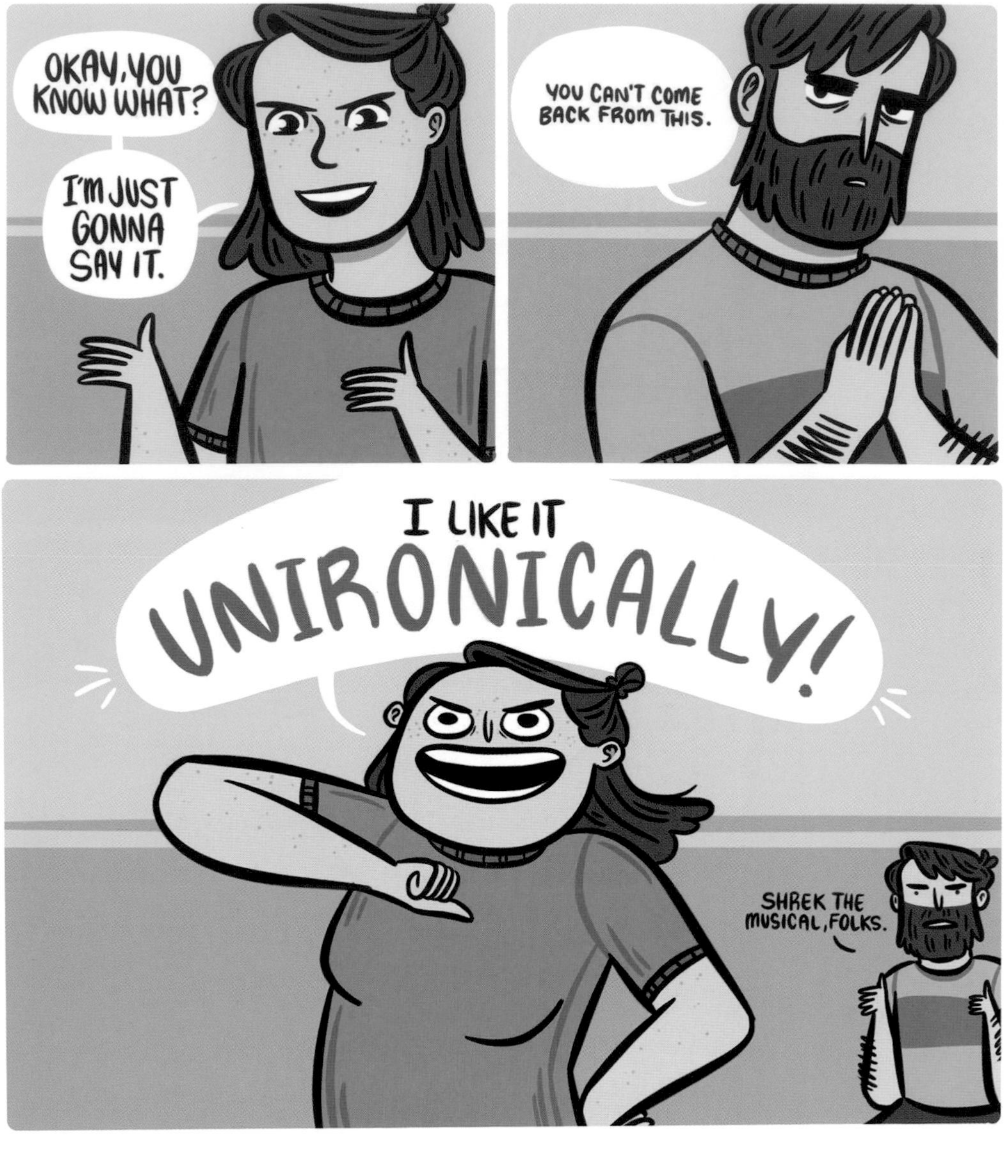
OKAY, YOU KNOW WHAT?
I'M JUST GONNA SAY IT.
YOU CAN'T COME BACK FROM THIS.
I LIKE IT UNIRONICALLY!
SHREK THE MUSICAL, FOLKS.

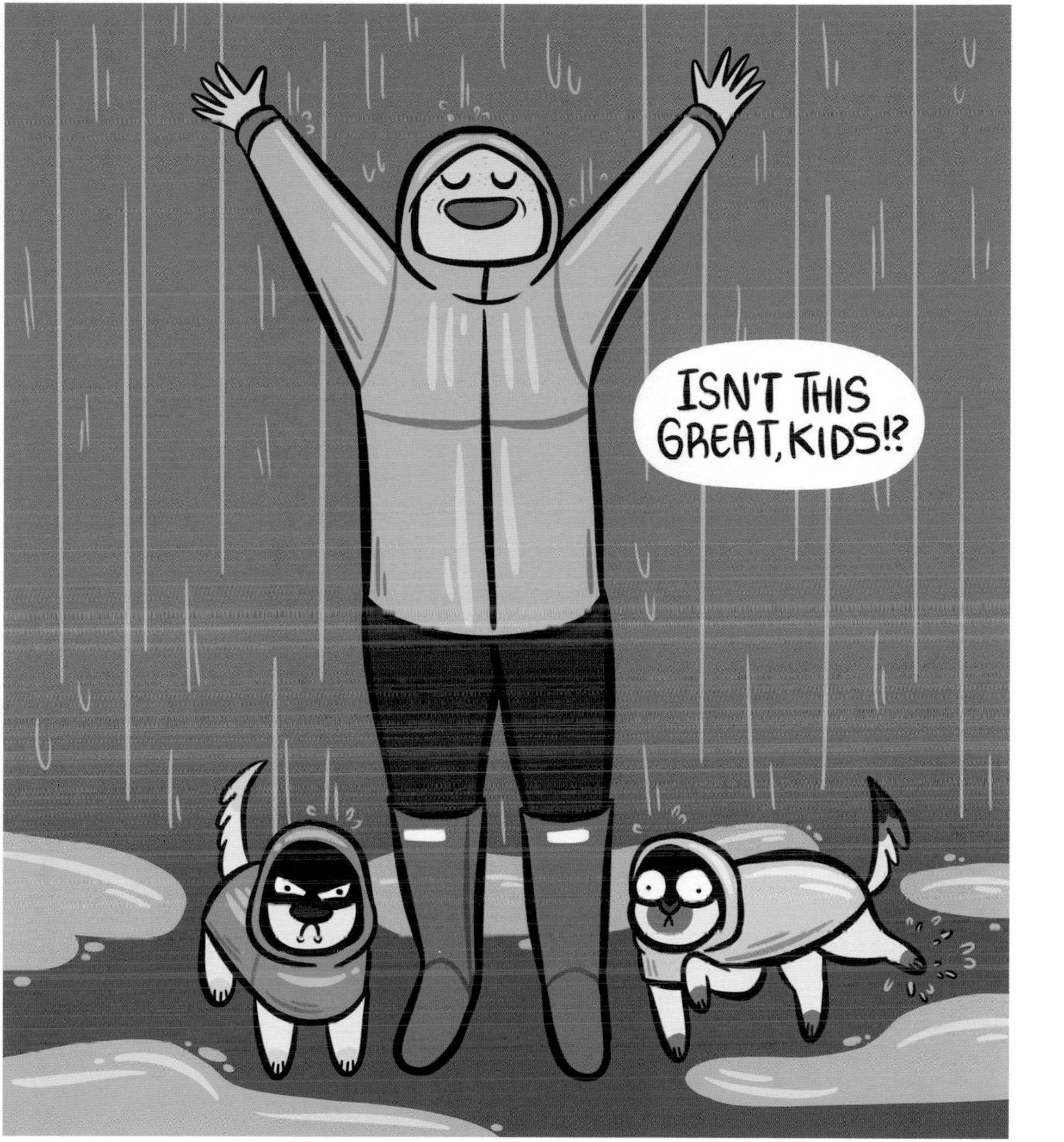
ISN'T THIS GREAT, KIDS!?

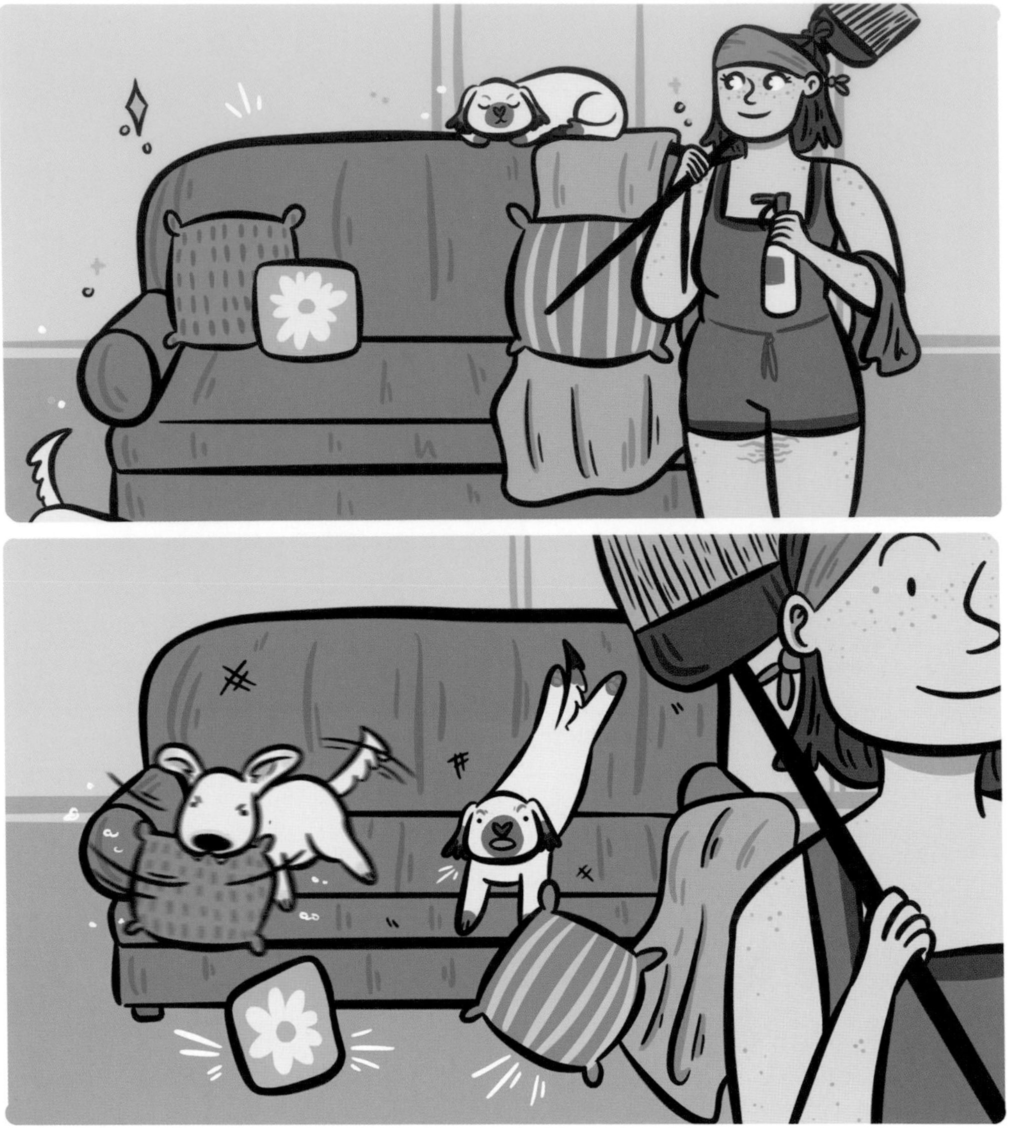

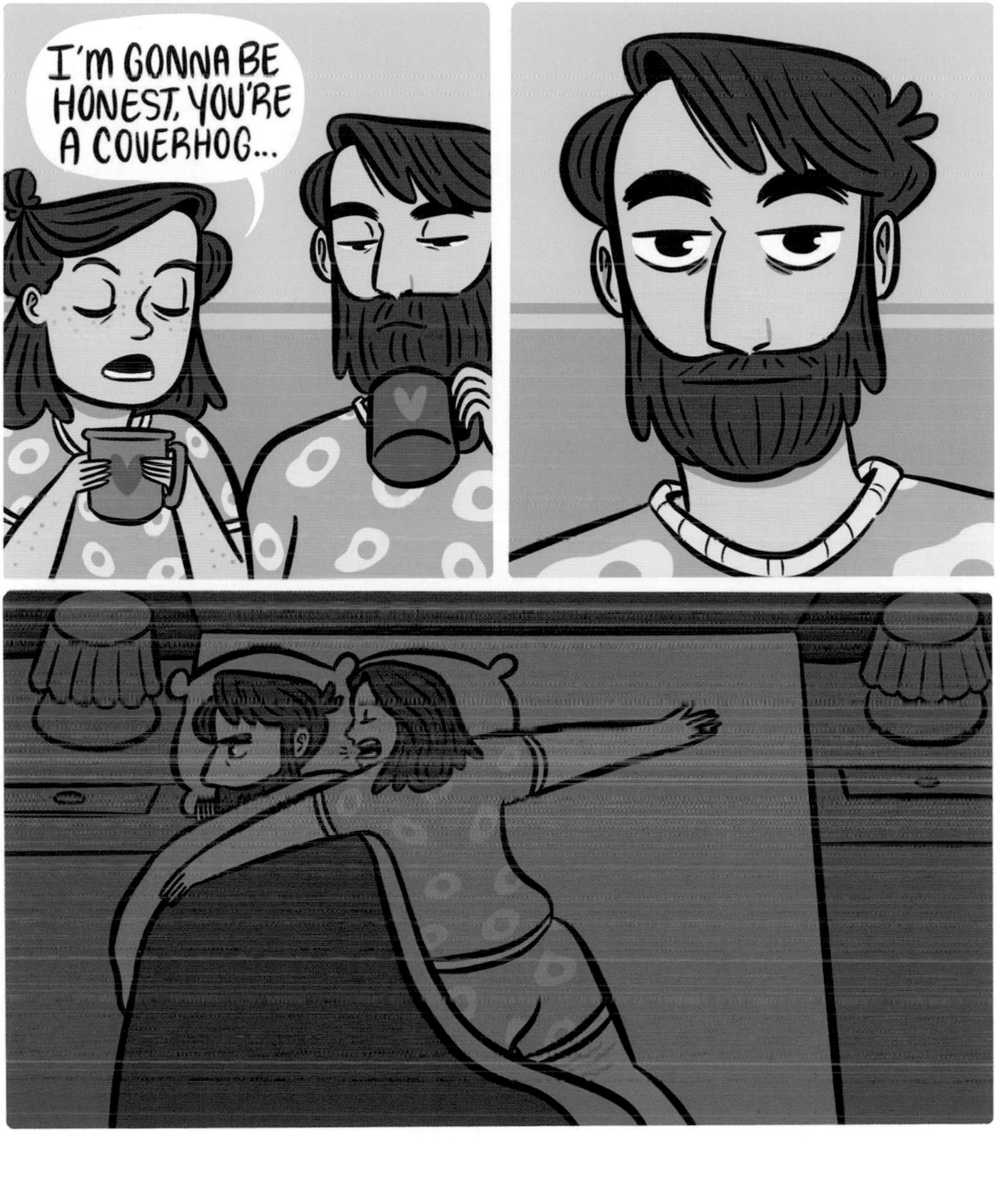
I'M GONNA BE HONEST, YOU'RE A COVERHOG...

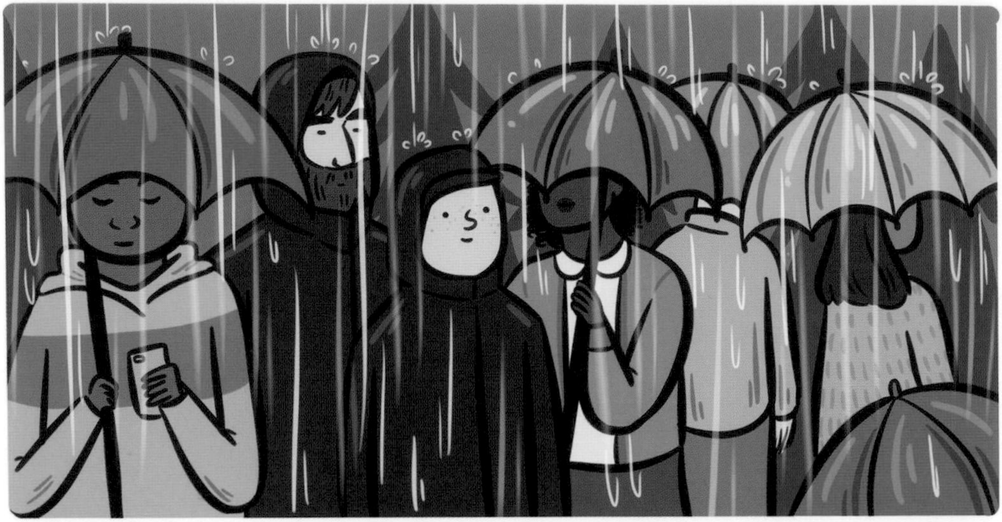

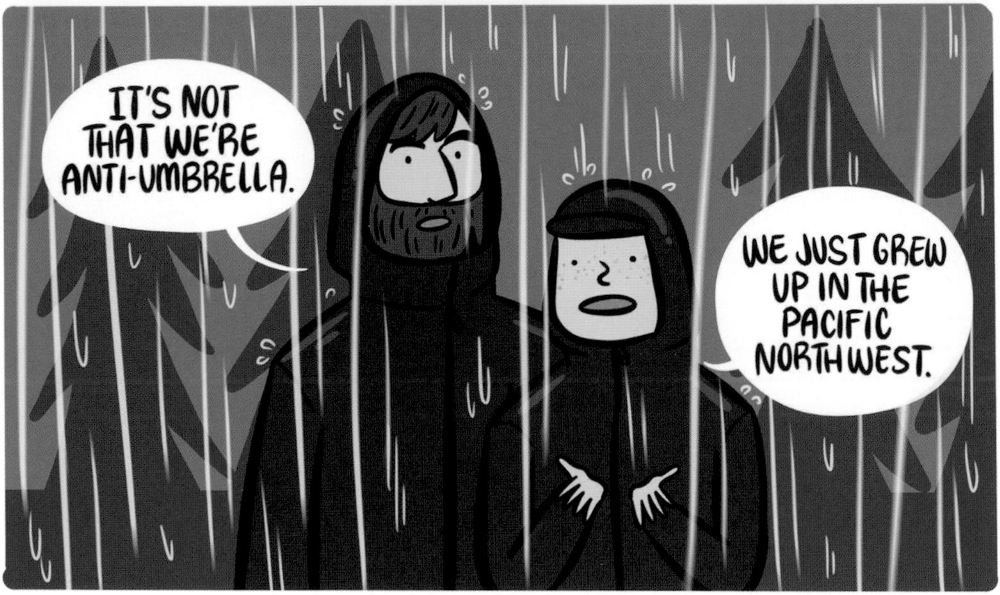
IT'S NOT THAT WE'RE ANTI-UMBRELLA.
WE JUST GREW UP IN THE PACIFIC NORTHWEST.

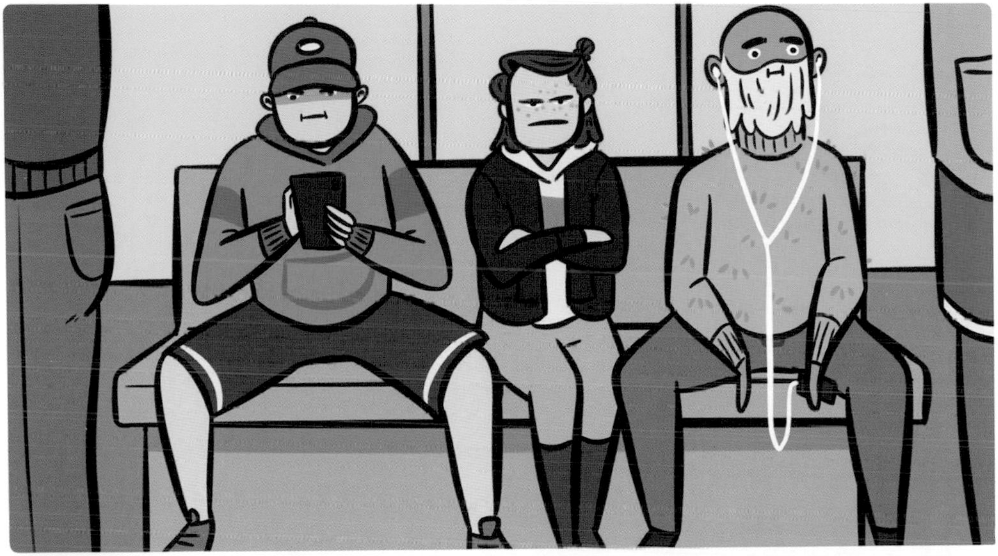

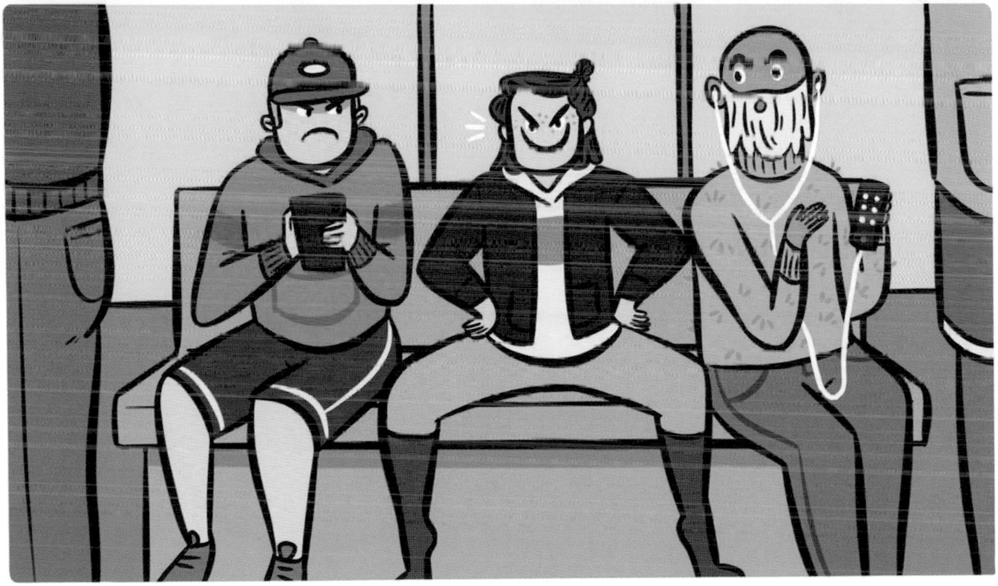

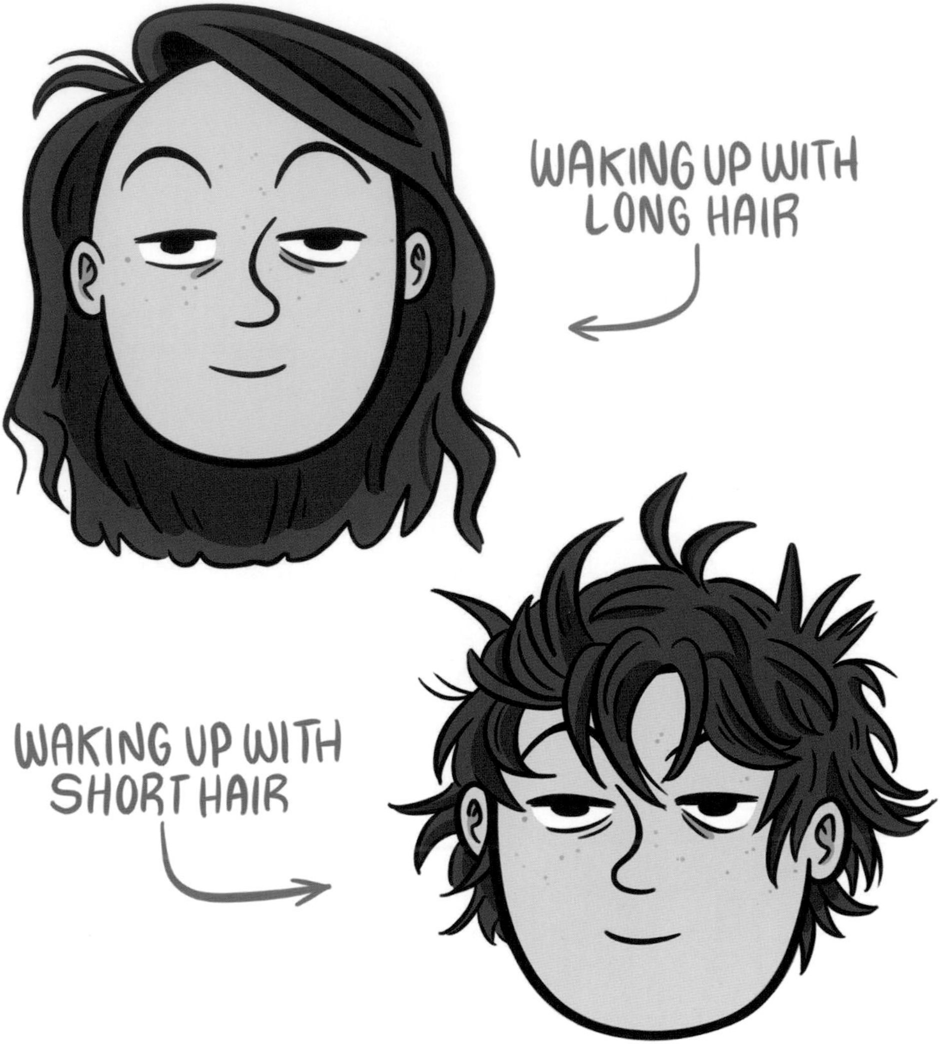
WAKING UP WITH LONG HAIR
WAKING UP WITH SHORT HAIR

THE BEST PART OF CHOPPING OFF LONG HAIR

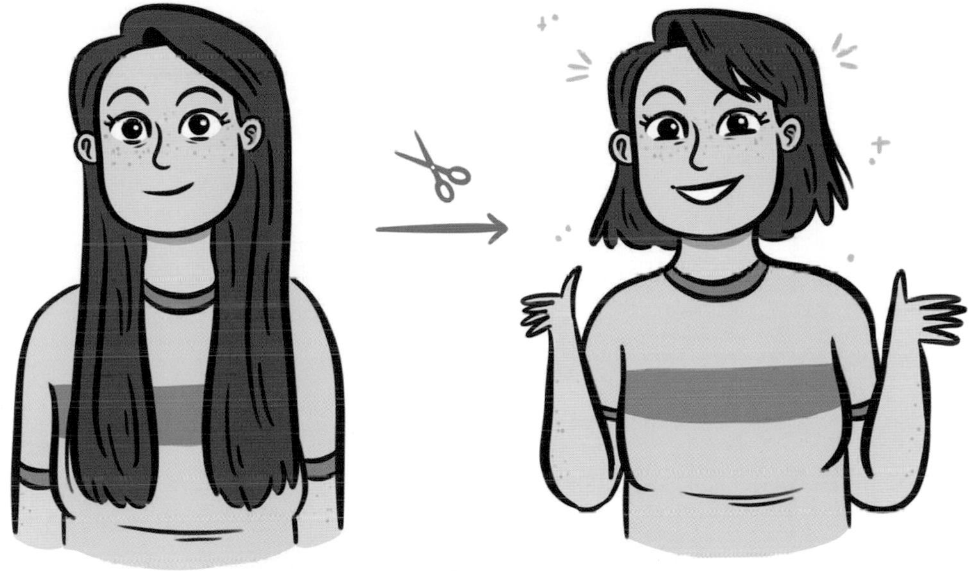

IS THE FIRST SHOWER

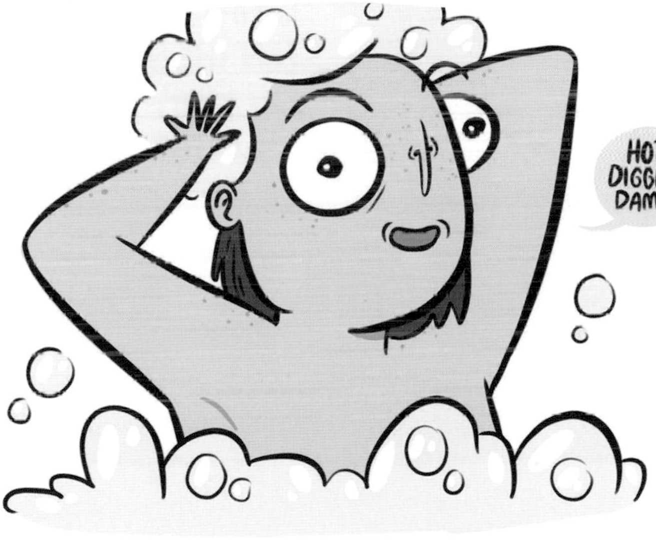
HOT DIGGITY DAMN

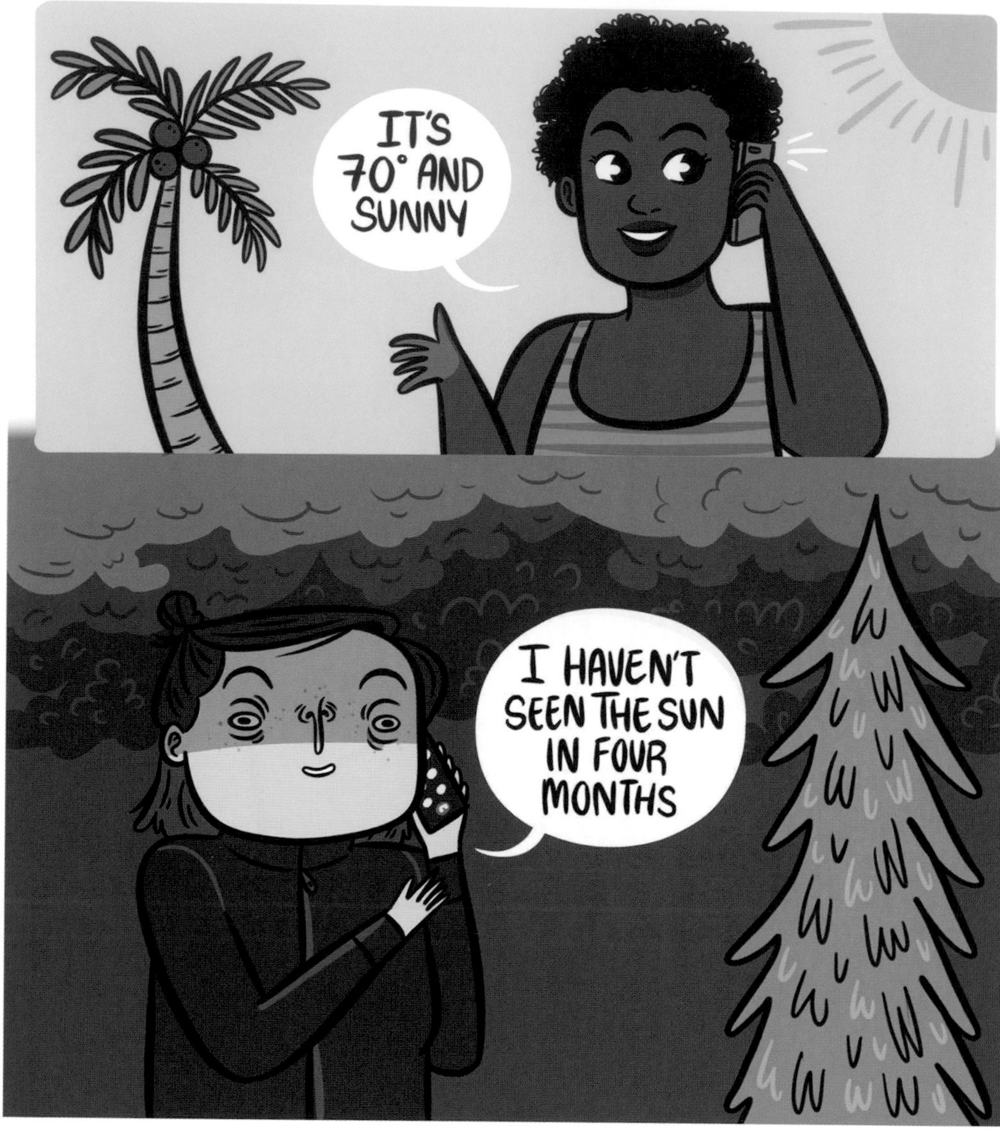
IT'S 70° AND SUNNY
I HAVEN'T SEEN THE SUN IN FOUR MONTHS

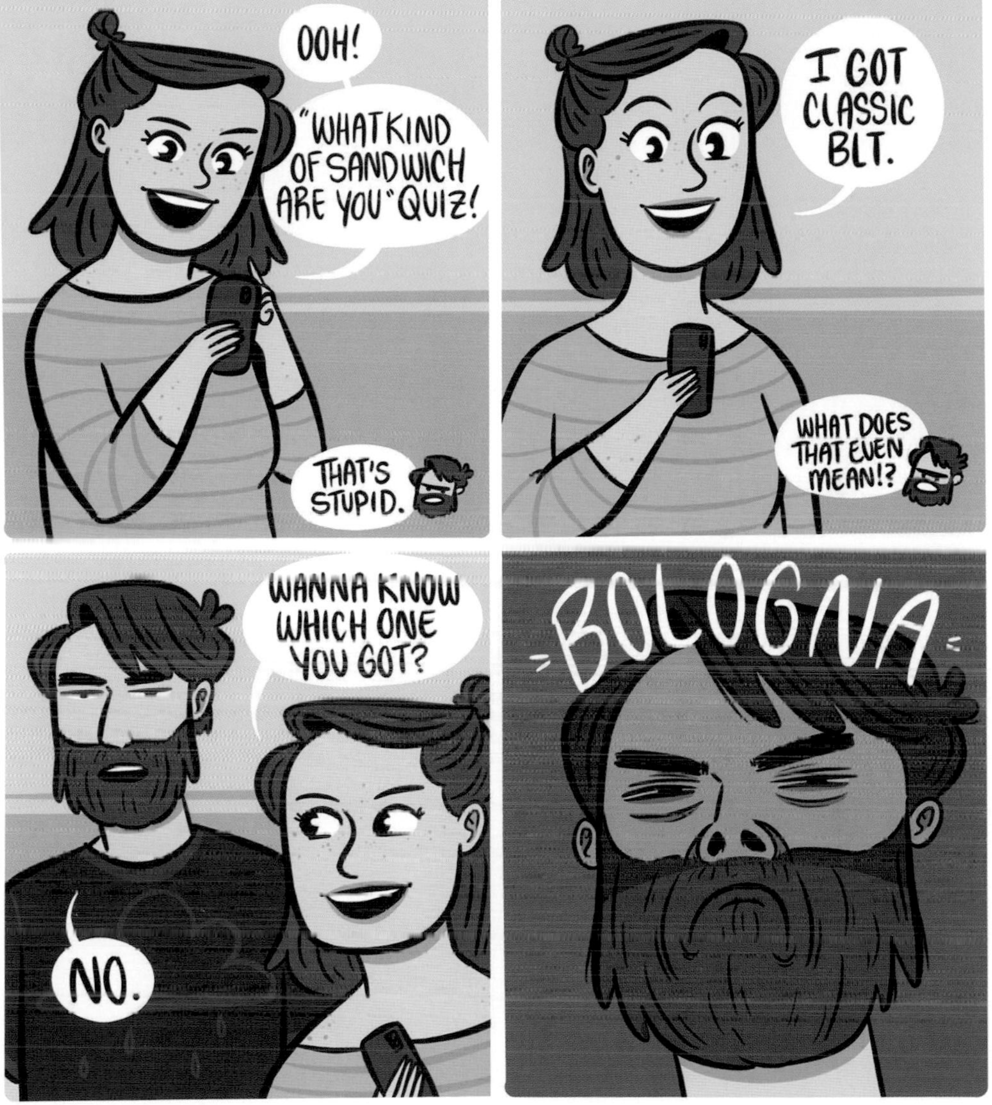
OOH!
"WHAT KIND OF SANDWICH ARE YOU" QUIZ!
THAT'S STUPID.
I GOT CLASSIC BLT.
WHAT DOES THAT EVEN MEAN!?
WANNA KNOW WHICH ONE YOU GOT?
NO.
BOLOGNA

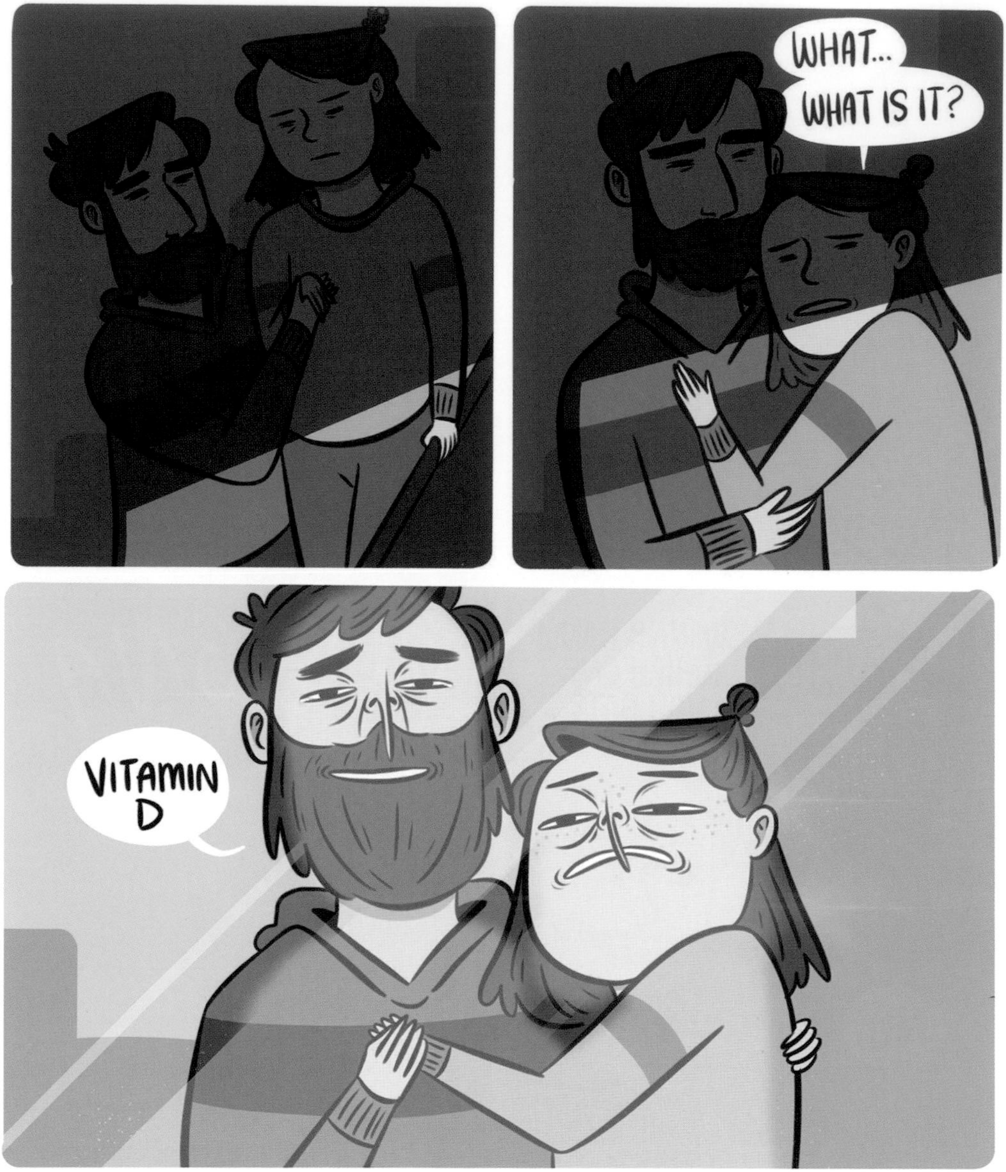
WHAT...
WHAT IS IT?
VITAMIN D

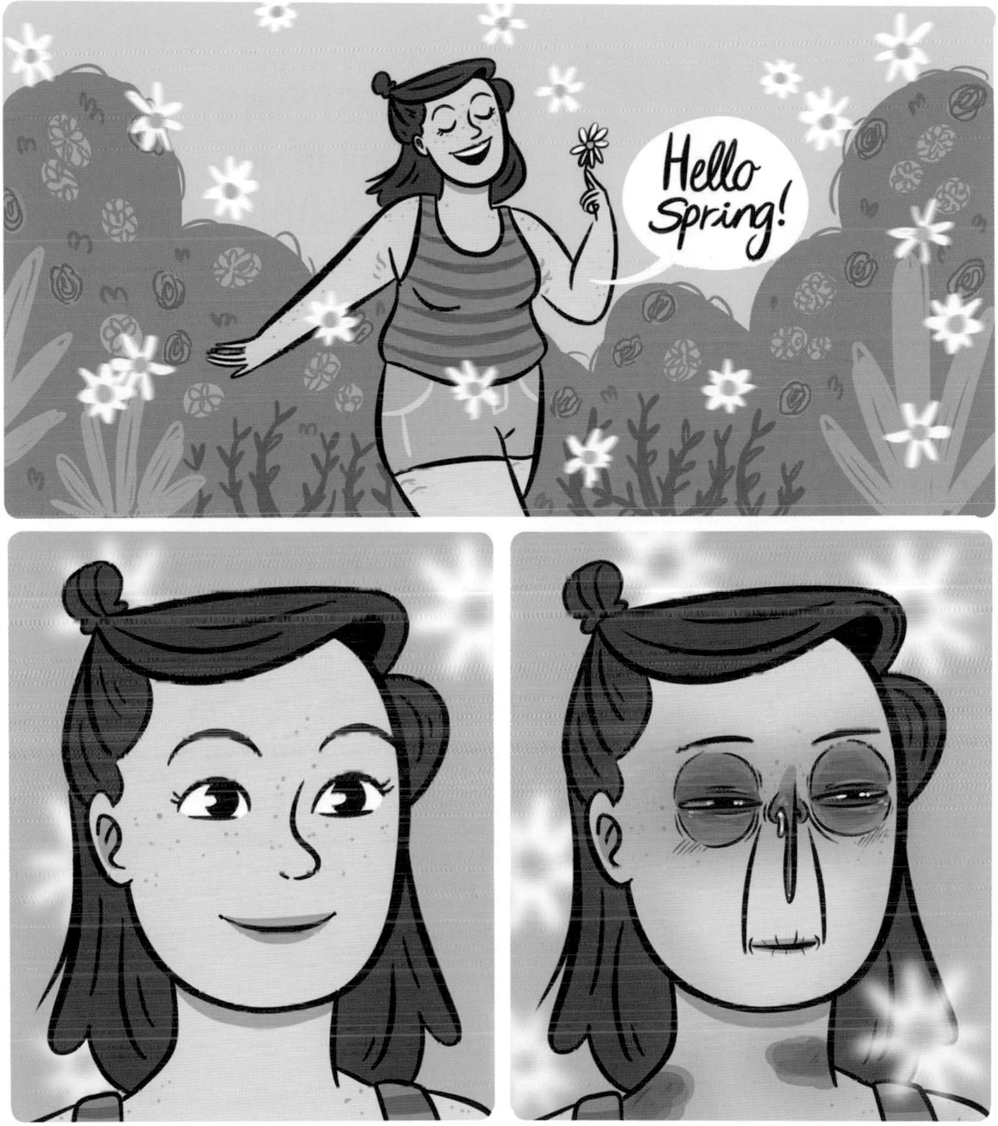
Hello Spring!

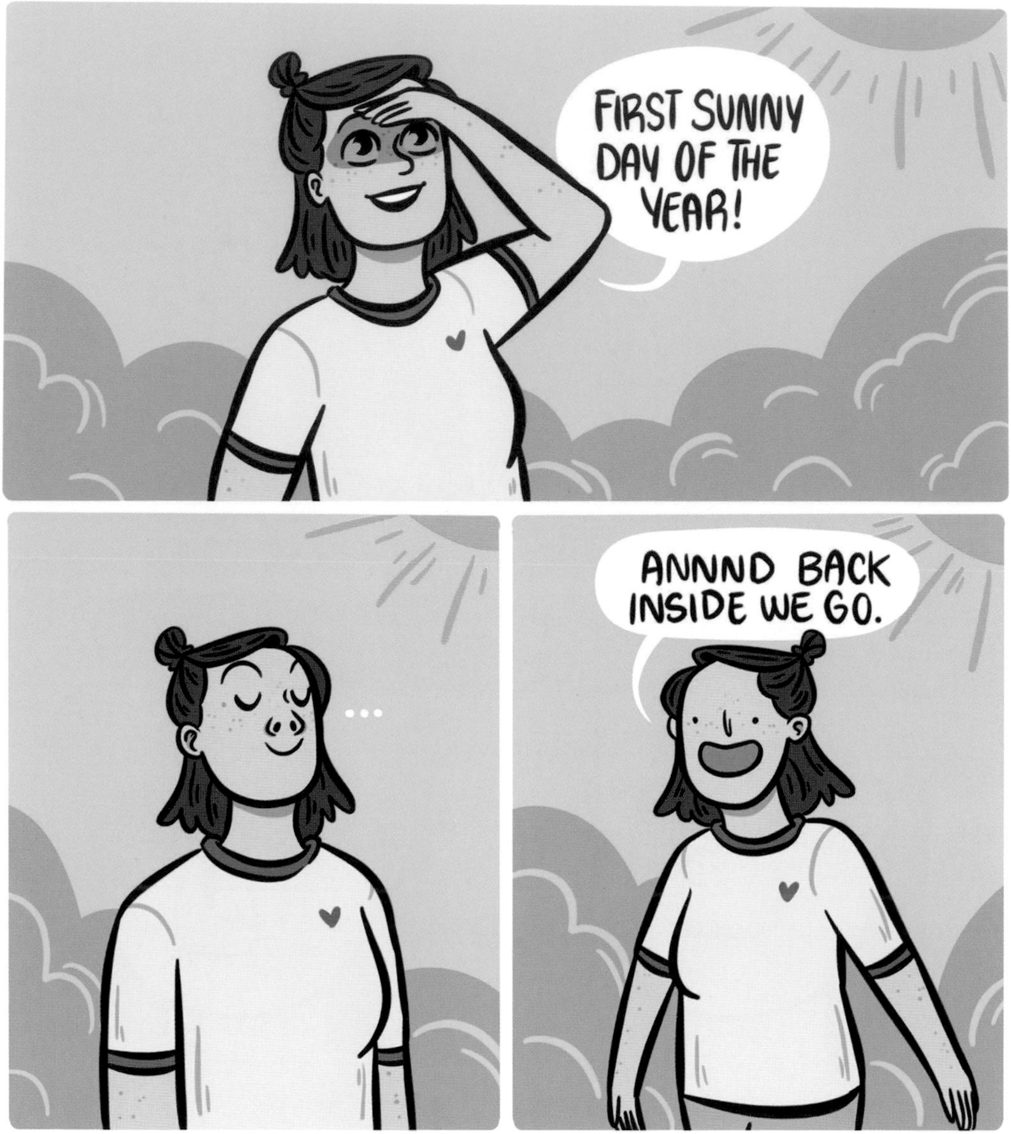
FIRST SUNNY DAY OF THE YEAR!
...
ANNND BACK INSIDE WE GO.

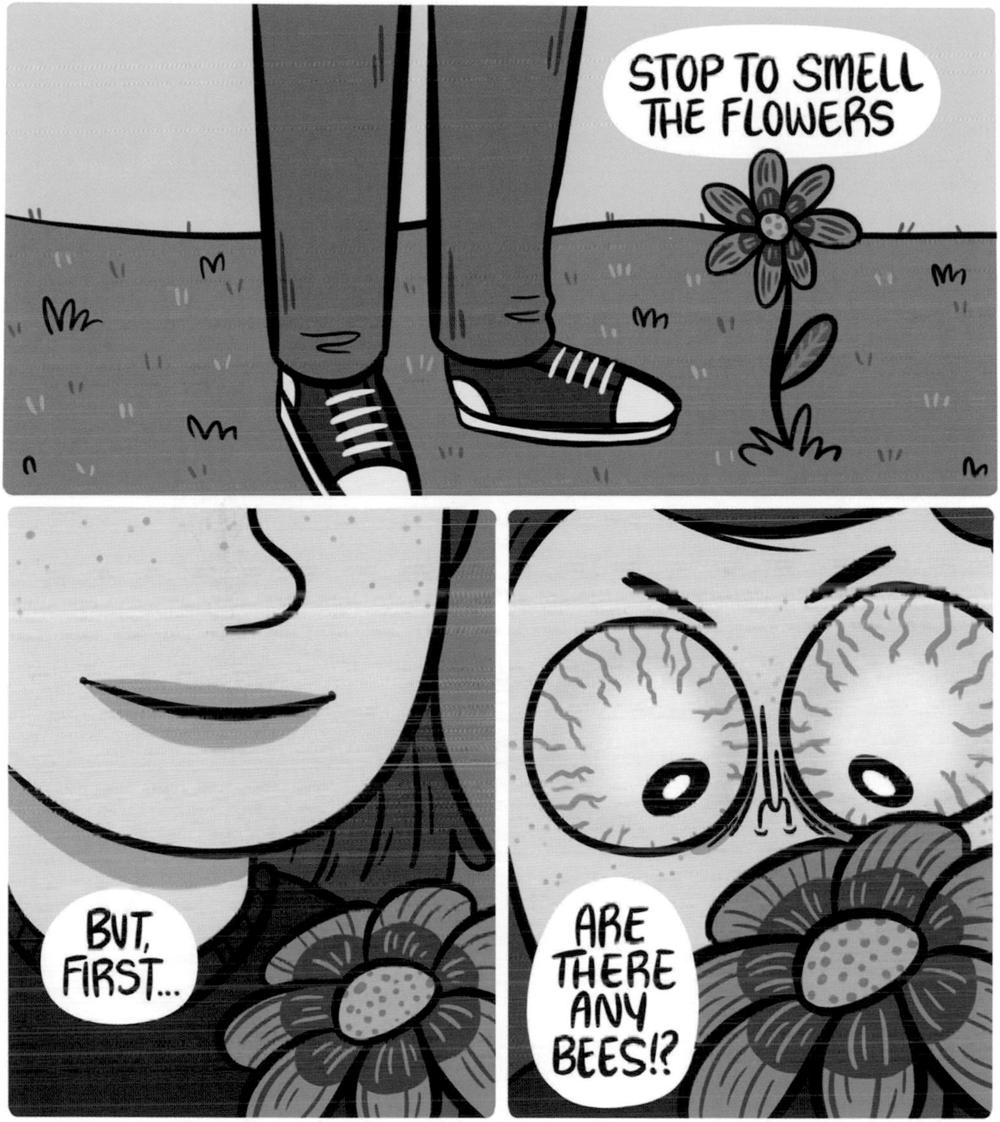
STOP TO SMELL THE FLOWERS
BUT, FIRST...
ARE THERE ANY BEES!?

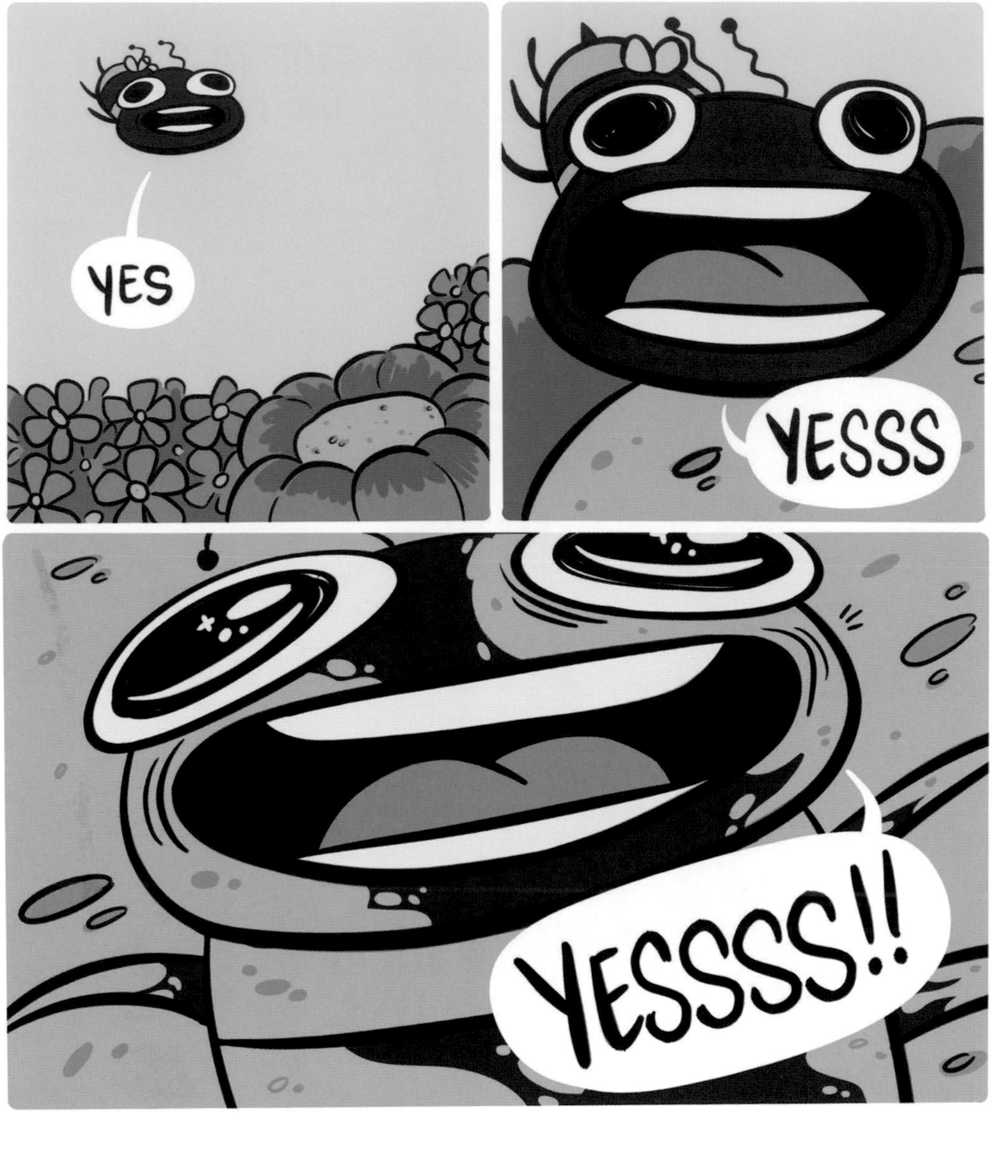
YES
YESSS
YESSSS!!

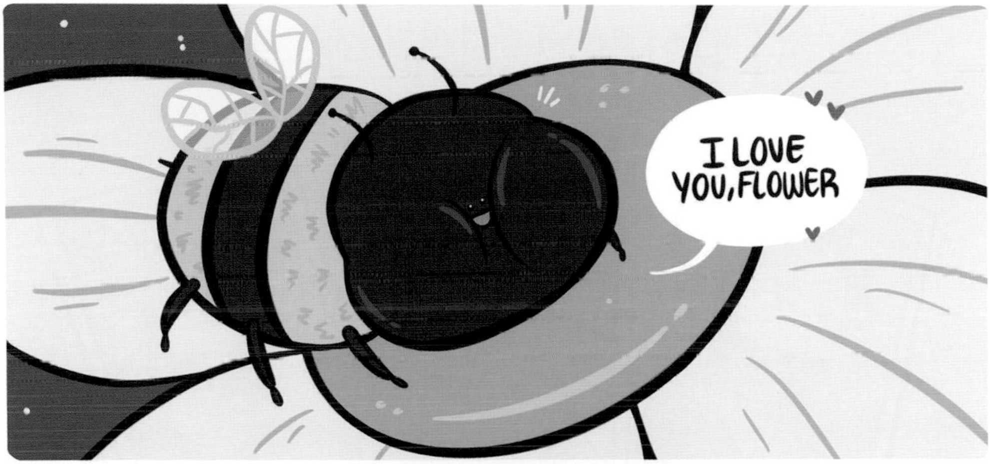
I LOVE YOU, FLOWER

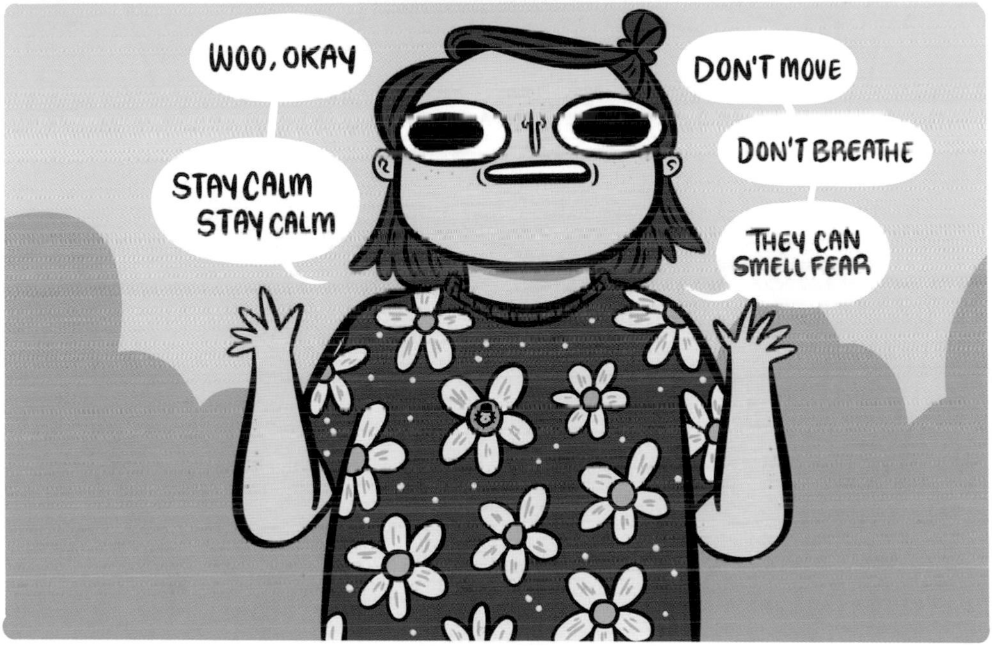
WOO, OKAY
STAY CALM STAY CALM
DON'T MOVE
DON'T BREATHE
THEY CAN SMELL FEAR

PHOTOS I HAVE OF HIM:

PHOTOS HE HAS OF ME:

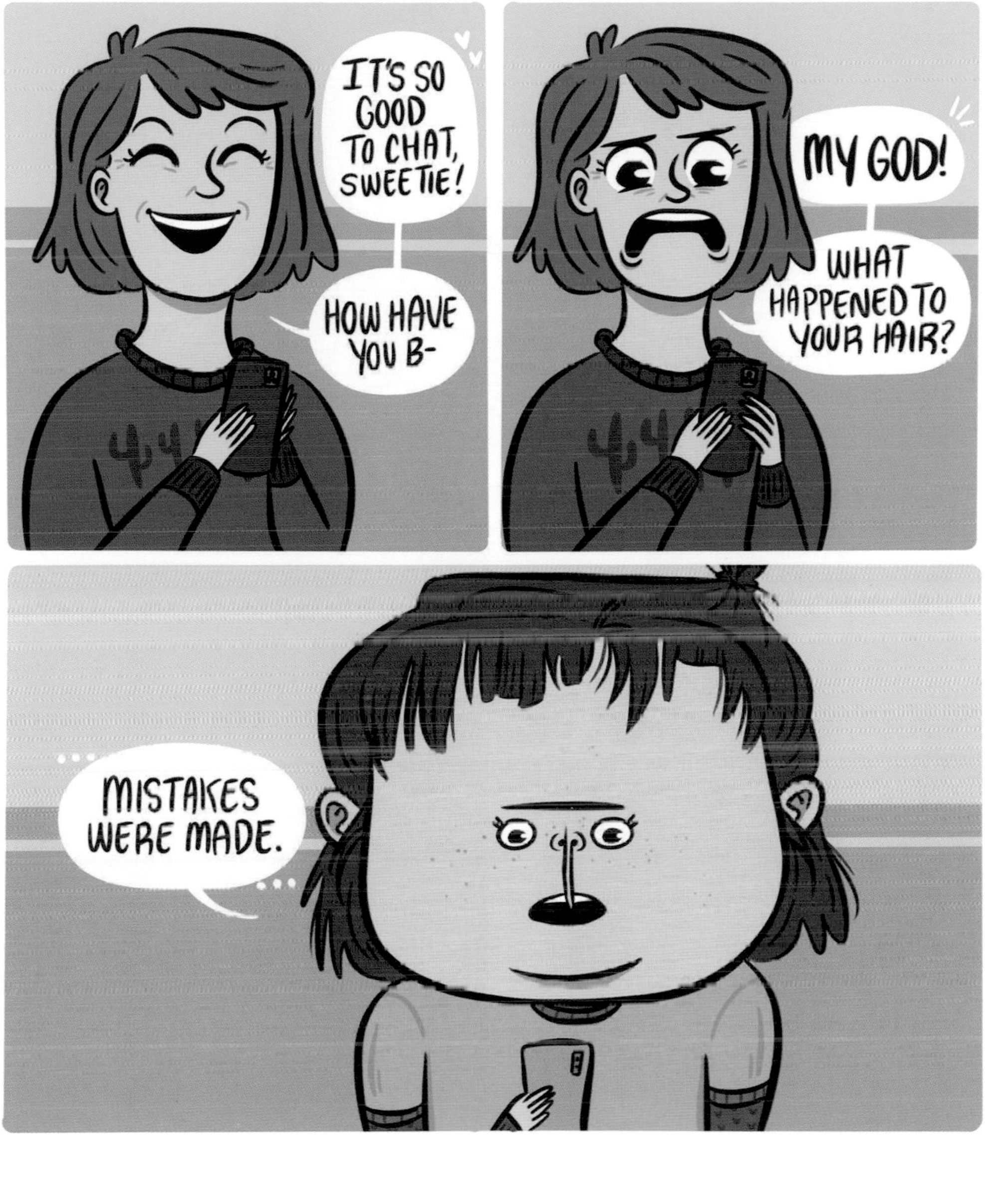
IT'S SO GOOD TO CHAT, SWEETIE!
HOW HAVE YOU B-
MY GOD!
WHAT HAPPENED TO YOUR HAIR?
MISTAKES WERE MADE.

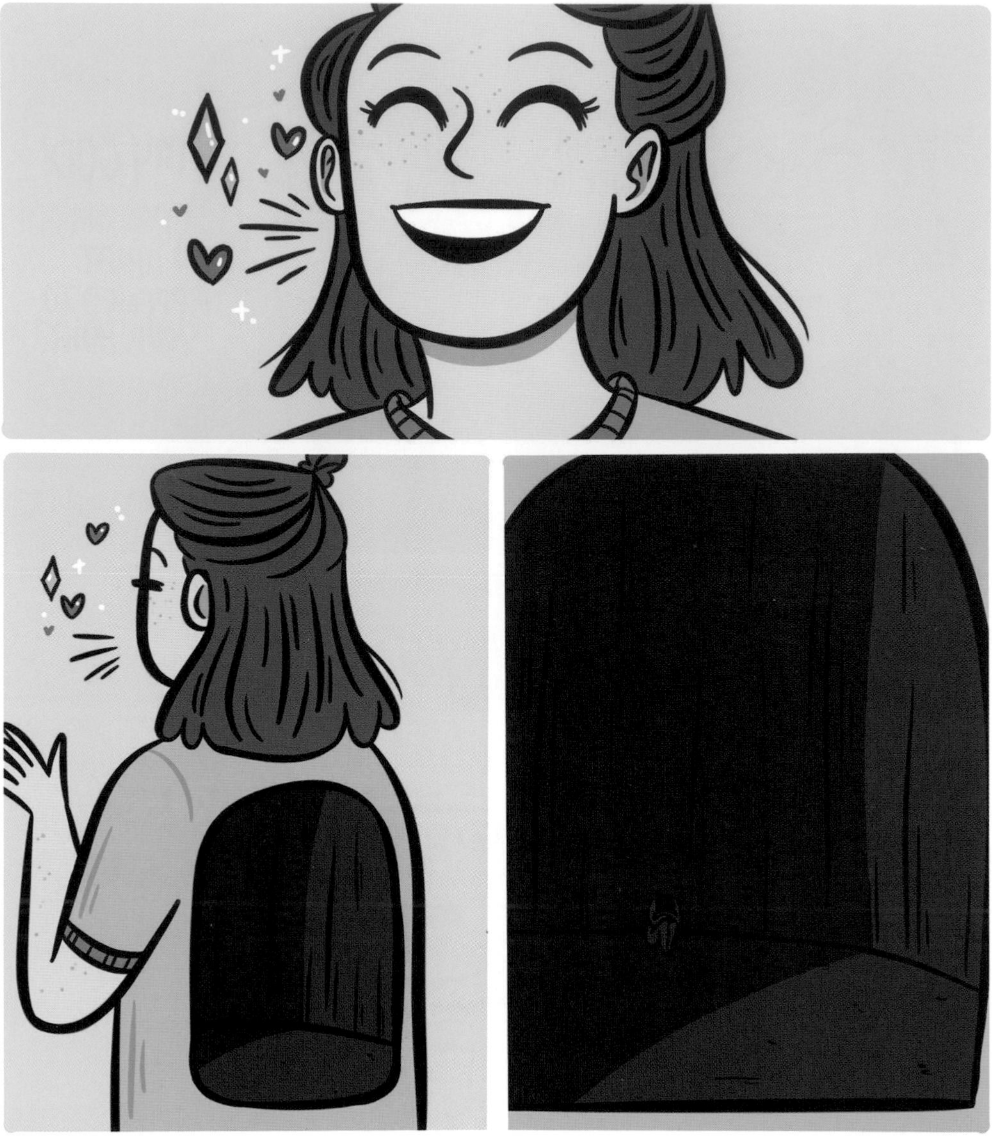

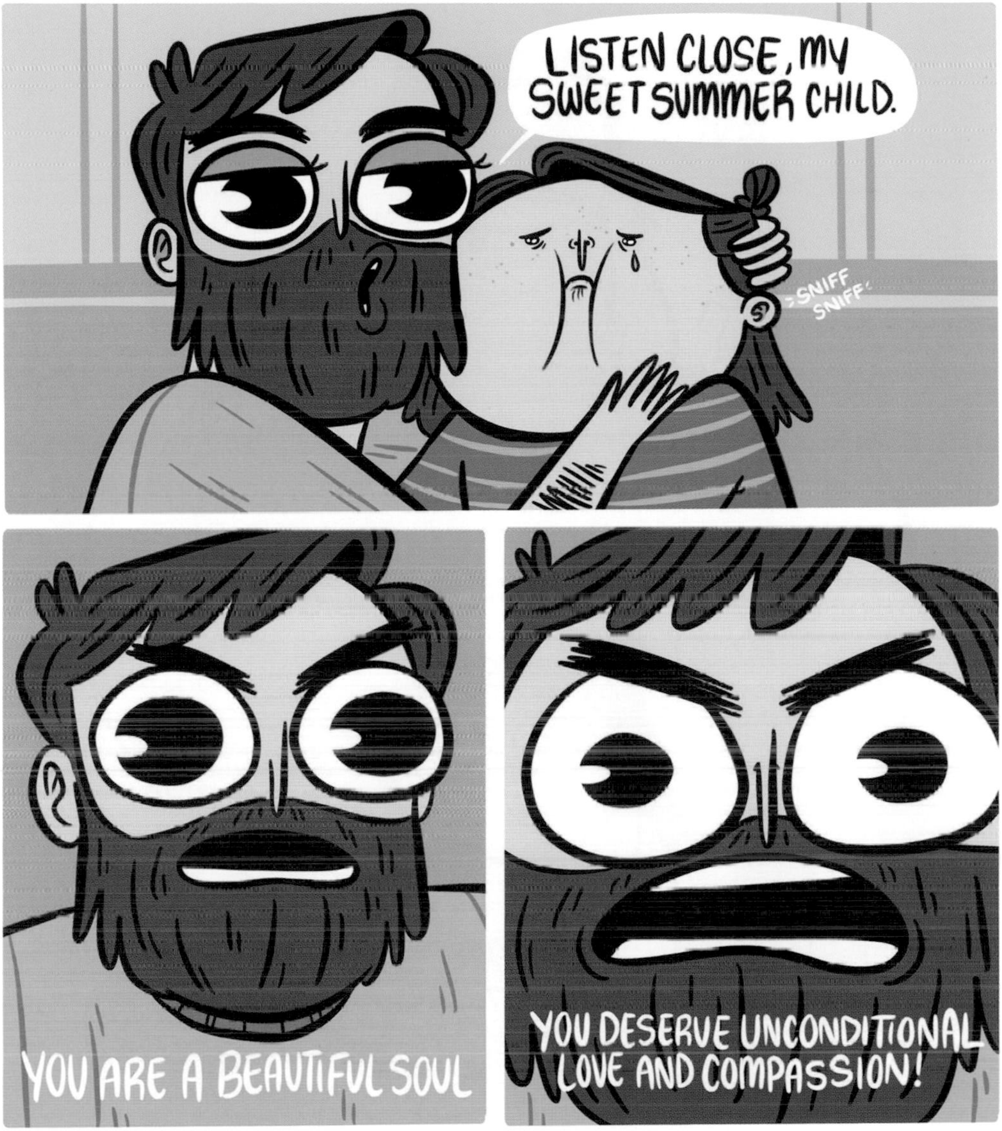
LISTEN CLOSE, MY SWEET SUMMER CHILD.
SNIFF SNIFF
YOU ARE A BEAUTIFUL SOUL
YOU DESERVE UNCONDITIONAL LOVE AND COMPASSION!

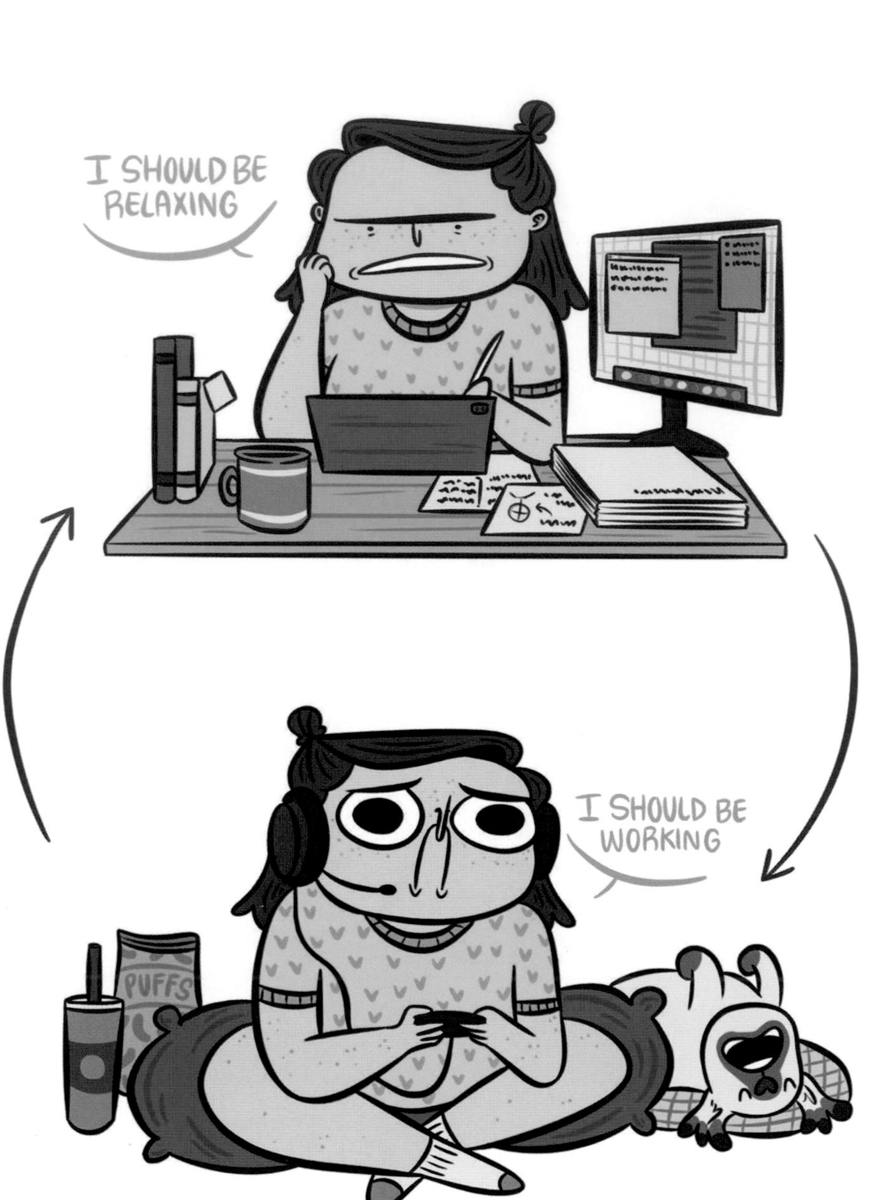
I SHOULD BE RELAXING
I SHOULD BE WORKING
PUFFS

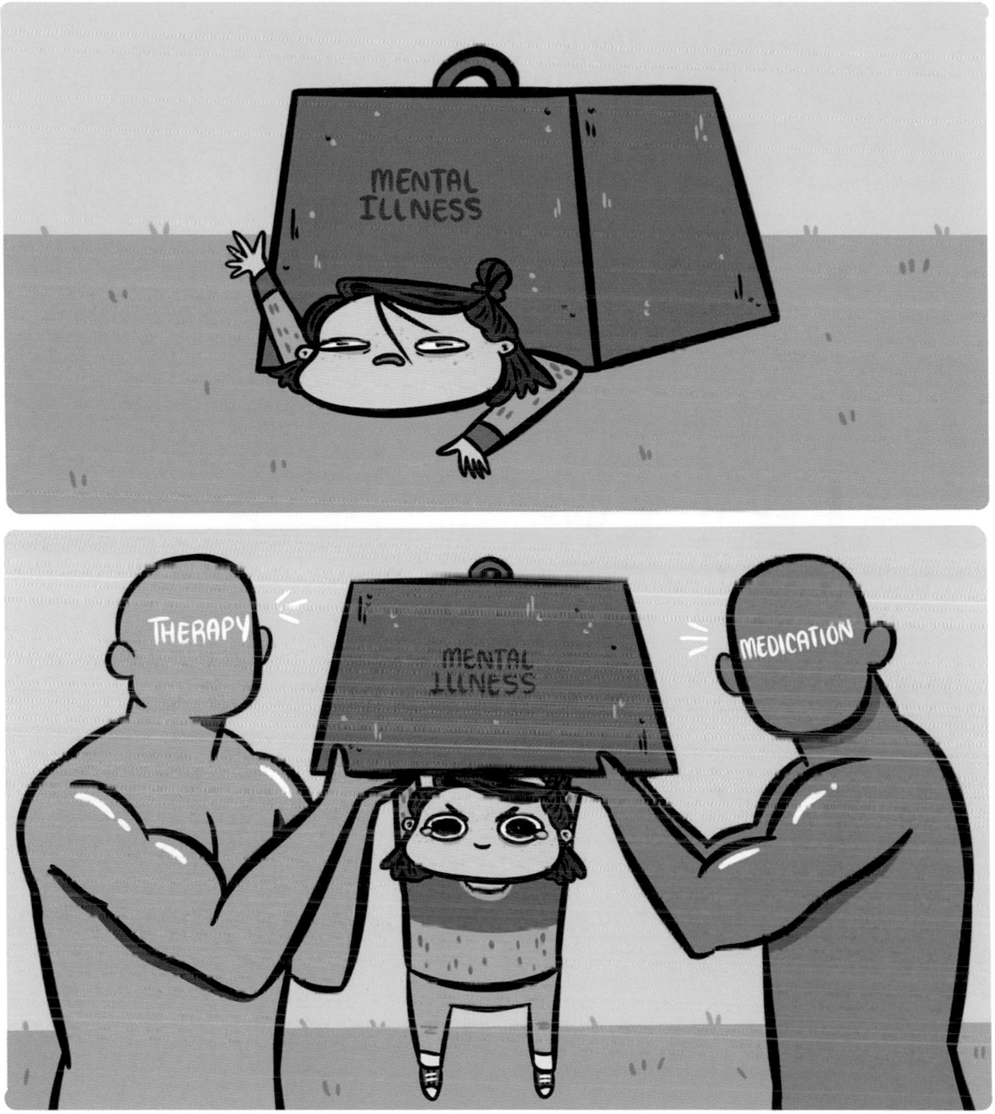
MENTAL ILLNESS
THERAPY
MENTAL ILLNESS
MEDICATION

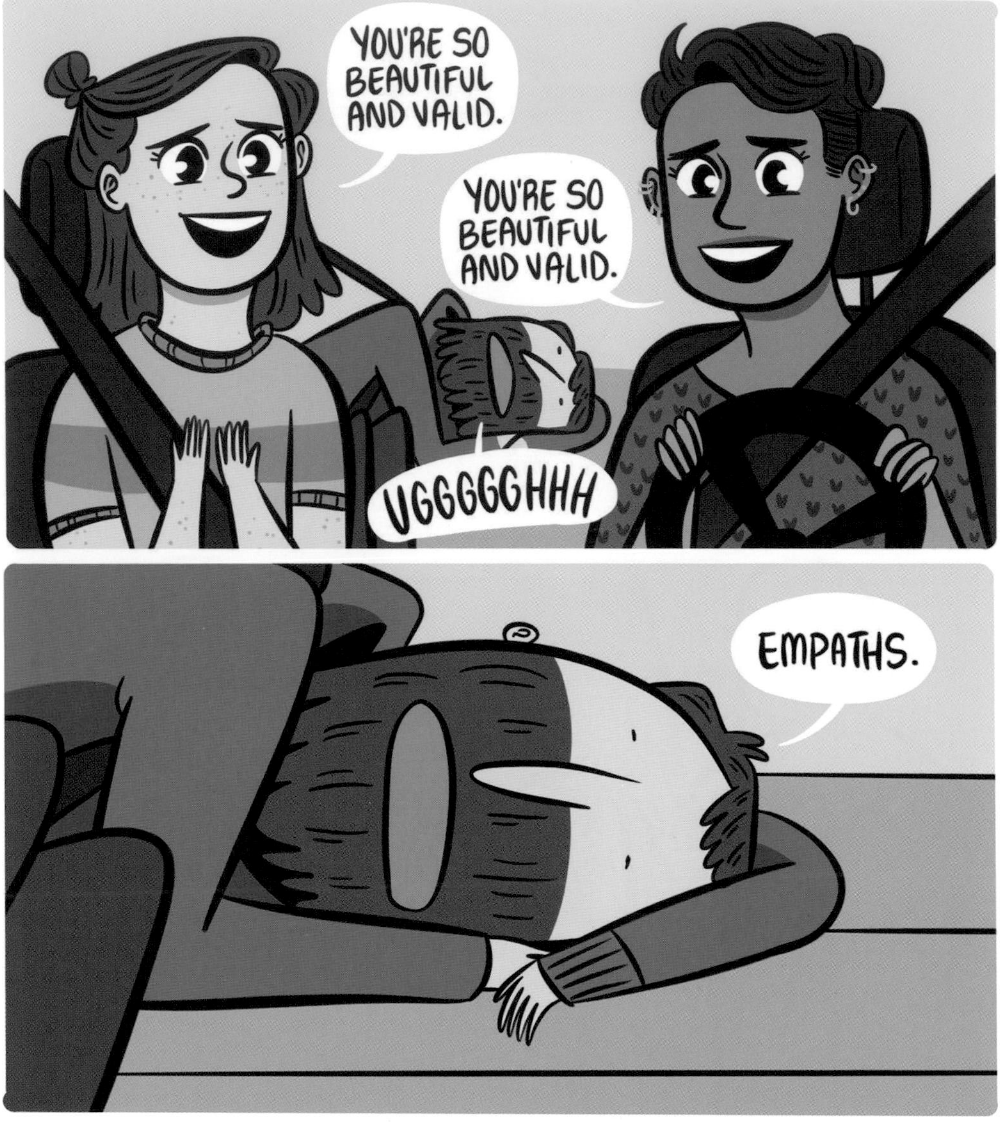
YOU'RE SO BEAUTIFUL AND VALID.
YOU'RE SO BEAUTIFUL AND VALID.
UGGGGGHHH
EMPATHS.

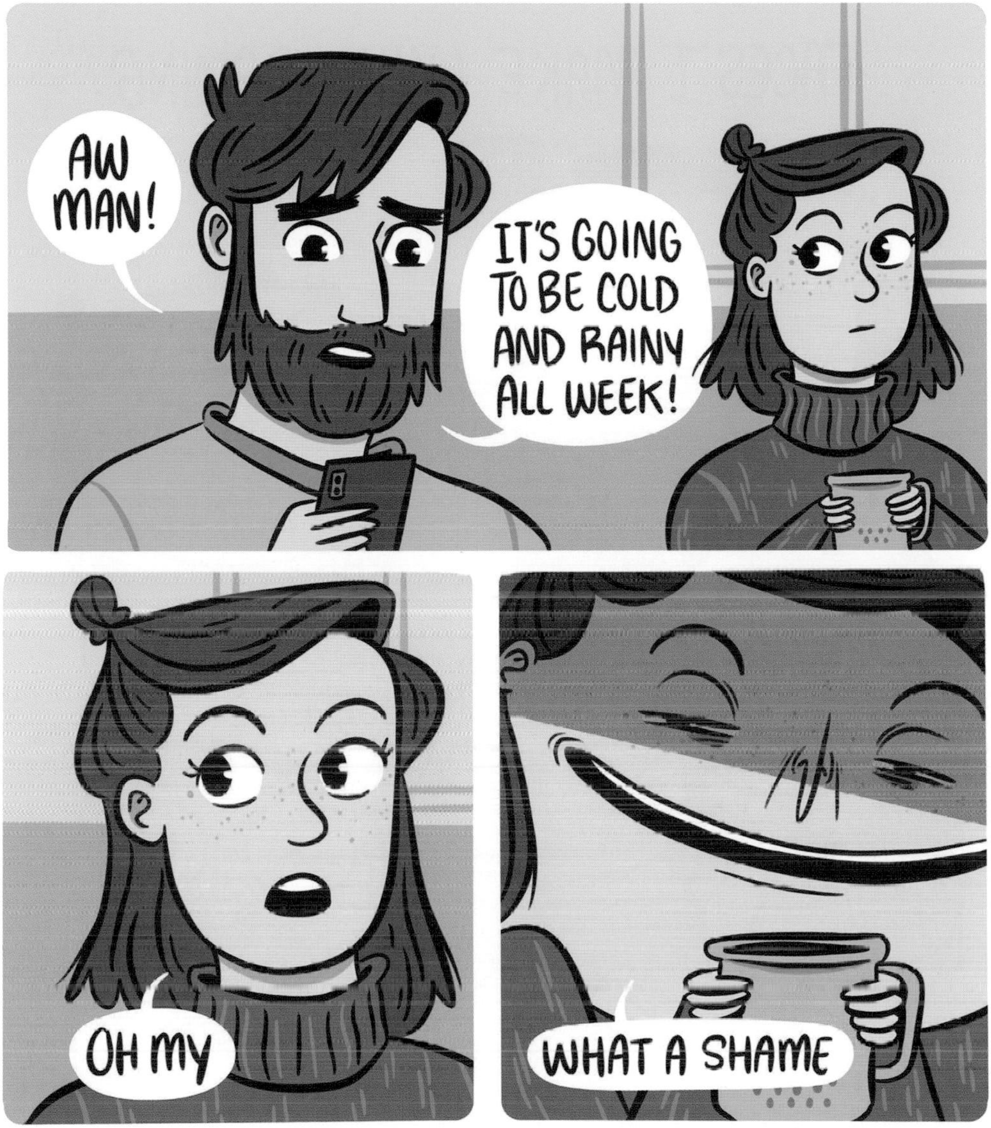
AW MAN!
IT'S GOING TO BE COLD AND RAINY ALL WEEK!
OH MY
WHAT A SHAME

FACES I MAKE WHILE GAMING:

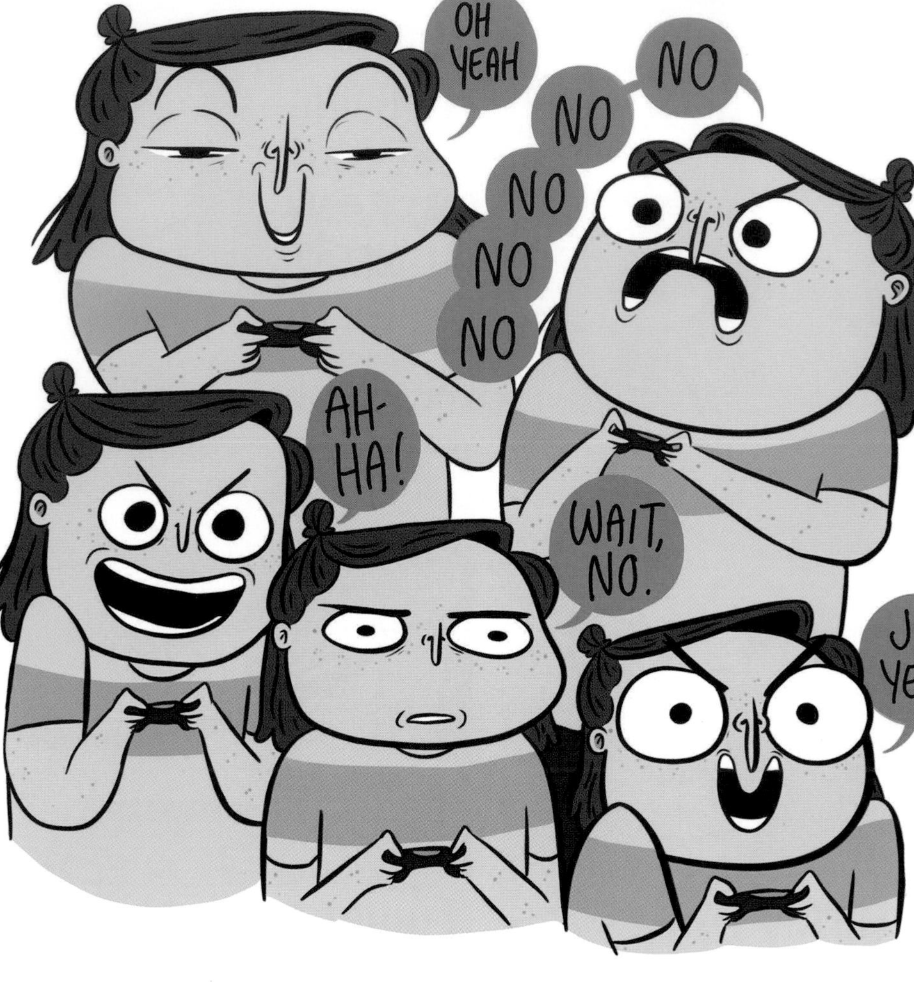
OH YEAH
NO
NO
NO
NO
NO
AH-HA!
WAIT, NO.
JK! YES!

TWO KINDS OF DND NOTETAKERS:

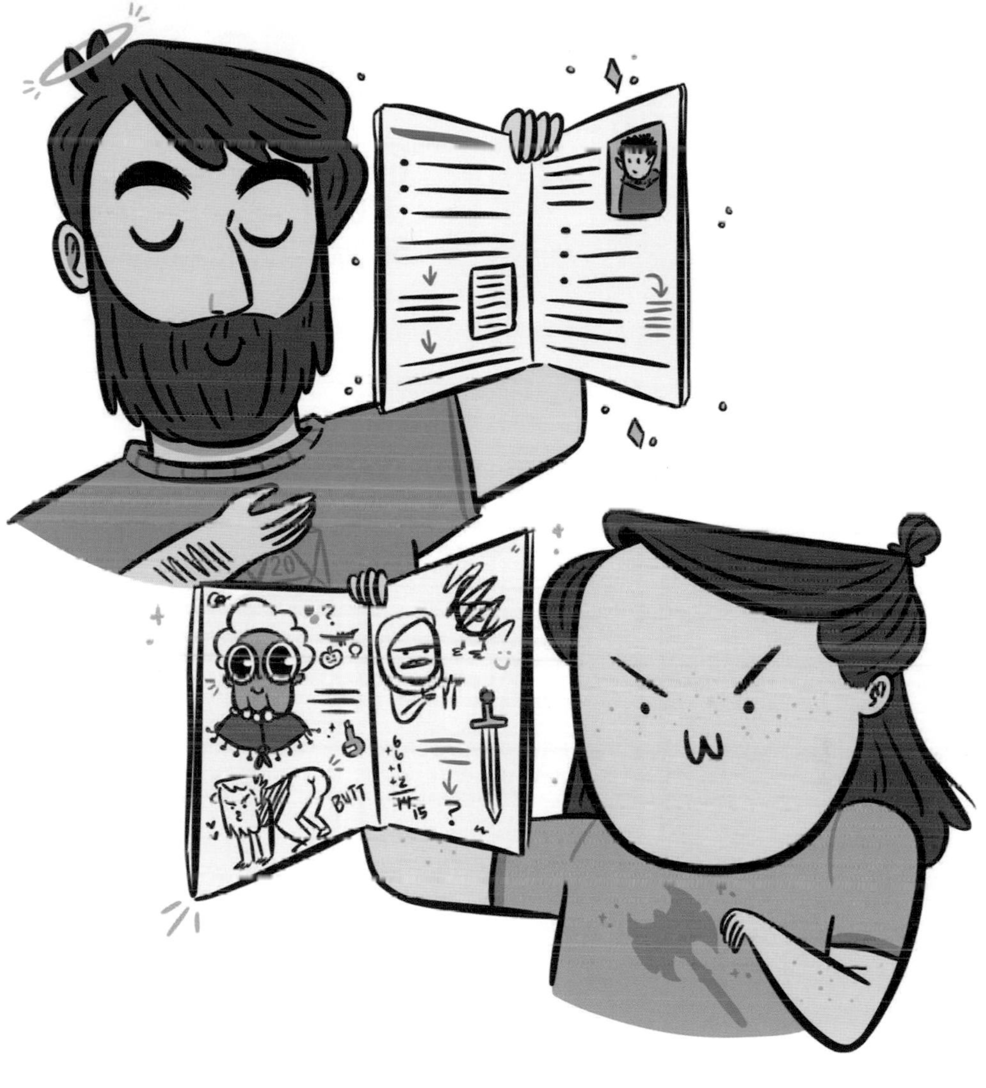
BUTT

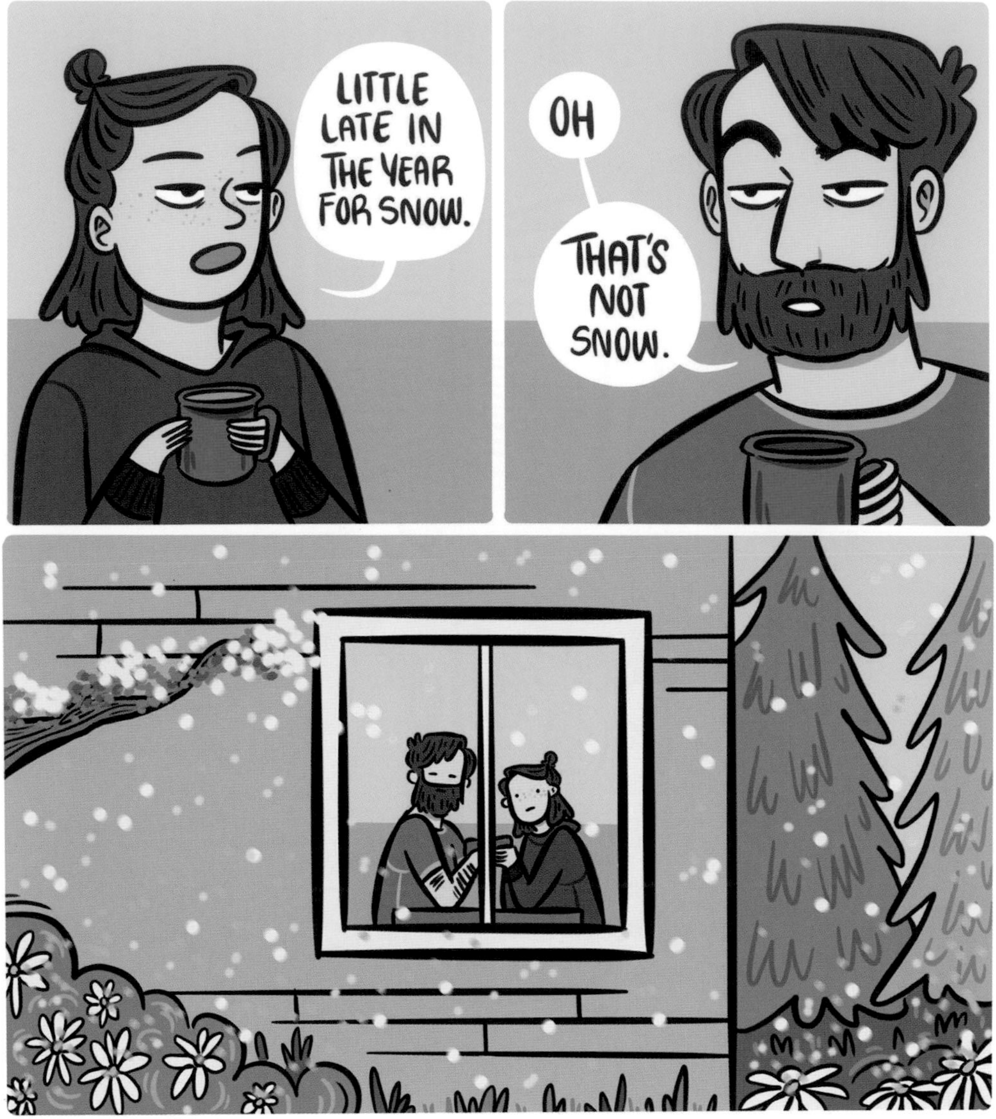
LITTLE LATE IN THE YEAR FOR SNOW.
OH
THAT'S NOT SNOW.

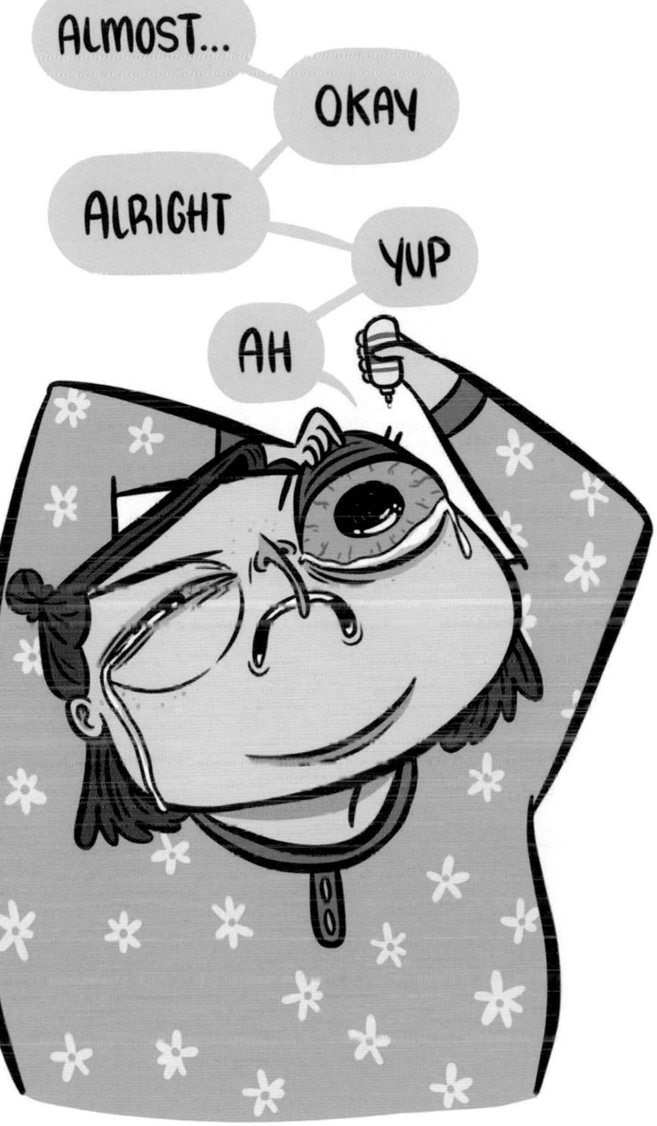
ALMOST...
OKAY
ALRIGHT
YUP
AH

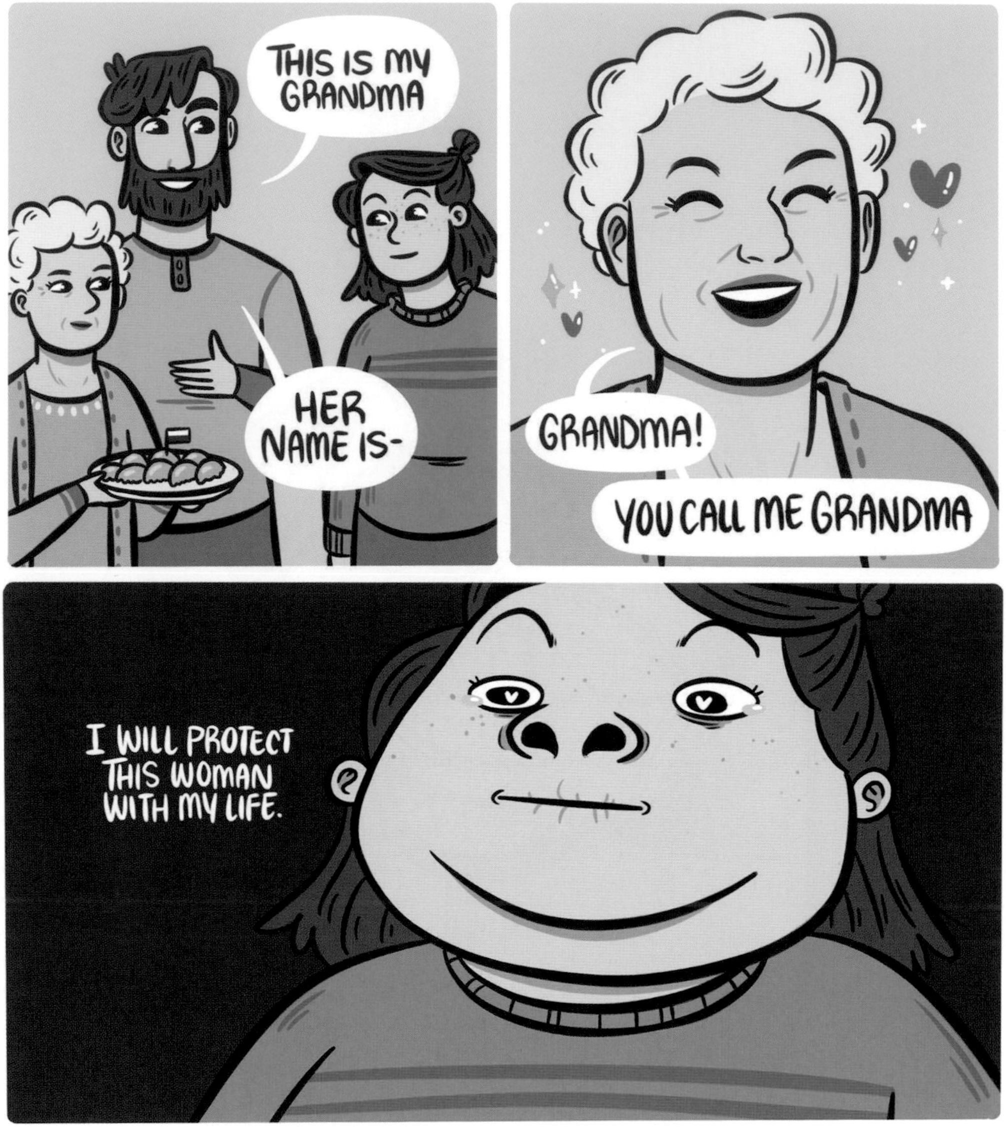
THIS IS MY GRANDMA
HER NAME IS-
GRANDMA!
YOU CALL ME GRANDMA
I WILL PROTECT THIS WOMAN WITH MY LIFE.

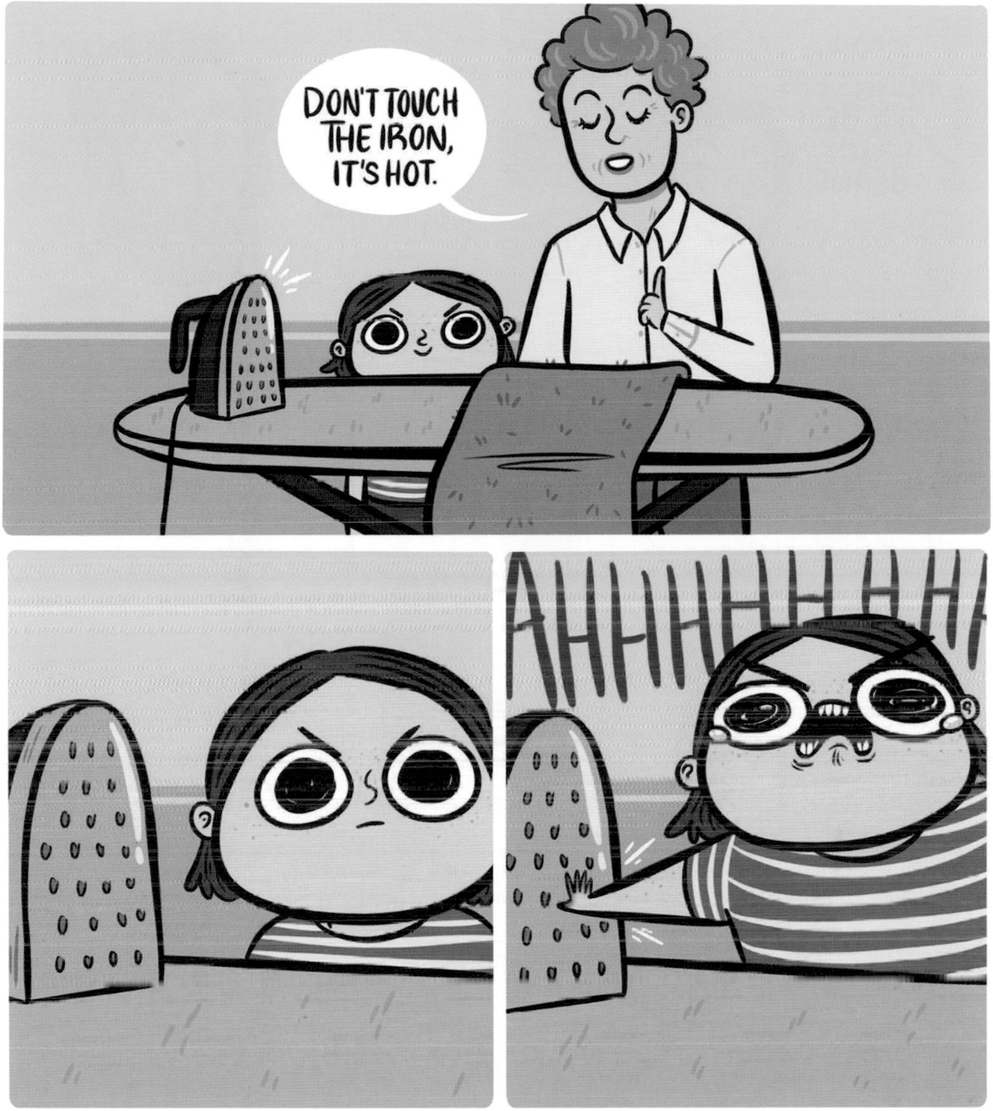
DON'T TOUCH THE IRON, IT'S HOT.
AHHHHHHHH

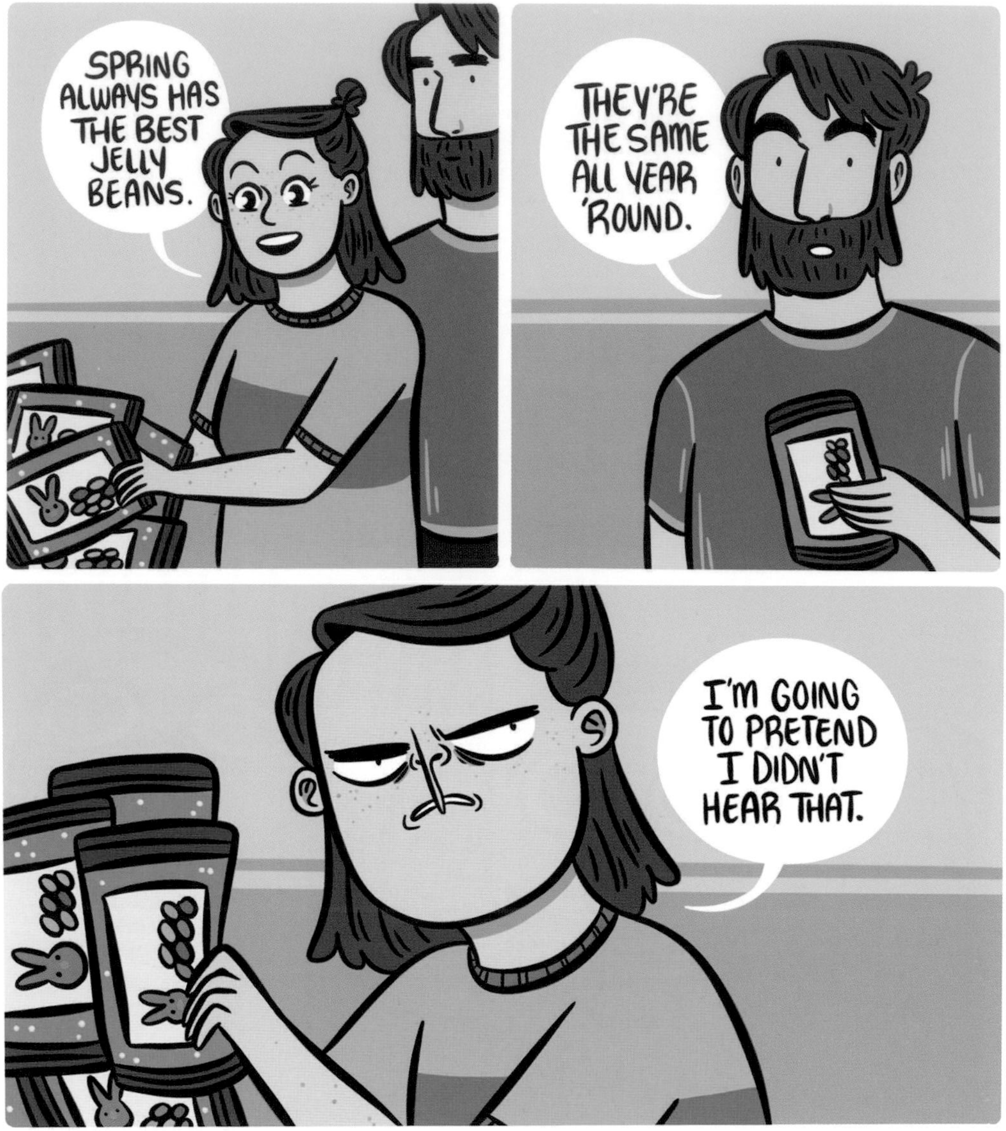
SPRING ALWAYS HAS THE BEST JELLY BEANS.
THEY'RE THE SAME ALL YEAR 'ROUND.
I'M GOING TO PRETEND I DIDN'T HEAR THAT.

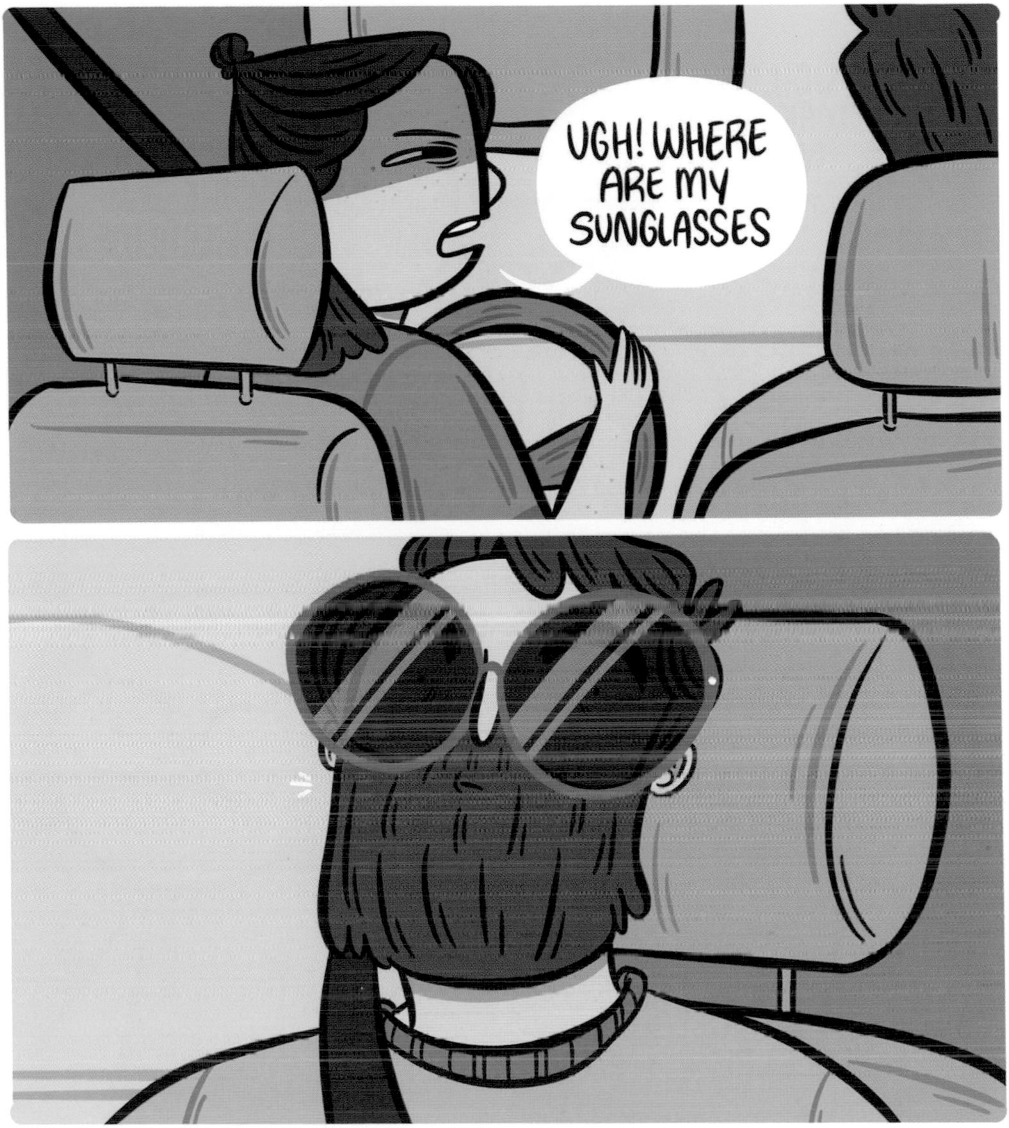
UGH! WHERE ARE MY SUNGLASSES

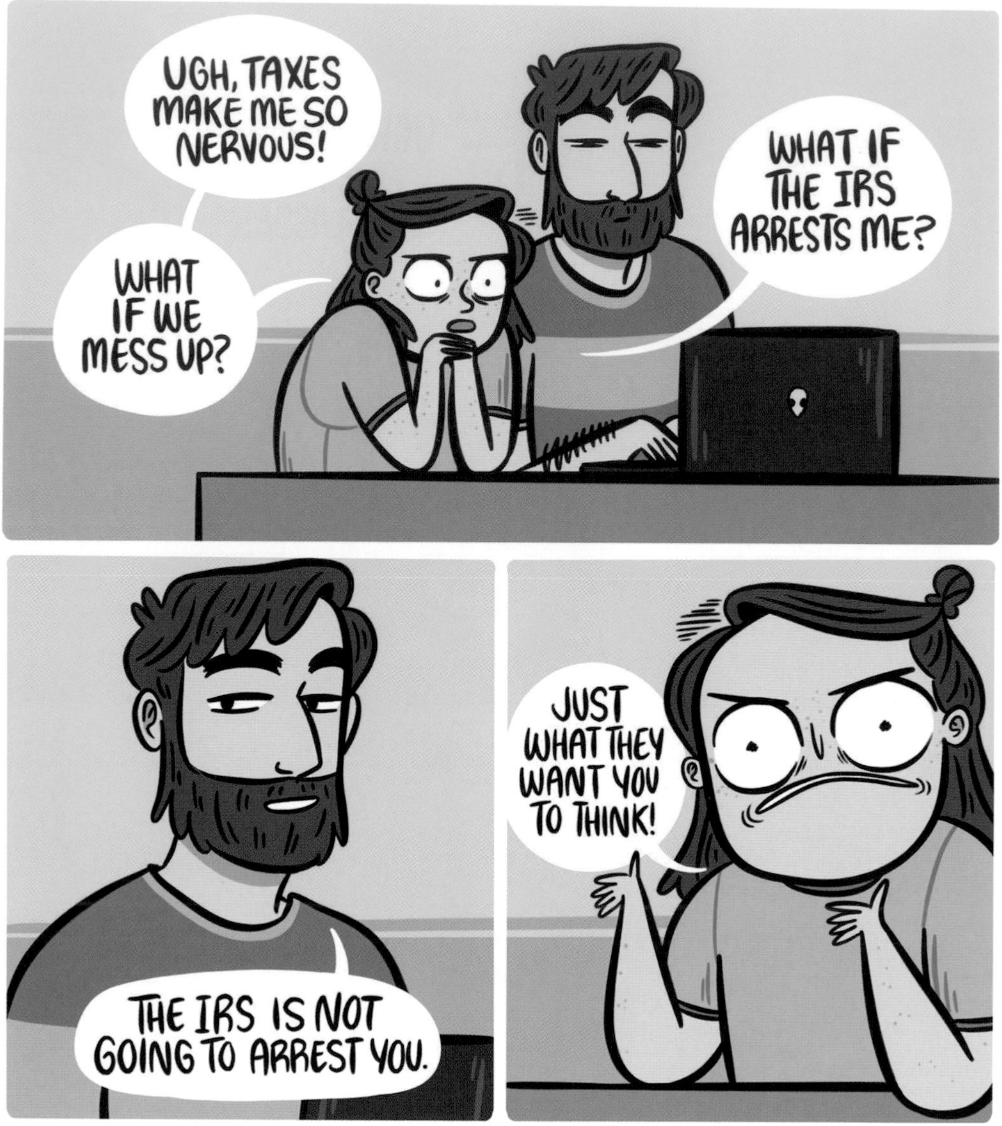
UGH, TAXES MAKE ME SO NERVOUS!
WHAT IF WE MESS UP?
WHAT IF THE IRS ARRESTS ME?
THE IRS IS NOT GOING TO ARREST YOU.
JUST WHAT THEY WANT YOU TO THINK!

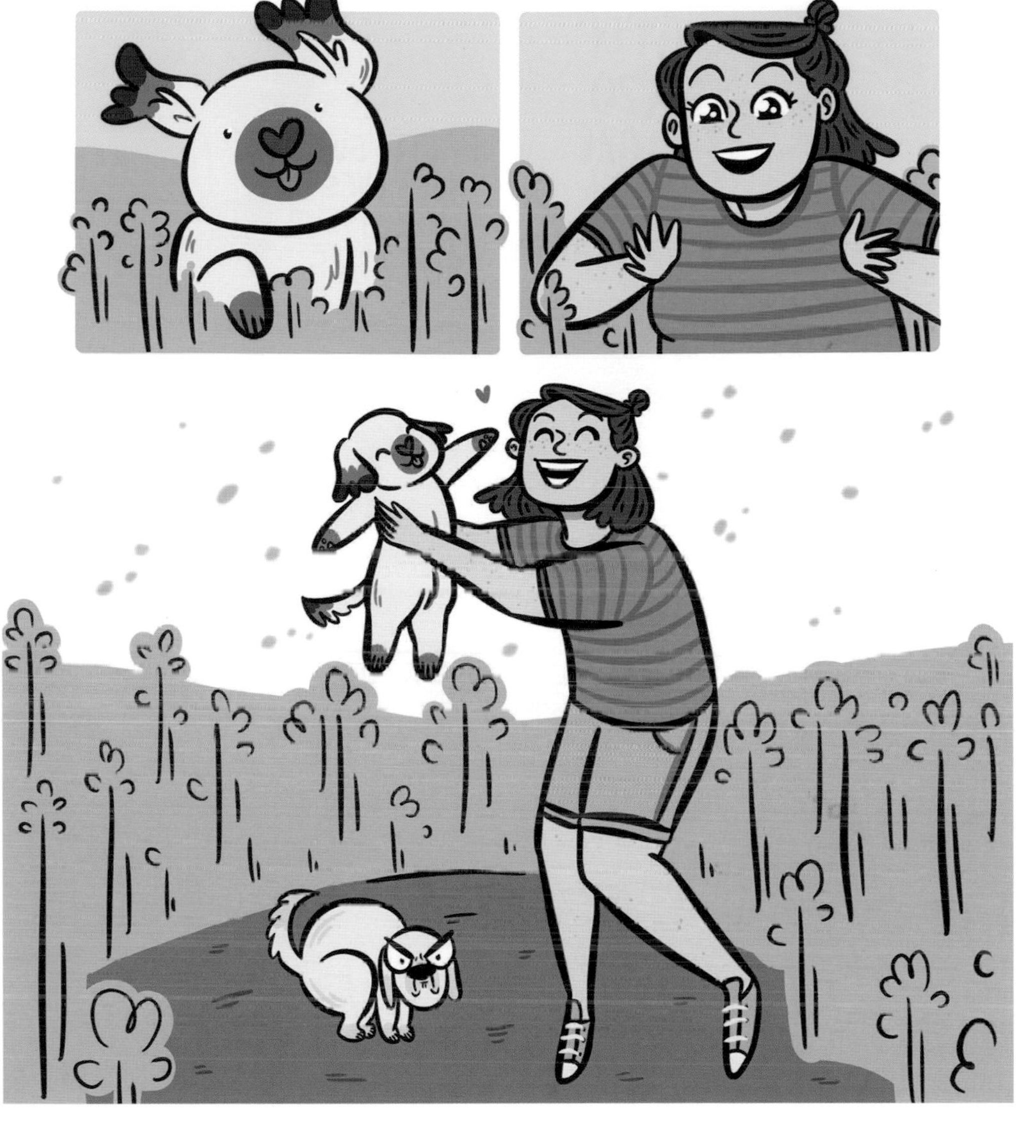

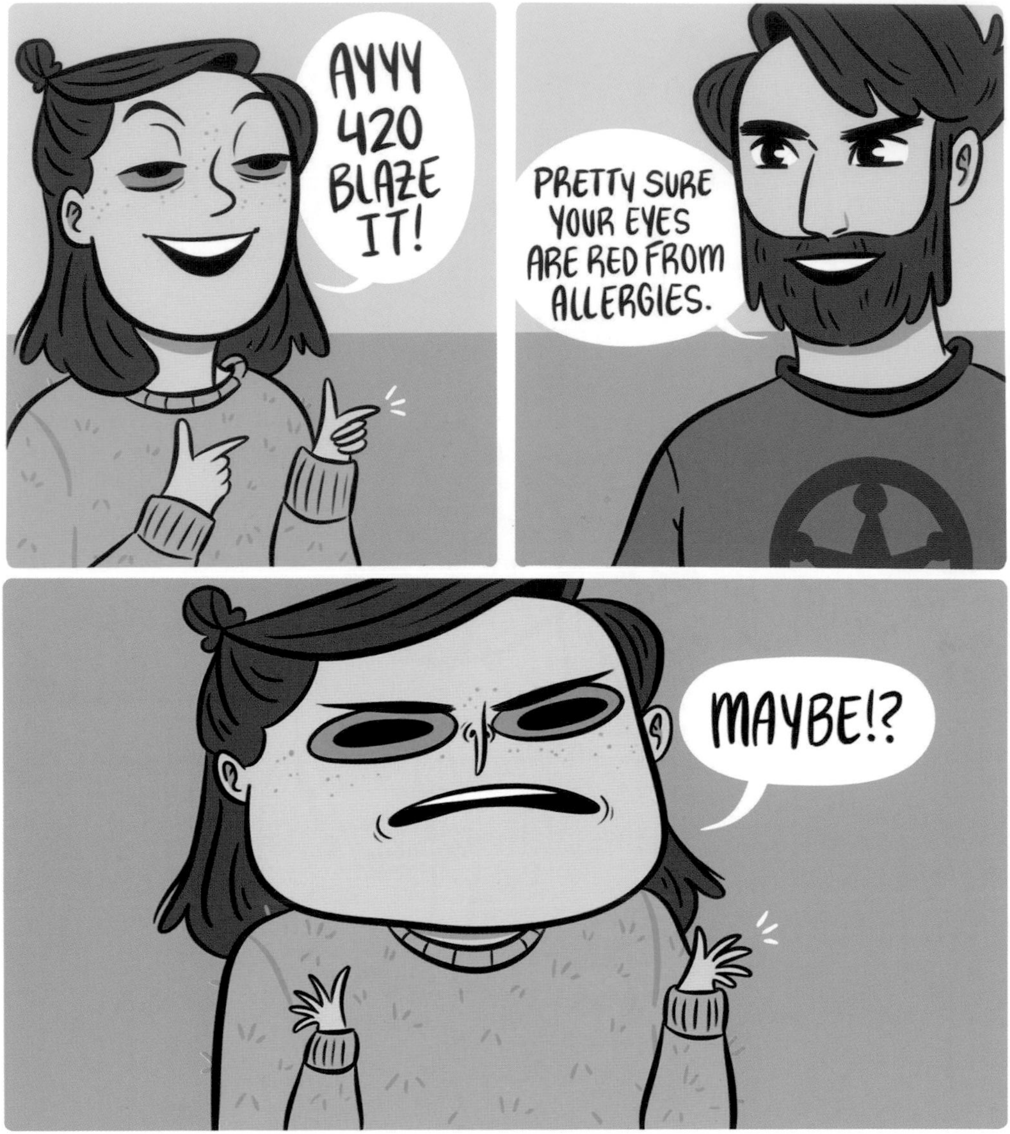
AYYY 420 BLAZE IT!
PRETTY SURE YOUR EYES ARE RED FROM ALLERGIES.
MAYBE!?

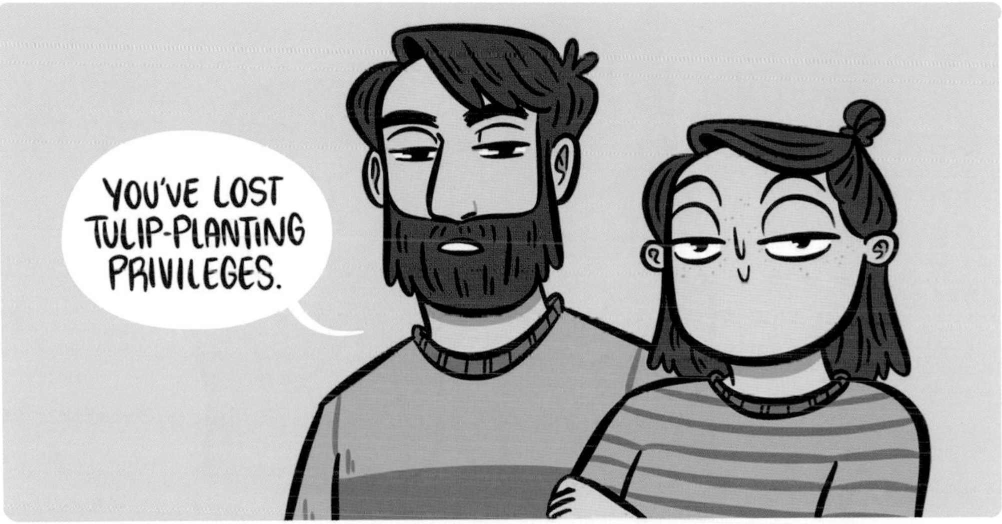
YOU'VE LOST TULIP-PLANTING PRIVILEGES.

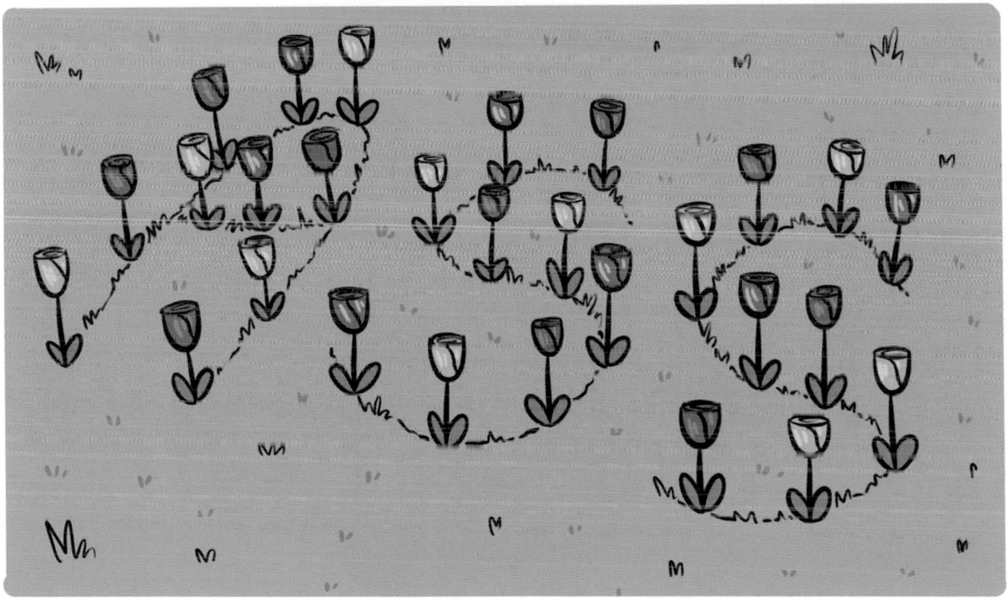

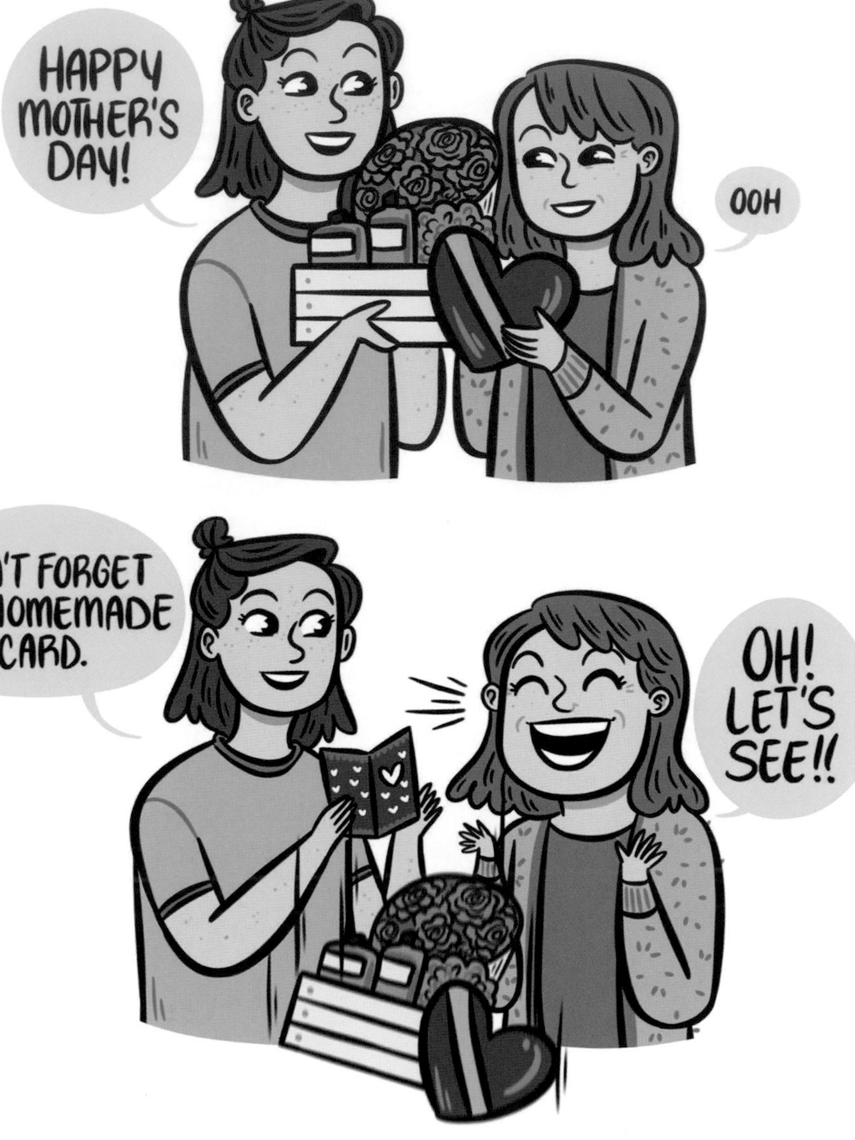
HAPPY MOTHER'S DAY!
OOH
DON'T FORGET THE HOMEMADE CARD.
OH! LET'S SEE!!

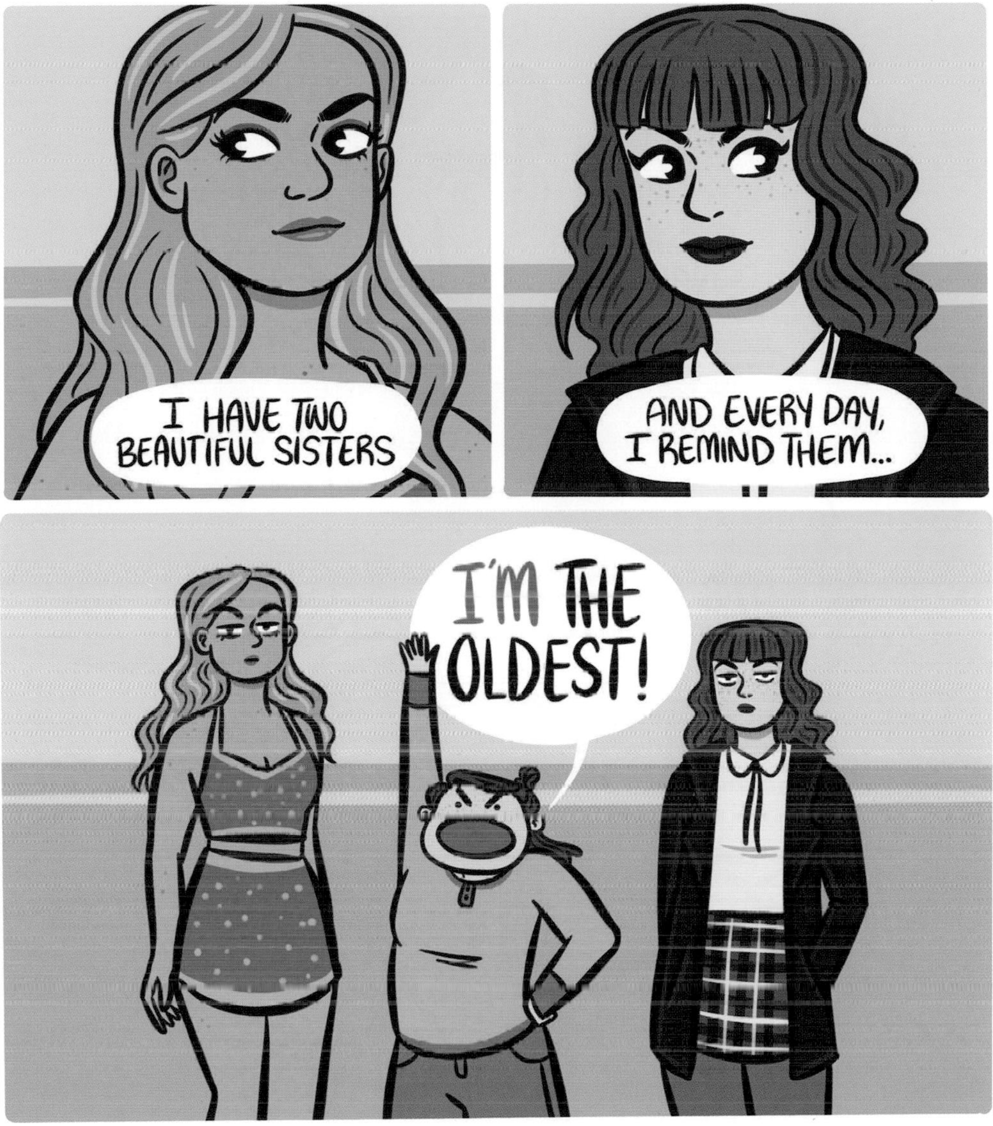
I HAVE TWO BEAUTIFUL SISTERS
AND EVERY DAY, I REMIND THEM...
I'M THE OLDEST!

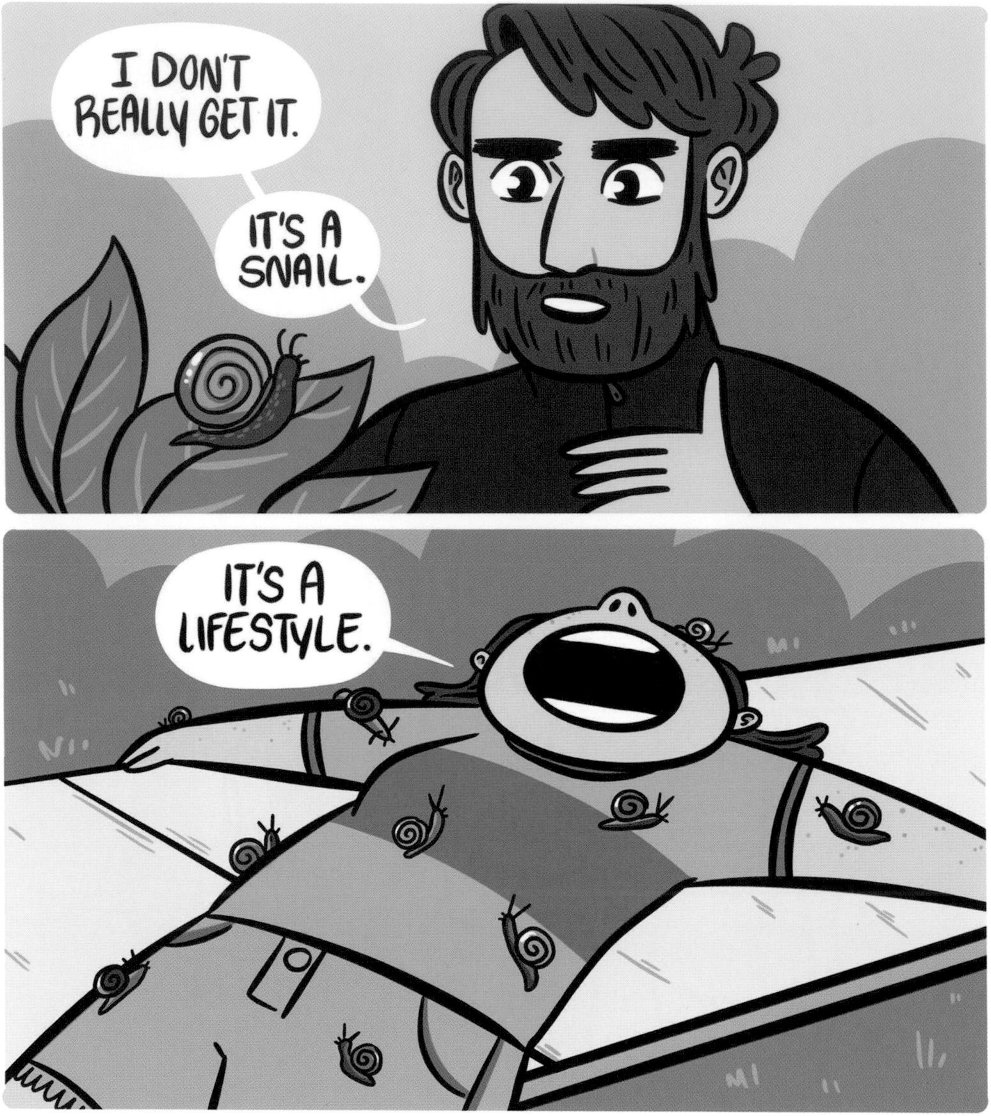
I DON'T REALLY GET IT.
IT'S A SNAIL.
IT'S A LIFESTYLE.

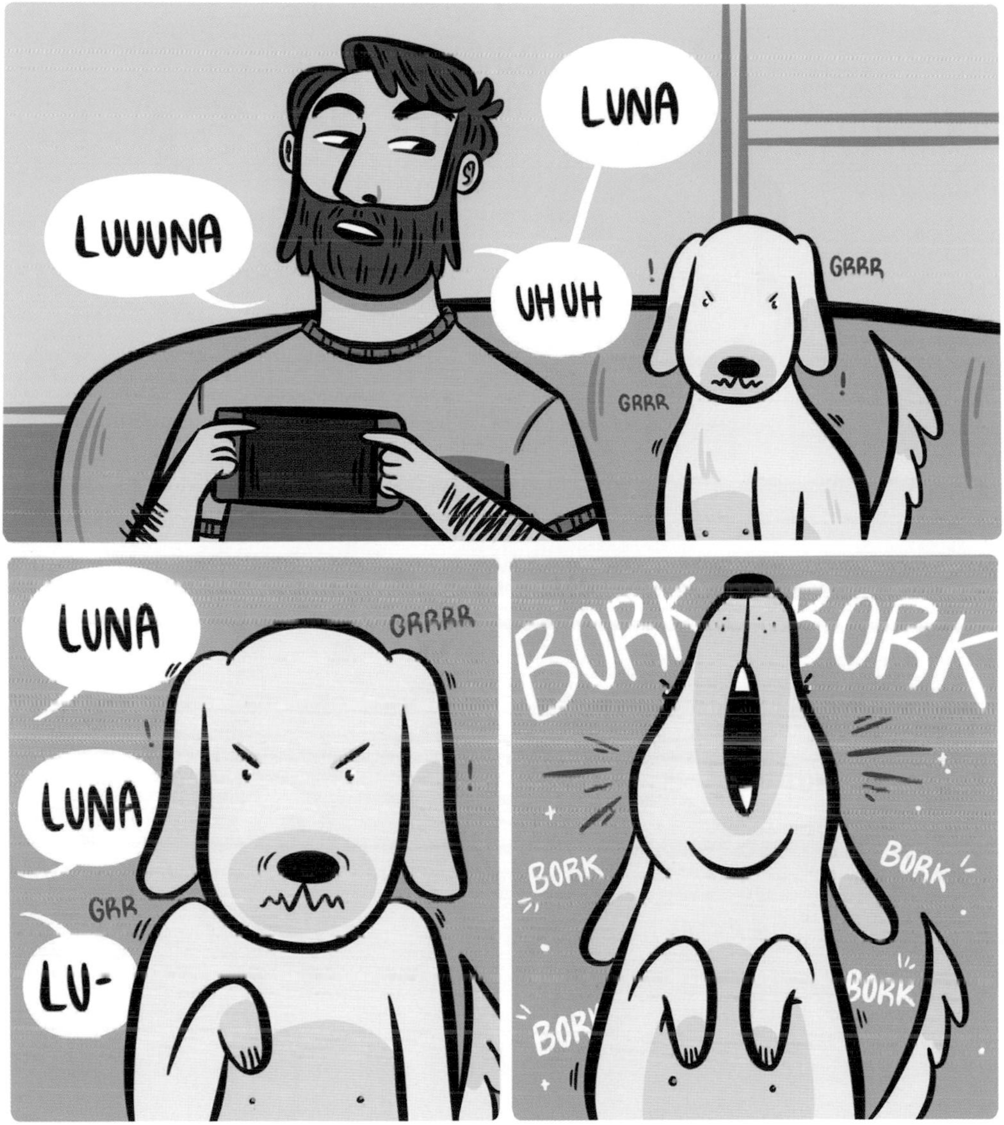
LUUUNA
LUNA
UH UH
GRRR
GRRR
LUNA
GRRRR
LUNA
GRR
LU-
BORK BORK
BORK
BORK
BORK
BORK

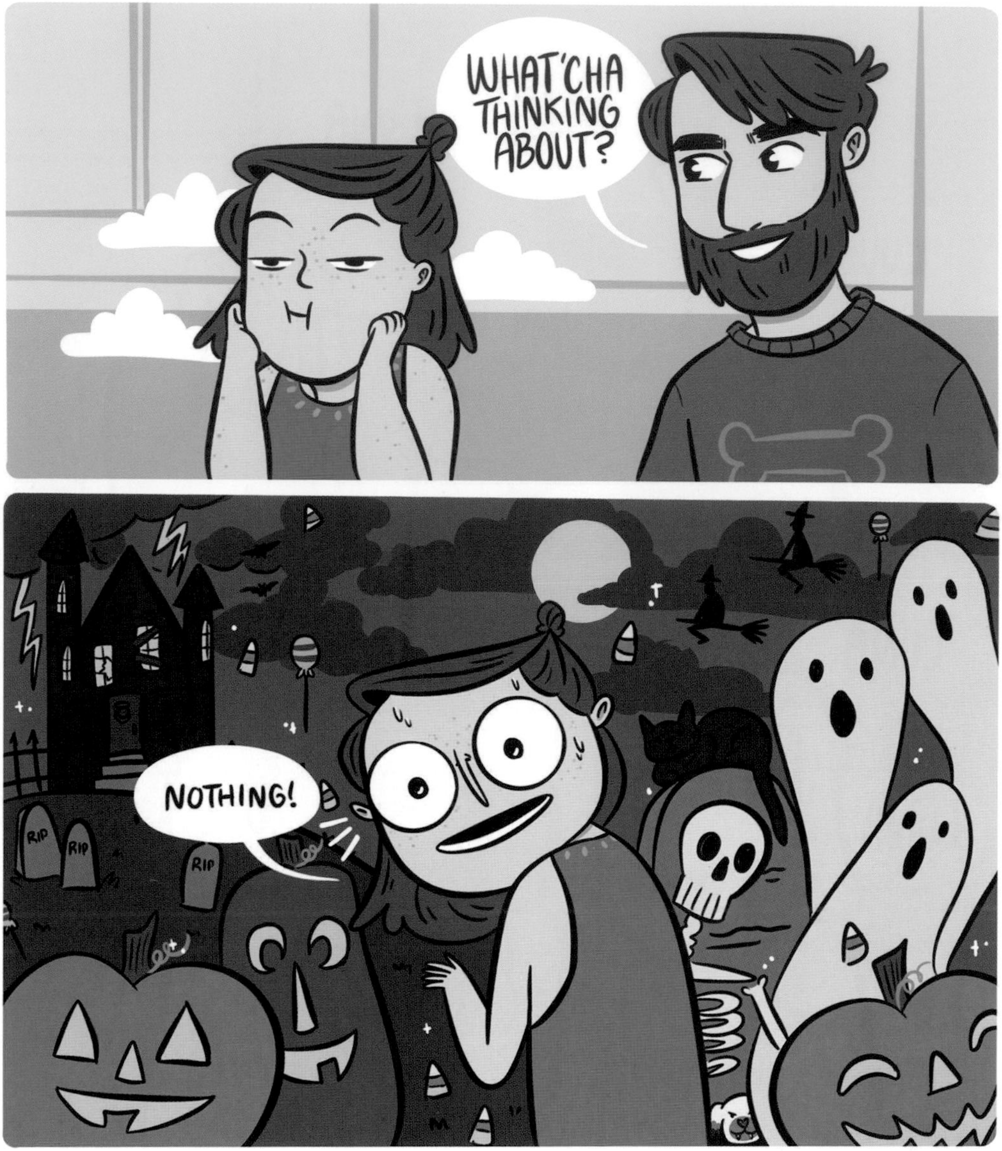
WHAT'CHA THINKING ABOUT?
NOTHING!

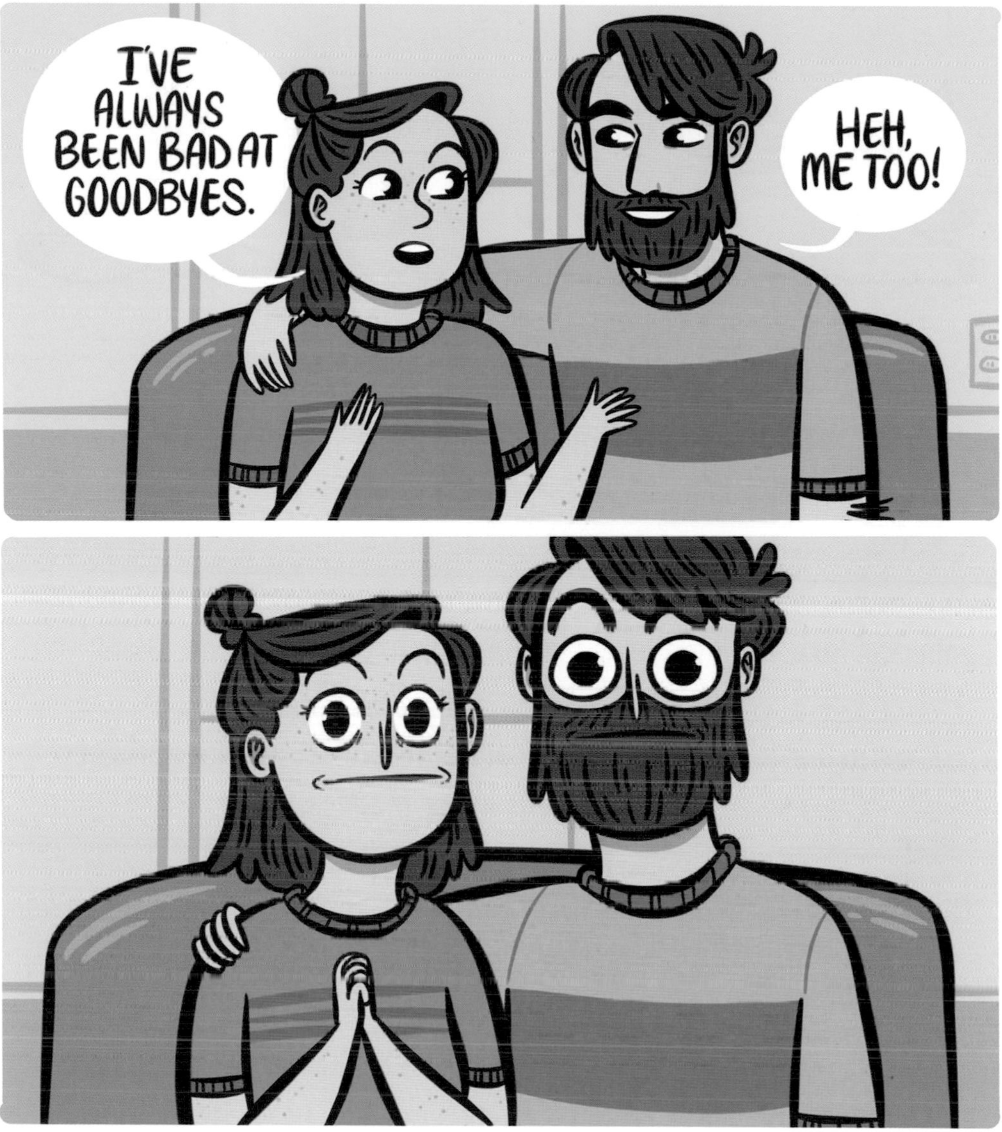
I'VE ALWAYS BEEN BAD AT GOODBYES.
HEH, ME TOO!

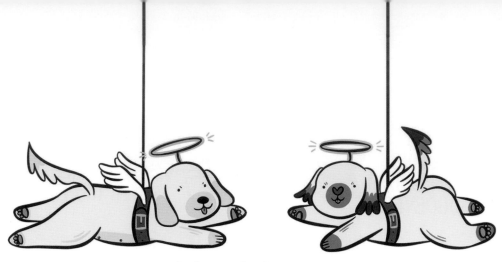

Acknowledgments

Thank you to my husband and better half, Carson.
We go together better than sprinkles on a peanut butter sandwich.

To my friends and family who have shown me the meaning of unconditional patience, love, and kindness, I wouldn't be here without you. Thank you.

A warm thank you to my agent, Laurie Abkemeier, for her guidance throughout this entire process.

Thank you to my editor, Patty Rice, and all the amazing folks at Andrews McMeel Publishing.

Finally, this book would not have been possible if it wasn't for the amazing community of ArtbyMoga readers. From the bottom of my heart, thank you, thank you, thank you.

Meg Adams is a comic artist and illustrator from Bend, OR.

Aside from art, she loves basking in the glory of her husband, taking her sweet pups out on adventures, and disappointing her parents.

(It's a joke, guys.)